The Ghosts of Iwo Jima

Joseph G. Dawson III, General Editor

TEXAS A&M UNIVERSITY PRESS   COLLEGE STATION

The Ghosts of Iwo Jima

ROBERT S. BURRELL

The paper used in this book meets the minimum
requirements of the American National Standard
for Permanence of Paper for Printed Library
Materials, Z39.48–1984.
Binding materials have been
chosen for durability.

Library of Congress Cataloging-in-Publication Data

Burrell, Robert S., 1970–
    The ghosts of Iwo Jima / Robert S. Burrell.
        p. cm.—(Texas A&m university military history series ; no. 102)
    Includes bibliographical references and index.
    ISBN 1-58544-483-9 (cloth : alk. paper)
    1. Iwo Jima, Battle of, Japan, 1945.   2. United States. Marine Corps—
History—World War, 1939–1945.   3. Marines—United States.
I. Title.   II. Texas A&M University military history series ; 102.
D767.99.I9B87   2006
940.54'2528—dc22   2005025902

    Nearly all the photographs and maps in this work derive from government
sources, most from the Marine Corps University Research Archives. Dr. Jim Ginther
graciously provided them in digital format. Special Collections, Nimitz Library, U.S.
Naval Academy, was another source of government photos. A few other government photos came from Naval Historical Center, National Archives, White House
Photo Office, and the Library of Congress. The first map, depicting the command
arrangement in the Pacific Theater, is from the U.S. Military Academy, West Point.
The second map, depicting Pacific strategy, was published in Haywood S. Hansell
Jr.'s *Strategic Air War against Japan* (1980). The third map, showing Iwo Jima defenses,
derives from Whitman S. Bartley's *Iwo Jima: Amphibious Epic* (1954). A diagram similar
to the figure showing the proposed organization of the unified armed forces can also
be found in Demetrios Caraley's *Politics of Military Unification: A Study of Conflict and
the Policy Process* (1966).

This work is dedicated to Sergeant Lynn Elverton Claflin from Headquarters Company, 3d Battalion, 27th Marines, who died at the battle of Iwo Jima on 28 February 1945. A blooded veteran of previous island campaigns, Lynn understood both the dangers of war and his responsibilities as a leader of the Marines. After being seriously wounded, he refused medical treatment, preferring instead to carry out his duty of leadership. Like Lynn, many other combatants sacrificed themselves to safeguard the lives of friends.

You are not forgotten.

Greater love hath no man than this,
that a man lay down his life for his friends.
(JOHN 15:13)

Contents

Illustrations

Maps

Figures

Photographs

Tables

Acknowledgments

Although the ideas expressed in this study are my own, I am honored to take a moment here to comment on the efforts of those institutions and individuals that made the publication of this work possible. First, I would like to express my appreciation to the U.S. Marine Corps. When I entered the Corps at eighteen years of age, I had a high school education and an uncertain future. I am forever indebted to those senior enlisted Marines who guided my transformation into a U.S. Marine. Foremost of these was my senior drill instructor, Sgt. R. G. Hoffman, who is now a sergeant major and a veritable legend on the drill field and in the Fleet Marine Forces. I will never forget his emphasis on self-discipline and meticulous attention to detail. My following four years of enlisted service in infantry, scout and target acquisition, and security forces engendered a profound appreciation for Marines at the tip of the spear. Much later on, the G.I. Bill and the Advanced Degree Program assisted me with both my undergraduate and graduate degrees. The culture, professionalism, and values of the Corps fundamentally changed my character and instilled in me many of the critical skills employed in this study.

While I pursued a graduate education at San Diego State University, Dr. William Cheek had the greatest impact on my ability to read history critically and write argumentatively. While challenging my narrow-mindedness, Dr. Cheek critiqued dozens of my essays, providing almost as much commentary on my weaknesses as I composed on the subject matter. Later, he repeated the same process on my revisions, and in the end, literally marked hundreds of pages. I have yet to meet another historian of Dr. Cheek's determination to understand the people we investigate as human beings—products of their environment and culture, and with strengths, weaknesses, and biases. I endeavor to uphold his standards of historical excellence.

During my research, I encountered many obstacles, and I remain grateful to those who helped me overcome them. Barbara Breeden and Barbara Manvel at the U.S. Naval Academy, Nimitz Library, as well as Carol Ramkey at the Marine Corps University Library, provided me with access to documents that were difficult to obtain. Mrs. Manvel, in particular, spent much time arranging interlibrary loans on my behalf, as well as providing research tips and reading a number of my rough drafts. Dr. Jim Ginther at Marine

Corps University Research Archives helped me sift through an enormous amount of information in Quantico, Virginia. In California, the staff at Curtis LeMay Library, March Field Air Museum, March Air Force Base, assisted me with papers related to the Twenty-First Bomber Command. Dr. Richard Sommers from the Military History Institute assisted with Army and Army Air Forces documents at Carlyle Barracks, Pennsylvania. Research assistant Jeff Sahaida helped me sift through the archives at the Air Force Historical Research Agency, Maxwell Air Force Base, Alabama. In Washington, D.C., Dave Giordano searched for documents related to Army Air Forces strategy at the National Archives, College Park, Maryland. In the Washington Navy Yard, Robert V. Aquilina of the Marine Corps History and Museums Division directed me to a host of information about Iwo Jima and subsequent events concerning the Marine War Memorial. Also at the Navy Yard, Mike Walker of the Naval Historical Center assisted me with the papers of Adm. Raymond A. Spruance and Adm. Chester W. Nimitz, as well as official Navy planning and intelligence information. As well, Ken Johnson at the Navy Historical Center provided me with a complete list of Navy records available at the National Archives—a valuable tool. In Maryland, Gary LaValley helped me search through the photo collection at the Special Collections and Archives Division, Nimitz Library, U.S. Naval Academy. I would also like to thank Iwo Jima veteran James C. Carroll, who provided a "reality check" for some of my ideas and an interesting perspective on the employment of armor during the battle.

Scores of historians gave guidance and feedback throughout the written formulation of my argument. Dr. Owen Griffiths, Dr. Elizabeth Cobbs-Hoffman, and Dr. Michael Weiner gave generously of their time during the research and writing process at San Diego State University. My three-year teaching tour at the U.S. Naval Academy history department had an enormous impact on the revision of my later work and the direction of my research. Teaching Navy, Marine Corps, and Pacific war histories gave me a broader understanding of multiple events and Iwo Jima's relationship to them. More important, the energy, cooperation, and enthusiasm of the department faculty rivals the world's greatest learning institutions, and I took great advantage of this fact. The department chair for academic years 2002–2004, Dr. Mary Decredico, placed faith and confidence in me. The department chair for academic year 2005, Dr. David Peeler, consistently offered advice in response to my numerous queries. I would also like to thank the many other historians in the department who assisted me with my writing: Dr. Richard Abels, Dr. David Appleby, Dr. Robert Artigiani, Dr. Lori Bogle,

Lt. Jim Carroll, Dr. Phyllis Culham, Dr. Nancy Ellenberger, Capt. Timothy Feist, Dr. Scott Harmon, Dr. Fredrick Harrod, Lt. Cdr. Scott Herbner, Maj. Stuart Lockhart, Dr. Robert Love, Cdr. Jeff Macris, Dr. Daniel Masterson, Dr. William McBride, Maj. Chris Morton, Lt. Cdr. Joshua Segal, Dr. Craig Symonds, Dr. Ernest Tucker, Maj. Victor Tumilty, Capt. Ted Veggeburg, and Dr. Maochun Yu.

While working at the U.S. Naval Academy, I had the opportunity to interact with many leading historians outside the history department. In particular, Col. Jon T. Hoffman, deputy director of the Marine Corps Historical Center, reviewed my work and helped direct my research. Colonel Hoffman's enthusiasm for scholarship and professional guidance proved invaluable. Dr. Bruce Vandervort, editor of the *Journal of Military History*, patiently evaluated my arguments and solicited advice from outside readers for over a year. Additionally, Dr. Anne S. Wells, also with *Journal of Military History*, provided me with first-rate editorial comments. The U.S. Naval Academy's Shifrin Chair for academic year 2003, Dr. Victor Hansen, gave me critical feedback on ways to build a balanced perspective on controversial topics. Admiral Furusawa of the Japanese Military Self Defense Force introduced me to Col. Ken-ichi Arakawa, a senior research fellow at the Military History Department of the Japanese National Institute for Defense Studies. Colonel Arakawa researched and translated documents from Japanese.

Several family members and close friends read drafts of this work and gave me excellent feedback. Specifically, I would like to recognize my uncle and former Marine, Art Domingus; my stepfather and friend, Chris Claflin; my brother and Air Force first sergeant, Richard Burrell; and close family friend and Vietnam war hero, Sgt. Maj. Gene Davis. Regretfully, my mother passed away during my research and before the fruition of this study. I loved her very much, and I am sure she would have been proud. Lastly, my life would not be complete without the support of my wife and three sons; all my love goes out to Carmen, Joshua, Alexander, and Maximus. Thank you for your patience!

Preface

Imagine a young boy on a street corner in Washington, D.C. on a cold, windy morning. He has a newspaper in his hand and a bundle of the same at his feet. It is the middle of March 1945, and he shouts out the headline with all his adolescent might in an effort to overcome the noise of the bustling automobile traffic. "Iwo Jima casualties total twenty thousand wounded! Over four thousand dead, read all about it!"[1] Pedestrians stop to purchase the daily paper from the young lad with the customary dread at seeing the latest death toll of American sons lost overseas. Underneath the headline, an unidentified woman has written a letter to the Secretary of Navy, in which she pleads: "Please for God's sake stop sending our finest youth to be murdered on places like Iwo Jima. It is too much for boys to stand, too much for mothers and homes to take. It is driving some mothers crazy. Why can't objectives be accomplished some other way? It is most inhuman and awful—stop, stop."[2]

In the wake of Iwo Jima, the public voiced dismay at the cost of the operation. On 27 February the *San Francisco Examiner* had run a front-page editorial that bemoaned the heavy price in lives suffered in the battle. The article stated that the Navy's use of amphibious assault against strong Japanese positions led to "enormous and excessive casualties" that endangered long-term strategy by wasting manpower.[3] The newspaper further argued that General MacArthur should take command of all naval operations in the Pacific because "he SAVES THE LIVES OF HIS OWN MEN, not only for the future and vital operations that must be fought before Japan is defeated, but for their own safe return to their families and loved ones in the American homeland after the peace is won."[4]

Losses on Iwo Jima sprang to the forefront of American concerns in the spring of 1945, nearly four years into the bloody war. As the battle raged, casualty figures made the front page on a daily basis in nearly every major newspaper in the country. The body count obsessed the public as the toll quickly rose to extreme levels in a short period of time. Iwo Jima became the bloodiest battle in Marine Corps history. Moreover, it was one of the most costly American battles fought in World War II. Nearly a third of all Marines who died in World War II lost their lives on Iwo Jima.[5]

Journalists kept the public apprised of the obscenely destructive nature of the battle. One war correspondent stated that Iwo Jima was the "stiffest enemy fire yet faced in the Pacific War," and another reporter described the island as "eight square miles of unadulterated hell."[6] The inhospitable terrain kept the enormous physical damage confined within a limited space, which allowed photographers to publish some of the most disturbing pictures of the war. Newspapers and periodicals printed photos that corroborated journalists' accounts of the battle as a terror beyond imagination. In one picture that covered an entire page of the *San Francisco Examiner*, large numbers of Marines were strewn haphazardly on steep beaches of dark volcanic ash.[7] Bodies hunkered down amid craters, smoke, and burned wreckage so that the viewer could scarcely distinguish the living from the dead.

The passionate controversy over the casualties and necessity of the Iwo Jima operation dwindled after 1945. One of the main reasons was that the raising of the U.S. flag on Mount Suribachi, as photographed by Joe Rosenthal, became one of the most famous images of the twentieth century. Indeed, one recent popular writer called it "the most recognized, the most reproduced, in the history of photography."[8] The photograph won the Pulitzer Prize and turned the initial horror over casualty rates into nationalistic pride in collective effort and sacrifice. The war-tired population longed for an end to the dismal Pacific struggle, and rather than reflect on the enormous number of dead and wounded on Iwo Jima, it quickly chose to make heroes out of the young men in that glorious scene. The image of six young warriors planting the flag atop a bastion of Japanese strength affected public opinion immensely—increasing a sense of hope and optimism for a successful resolution to the conflict.

Marine journalist and historian Robert L. Sherrod, who served on Iwo Jima, shared his observations concerning America's preoccupation with Mount Suribachi. "In my opinion—and I find many Iwo types who feel the same way—the implications are all wrong. Iwo wasn't a matter of climbing the parapet and heroically planting the flag there. It was tortuous painful slogging northward on the porkchop shaped island, which eventually cost us 6,821 killed and 19,217 wounded. Suribachi was a symbol and it was nice to have our flag up there, but the action—and the horror—lay elsewhere—where three of the Rosenthal flag raisers . . . were killed."[9] In the glorification of Mount Suribachi, Americans have lost the context to understand Iwo Jima's importance to the war; undoubtedly, the public wanted to forget the hideousness of the battle, and the flag-raising served as a romantic diversion.

History has forgotten that not all the veterans or even the planners of the Pacific war agreed on the necessity of the battle. For example, during an interview concerning naval operations on Saipan, retired Adm. Charles Adair, a Navy captain in 1945 and a senior amphibious operations planner in the Pacific's Seventh Fleet, went off on an interesting tangent concerning Iwo Jima. At the end of his reflections, Adair said, "I don't think Iwo Jima should have been taken, because of the cost to take it. And I don't think the value was there. I don't think it was needed, and if every plane that landed on Iwo Jima, that had to critically, were added up, and the pilots were added up, I'll bet they wouldn't anywhere near total 25,000."[10] The trouble with current tales of Iwo Jima is that criticism like Adair's has ceased altogether, and over the years the legends of the battle have become America's reality.

The significance of Iwo Jima can be best explained through its two divergent histories, one tragic and the other triumphant, neither of which has been sufficiently addressed. On the one hand, most scholarship has accepted the U.S. military's explanation for the necessity of the terrible battle with little critical analysis. Not a single study has chronicled the multiple events leading up to the decision to seize Iwo Jima. The majority have started from the untested premise that the island was vital to U.S. war aims. Consequently, historians have not dealt with outstanding questions concerning why the United States attacked the island, nor have they evaluated to any great degree its value for subsequent operations. On the other hand, although iconography and myths of Iwo Jima have over-glamorized the battle, the veneration of Iwo Jima actually had much greater positive impact on the Marine Corps in the postwar era than has been previously suggested. In reality, American perception of Iwo Jima helped saved the Marines from extinction and continues to influence both the Corps and the nation today. Essentially, both of Iwo Jima's contrasting stories have yet to be fully told. This study undertakes that task.

PART 1

The Untold Truth

No single chapter, no single book could describe that battle. To tell the story of Iwo Jima, I would have to tell the individual story of every man in the assault force.

HOLLAND M. SMITH, *Coral and Brass, 1948*

CHAPTER 1   *Omission*

O n the morning of 19 February 1945, James Vedder, combat surgeon for 27th Regiment, 5th Marine Division, waited for his landing craft to touch the volcanic sands of Iwo Jima. Iwo Jima would serve as the doctor's first test in combat. Undoubtedly anxious, he could at least console himself with the thought that planners expected a two-day offensive, with a third day dedicated to mopping up enemy resistance.[1] U.S. commanders predicted that the assault force of 80,000 combat-hardened Marines could rapidly traverse an island neutralized from bombardment, either destroying the Japanese in their defensive positions or mowing them down in waves of desperate *banzai* attacks. That the Navy had originally scheduled these same three divisions for use in the Okinawa invasion just thirty days later demonstrated that it did not, at least initially, consider the operation very difficult.[2] At 0830, battleships, cruisers, and destroyers leveled their massive guns on the beachhead of Iwo Jima and blasted the landscape with the largest preparatory bombardment to date. The violent explosions ashore quickly shrouded the visible topography of the island in smoke and debris. Little did Vedder know that U.S. commanders had severely underestimated the defenses on Iwo Jima, incorrectly assumed Japanese defensive strategy, and overrated the effects of technological and numeric superiority. The men of the 109th Japanese Infantry Division, in their meticulously designed fortifications, were poised to skillfully defend Sulfur Island (the literal translation of the Japanese name "Iwo Jima") from the 3d, 4th, and 5th Marine Divisions, resulting in the most appalling contest of the Pacific War. With a bare twenty months of military experience, Dr. Vedder was about to face thirty-three days of the most horrific carnage imaginable as American boys and amphibious veterans fed the "meat-grinder" on Iwo Jima.[3] Vedder hit the beach just minutes behind the first waves of troops, attempting to exercise compassion in hell.

Peacetime forgets that wartime accounts of misery, destruction, and death can be amazingly direct, detailed, and diverse. On the lunar landscape of Iwo Jima, Vedder treated wounds that mangled faces, shattered jaws, and split skulls wide open. He frequently attempted to care for American boys with missing limbs, wounds so devastating that no healing was possible. He witnessed Marines and sailors die most violently from massive artillery and mortar rounds, as well as from unexpected and precise Japanese marksmanship. He looked after sanitation aspects of hundreds of decomposing corpses. The same insects that infested the dead infiltrated the eyes, ears, and nostrils of the living; or worse, they contaminated food designated for human consumption. In all this horror, his job became almost routine, allowing for times of humor and even small moments of happiness. However, in a 220-page narrative dedicated to the battle, combat surgeon James Vedder made no mention whatsoever of an American flag raised on top of Mount Suribachi. Perhaps that "omission" constitutes the most important evidence of all . . .

Nearly everyone has heard of Iwo Jima and recognizes the monumental icon of six U.S. servicemen raising the American flag on top of Mount Suribachi in 1945. The public generally understands that this image symbolizes patriotism and valor, even though the picturesque scene greatly distorts the miserable experiences of the combatants. Operation Detachment (the code name for the U.S. war plan to invade Iwo Jima) was the largest U.S. Marine

THE UNTOLD TRUTH

Corps operation ever conducted and cost the lives of over 25,000 Americans and Japanese. However, the public has failed to realize that, tragically, the decision of the Joint Chiefs of Staff to seize Iwo Jima cost thousands of American lives for an objective that never fulfilled the intended purposes—a truth that has been unaddressed by historians for over sixty years. The valuable lessons of Iwo Jima lie covered and dormant, buried under myth and legend.

A more detailed look into the planning for Iwo Jima demonstrates that the service rivalry resulting from the dual advance of the U.S. Navy and the U.S. Army in the Pacific heavily influenced the decision to initiate Operation Detachment. Rather than waiting for the Army to complete its seizure of the Philippines in 1944 and release the ground forces needed to invade Formosa, the Navy made a hasty change in plans to seize Okinawa instead and thereby continue its northward advance. Although Okinawa satisfied the Navy's purposes, the objective of seizing Iwo Jima actually derived from Army Air Forces strategy. The intent was to improve poor performance of the B-29 Superfortress by providing fighter support from Iwo Jima. These combined objectives of Okinawa and Iwo Jima ensured approval by the Joint Chiefs of Staff. This alliance between the Navy, which was seeking to outflank the Army, and the Army Air Forces, which wanted to prove the case for strategic bombing in order to create an independent postwar service, satisfied their respective interests. However, the Marine Corps, which predominantly paid the heavy price for carrying out Operation Detachment, remained excluded from the decision-making process. When fighter operations from Iwo Jima failed, the military sought additional reasons to justify the costly battle, and historians have unfortunately perpetuated these illusions.

Far from glorious, combat on Iwo Jima was perhaps the most brutal, tragic, and deadly in American history. Scholars have never yet sufficiently addressed the strategic decisions and ensuing justifications for Iwo Jima. The major weakness in the conduct of the Pacific War resided in the inability of the Joint Chiefs of Staff to unify the efforts of the Army and Navy. Consequently, the Army, Navy, and Army Air Forces conducted separate and competing campaigns against Japan. Operation Detachment derived from Army Air Forces strategy, brought about by the need to improve disappointing B-29 operations, in an atmosphere of fierce competition, and with the fear of losing autonomy. At the cost of thousands of lives, Operation Detachment resulted in an airbase of questionable value, with a price that neither the public, nor the military, could swallow.

Nearly every book, journal article, encyclopedia entry, and Web site that addresses the battle justifies the nearly 7,000 American dead with the "emergency landing theory." Essentially, the theory argues that 2,251 B-29 Superfortresses landed on Iwo Jima; each Superfort carried eleven crewmen; accordingly, Operation Detachment saved the lives of 24,761 Americans. But the emergency landing theory does not stand up to scrutiny. The absurdity of the claim demonstrates the extent to which the battle has been misunderstood. Rather than saving the lives of U.S. airmen, Operation Detachment may have actually detracted from U.S. war efforts to defeat Japan. If we view the Pacific war through the lens of Iwo Jima, its most important lessons may emerge.

Theirs not to make reply,
Theirs not to reason why,
Theirs but to do and die:
Into the valley of Death
Rode the six hundred.

"The Charge of the Light Brigade,"
ALFRED, LORD TENNYSON, *1870*

It is not within our providence to evaluate the cost in money,
time, equipment, or, most of all, in human life. We are told
what our objective is to be and we prepare to do the job,
knowing that all evaluations have been considered by
those who give us our orders.

LT. GEN. HOLLAND M. SMITH, USMC,
March 1945

CHAPTER 2   *Fateful Decision*

I n late winter 1944 Raymond A. Spruance resumed command of the
Navy's Pacific Fleet. As routinely became the case, the Pacific Fleet
automatically reverted to the name Fifth Fleet under Spruance's supervision, although the Navy dubbed the same armada the Third Fleet while
under Adm. William Halsey's direction. Spruance and Halsey rotated into
this position of command—"the same horse with different drivers," or so the
saying went. A seasoned naval officer, Spruance was a quiet but ambitious
man. His service to country since 1906 had led him to numerous command
positions. He was a meticulous commander, who at times proved willing to
take calculated risks. Spruance's string of victories in the Pacific equaled or
perhaps surpassed those of any of the great naval leaders in world history. His

aggressive leadership had led to the U.S. Navy's most important victory, at the Battle of Midway in 1942. He had commanded the Navy's amphibious assaults in the Gilbert Islands, Marshall Islands, and Marianas Islands in 1943 and 1944. And he had destroyed what remained of Japanese naval air power at the Battle of the Philippine Sea in 1944. Naval historian Samuel Eliot Morison described Spruance as "one of the greatest fighting and thinking admirals in American naval history."[1] Due to his recognized intelligence and thoughtful demeanor, Spruance had gained the respect of just about everyone in the U.S. Navy.

In early 1945 Commander in Chief of the U.S. Navy, Adm. Ernest J. King, charged Spruance with the leadership of one of the largest fleets ever assembled, with the goal of seizing the island of Iwo Jima. Spruance's vast naval experience could not lighten the heavy weight placed on his slender shoulders. From his flagship at Ulithi, Spruance could observe hundreds of ships assembling for Operation Detachment. Like a giant pretzel with holes in the middle, Ulithi's coral reef encircled magnificent bays, leaving room for hundreds of vessels to resupply in its protected harbor. A quarter of a million men prepared for one of the greatest amphibious assaults in history. The bustling scene of vessels hastily taking on supplies gave the admiral time for pause. Items being loaded included food, clothing, trucks, artillery, tanks, ammunition, medicine, and units of whole blood. Disturbingly, Marine Gen. Holland M. Smith was predicting large numbers of casualties. As the day of the assault approached, Spruance's doubts about the necessity of seizing the island grew. The Commanding General of the Twenty-First Bomber Command, Curtis LeMay, had boarded the USS *Indianapolis* earlier on 27 January. Perhaps the admiral's guest could calm his fears.

Spruance's visitor, the colorful LeMay, had stood apart as a prominent supporter of strategic air power ever since his highly publicized flight in 1937 when, during an exercise, he had sunk the U.S. Navy's battleship USS *Utah* off the coast of California with a B-17 bomber. First as a member and eventually as the commander of the Eighth Air Force, LeMay attacked strategic targets in Europe from secure bases in England. During those years, he was forced to face the harsh reality that America's technological fascination with air power did not always live up to expectations. Much to his dismay, his bombers had difficulty hitting desired targets with precision, and the German *Luftwaffe* (German Air Force) took a devastating toll on American aircrews. Yet LeMay demonstrated a particular genius for training aircrews to compensate for the limitations in aircraft design, and he developed a pragmatic doctrine of massed formations that made strategic bombing more

THE UNTOLD TRUTH

effective in Europe while decreasing the losses to airmen. Consequently, by 1944, many viewed the general as the "fastest burning rocket in the AAF [Army Air Forces]."[2]

The Army Air Forces' prized B-29 Superforts finally rolled off the assembly lines and began operating out of both Indian and Chinese bases in the Twentieth Bomber Command in June 1944. The war had passed its climax, a condition that put more pressure on Chief of Staff of the Army Air Forces Henry H. "Hap" Arnold (Hap being short for "happy") to produce convincing strategic results quickly. General Arnold desperately desired to demonstrate the importance of strategic air power. To call operations in the Burma-India-China theater challenging would be an enormous understatement. The logistics involved posed the greatest difficulty. Lack of heavy equipment meant that thousands of Chinese peasants built and maintained airfields by hand. Flying out of India required bombers to climb over the Himalayan Mountains on each mission. Transporting supplies by air instead of by sea severely limited the amount of tonnage that could be shipped and required the constant use of a large percentage of the available aircraft. To complicate matters, the distances involved in supporting B-29s halfway around the world from the United States proved problematic. The Twentieth Bomber Command attempted precision daylight bombing of mainland Japan from Indian bases, but the meager results did not satisfy Arnold. Irrespective of geographical problems, the B-29 Superfortress, at this early stage in its deployment, failed to live up to expectations due to poor training of aircrews and persistent maintenance issues with the aircraft. The Army Air Forces' vision for the future of modern warfare, the devastating application of precision bombing from high altitudes, proved premature.[3]

Arnold was concerned about the negative publicity over the poor performance of the B-29 because it endangered his quest for an independent air force.[4] Although publicity issues mattered to senior officers in the Army and Navy, for Arnold it was a major preoccupation. In the words of historian Michael Sherry, publicity had been "made critical by the air force's declining chance to win the war on its own and to secure favorable coverage in the face of accelerating ground and naval operations."[5] Arnold transferred LeMay to China in late 1944 to improve the effectiveness of the B-29, and LeMay committed himself to make that happen, demanding that his pilots hit targets, regardless of dangers to aircraft and crew.[6]

Due to logistical concerns and the deteriorating situation of U.S. allies in China, Arnold decided to consolidate all his Superfortress resources in the Marianas Islands under the Twenty-First Bomber Command and sacrifice the efforts of the Twentieth Bomber Command in India. Initially, Arnold gave the Twenty-First Bomber Command in the Marianas to Gen. Haywood Hansell. However, it soon became clear that General LeMay in China and General Hansell in Saipan advocated different approaches in employing the B-29. General Hansell repeatedly attempted to make the Superfortress achieve the function for which it was designed—precision high-altitude bombing during daylight hours—the poor results of which continued to frustrate him. An Air Force study later described General Hansell as "inflexible in outlook and reluctant to innovate. Most particularly, he clung to the dogma of precision bombing when it was becoming apparent that high-altitude winds over Japan precluded the effective use of this concept with existing technology."[7] Operating from Twentieth Bomber Command in the Burma-India-China theater, LeMay, in contrast, demonstrated more flexible views by accepting the inherent deficiencies in the B-29's design and experimenting with both night bombing and incendiary attacks.

Arnold decided to replace the conservative Hansell with the ambitious LeMay in January 1945, giving LeMay the responsibility for strategic bombing against Japan. Arnold ensured that LeMay understood that the Army Air Forces' future rested in his hands. According to an Air Force study, "LeMay felt the pressures of time and urgency ('General Arnold needed results,' he said) to avoid a ground invasion of Japan and, in the bargain, insure the survival of the strategic air command concept."[8] With the end of the war in sight, Arnold "pushed more and more for decisive results to support his dream of an independent air service."[9]

So this was the situation with the B-29 in January 1945 when Adm. Raymond Spruance surveyed preparations for the invasion of Iwo Jima from his flagship at Ulithi Atoll. General LeMay had taken over the Twenty-First Bomber Command less than two weeks earlier when Admiral Spruance sat down with him on the USS *Indianapolis*. Without hesitation Spruance asked the first question on his mind: "What do you think about the value of Iwo Jima?" LeMay responded, "Oh! But it is going to be a tremendous value to me. Without Iwo Jima I couldn't bomb Japan effectively."[10] Having worried about the operation for over two months, the uneasy admiral felt reassured by the younger LeMay's confidence. Indeed, it took a load off his mind.[11] The conversation quickly turned to other matters.

Criticizing the conversation between Spruance and LeMay, Adm. Charles Adair, a captain in 1945 and one of the Pacific Fleet's chief planners, doubted LeMay's competency to influence overall U.S. strategy. "Now, how much of an expert is General LeMay?" he wondered. LeMay "had been in the area ten days. I wonder how much he knew about Guam, and how much he knew about Tinian, how much he knew about Iwo Jima, and how much he knew about a lot of things, really. But here he is . . . and if anybody should ask him, 'Do you need Iwo Jima or not?,' I can imagine he would say, 'Yes, we need it.' Now why did we need it?"[12]

Admiral Spruance's conversation with General LeMay and Admiral Adair's speculations only scratch the surface on a host of intriguing issues that require further investigation. Months earlier, Spruance was one of three admirals who proposed Operation Detachment to the Chief of Naval Operations, Adm. Ernest J. King. With less than a month left before D-Day and with the operation in full swing, why did Spruance openly express doubts about the island's value? And why did he do so to an Army Air Forces general? How had this situation developed? The answers lie in the planning and organization of the Pacific War—in the years that led to a fateful decision.

Service Rivalry in Pacific Strategy, 1942–43

The most decisive impact on the planning and conduct of Operation Detachment originated from the organization of the U.S. command structure early in the war. After defeat at Pearl Harbor, the U.S. military command organization was still clearly divided between land and sea operations with little coordination between the two. The Joint Board, the U.S. general planning body that included both services, discovered that it did not have the proper authority or organization to work in concert with the British Chiefs of Staff Committee. To integrate differing aspects of land, air, and sea power, the British Chiefs of Staff consisted of army, air force, and naval officers. By emulating their British counterparts, the U.S. Army and Navy created the Joint Chiefs of Staff in January 1942. By the summer of 1942, the Joint Chiefs of Staff consisted of Adm. Ernest J. King (Chief of Naval Operations), Adm. William D. Leahy (Presidential Chief of Staff), Gen. George C. Marshall (Army Chief of Staff), and Gen. Henry H. Arnold (Commander of the Army Air Forces). When the U.S. Joint Chiefs of Staff and the British Combined Chiefs of Staff met, the two merged into the Combined Chiefs of Staff, which planned, approved, and coordinated allied operations against Germany, Italy, and Japan.

Although made up of four members, the Joint Chiefs of Staff did not distribute its power equally. General Marshall and Admiral King remained the senior directors of the Army and Navy. Consequently, General Arnold and Admiral Leahy usually followed the lead of their own service's director.

Nevertheless, the composition of the Joint Chiefs of Staff changed the power structure of the U.S. military. The Army Air Forces had struggled for many years to become a separate service, similar to the British Royal Air Force.[13] However, the Army and Navy had suppressed the Army Air Forces' effort, preferring to subjugate air power in support of naval and land operations. Now General Arnold had attained a seat at the table with General Marshall and Admiral King. The Army Air Forces expanded its semi-autonomy over the next two years, which complicated the traditional rivalry between the Army and Navy. Equally important, the rapidly expanding Marine Corps remained disenfranchised in the decision making process.[14] The dynamics of this power-sharing arrangement would eventually have profound effects on the decision and conduct of Operation Detachment.

Often to the dismay of both his colleagues and the British Chiefs of Staff, Admiral King regarded Japan and not Germany as America's primary military responsibility. Fearing the loss of the remainder of their possessions in the area, the British, to King's satisfaction, finally acquiesced to total U.S. control of the Pacific. Unfortunately, the Joint Chiefs of Staff could not agree on the choice of a U.S. commander in the Pacific. Opinionated and ambitious, King abhorred the thought of subordinating the Navy to the Army in what would primarily be a naval conflict. Nonetheless, the plausible choice for unified leadership was Army Gen. Douglas MacArthur, whose experience, seniority, and popularity the Joint Chiefs of Staff could not overlook.

Perhaps no other American possessed better experience to organize a Pacific defense than MacArthur, but President Franklin Roosevelt's decision to bring him out of retirement in 1941 produced a host of additional conditions that influenced future policy. MacArthur boasted a strong personality. He was charismatic, persuasive, and accustomed to getting his way. Additionally, he had broad public support, giving him political clout at home. For over five years, MacArthur had built considerable personal interest in the defense of the Philippines and made numerous private bonds with members of its government.[15] Consequently, he resolved to protect the islands for reasons beyond their strategic value. Lastly, as a former Chief of Staff of the Army (1930–35), MacArthur had attained the highest position in the Army prior to the current Chief of Staff, George C. Marshall, who had been a colonel when MacArthur headed the Army. While both men held equal rank from 1941 onward, MacArthur's experience over his appointed superior produced a cooperative rather than a subordinate relationship between the two generals.

THE UNTOLD TRUTH

The Japanese surprise attack at Pearl Harbor, the worst naval defeat in American history, required the relief of Adm. Husband Kimmel from command of the Pacific Fleet in December 1941. In his place, the Navy had sent Chester Nimitz to take over the Pacific Fleet, a man described as an "excellent judge of character, robust of build and serene of temperament."[16] As opposed to MacArthur's bravado and narcissism, Nimitz appeared a fair-minded and amenable leader. Still, Nimitz remained firmly in command of his assets in the Pacific Fleet and sometimes clashed with the Chief of Naval Operations on its employment.

Whatever the merits of King's desire to prosecute a naval war in the Pacific with a Navy commander, MacArthur proved an obstacle to his aspirations. In the words of historian Russell Weigley, "MacArthur was too egotistical and in public and political esteem too powerful a personage to be subordinated to a Navy theater command, especially since Admiral King apparently disliked as well as distrusted him; while the Navy understandably refused to give control of the fast carriers and the ocean war in the Central Pacific to an Army general."[17]

In compromise between the two services, the Joint Chiefs of Staff divided the Pacific Theater into four areas: Southwest Pacific Area, North Pacific Area, Central Pacific Area, and South Pacific Area. The Southwest Pacific Area contained the most land mass and was given to General MacArthur. Nimitz controlled Central Pacific Area and North Pacific Area. Adm. Robert L. Ghormley commanded the South Pacific Area. Although both the Army and Navy served in each theater, the Pacific Ocean Areas (made up of the North, South, and Central areas) were predominantly Navy, and the Southwest Pacific Area was primarily Army. Since it limited the Army's advance on Japan, the most contentious partition of the Pacific would be the northern boundary between MacArthur's Southwest Pacific Area and Nimitz's Central Pacific Area—a line that crossed between the Philippine Islands and the large island of Formosa.

As theater commanders, Nimitz and MacArthur received direction from King and Marshall respectively, on behalf of the Joint Chiefs of Staff. In other words, the Joint Chiefs of Staff retained general authority over Pacific strategy. The Joint Chiefs generated war plans and approved each operation. Rather than providing unity, this command arrangement in Washington only complicated matters. The Joint Chiefs debated, compromised, or delayed on contentious issues. Secretary of War Henry L. Stimson succinctly stated the dilemma: "The Joint Chiefs of Staff was an imperfect instrument of top-level decision. Certainly it represented a vast improvement over anything that had existed before, and on the whole it was astonishingly successful, but it remained incapable of enforcing a decision against the will of any one of its members."[18] Slightly less generous, historian Ronald Spector used the word "monstrosity" to describe the combination of careerism and doctrinal differences that pervaded the arrangement.[19] The decision to split command in the Pacific Theater defied military principles and divided already scarce resources but ensured that Admiral King could prosecute the Navy's prewar plans across the Central Pacific relatively unhindered by Army influence. It is important to note that once the dual Army and Navy drives through the Central and Southwest Pacific collided in 1944 near the northern boundary line that separated them—the Formosa-Luzon area—the fierce debate over the command of future operations would result in the fateful decision to launch Operation Detachment.

Several problematic situations resulted from the Joint Chiefs of Staff's decision to prioritize service interests over unified strategy. In regard to the Marine Corps, a few cases had notable similarities to the misfortunes that plagued Operation Detachment and deserve explanation. To start with, the U.S. offensive campaign for Guadalcanal in the summer of 1942 resulted in the first major service rivalry–related fiasco since Pearl Harbor. At the outset, King quibbled with Marshall on the border between the Army's Southwest Pacific Theater and the Navy's South Pacific Theater. King's argument rested on his premise that MacArthur was unqualified to control carriers. But King's motivation for moving the line to the west was to ensure that the U.S. Navy retained command over the amphibious landing on Guadalcanal and the first major offensive of the war.

Highly annoyed by the Navy conducting operations in what was originally designated as his theater, MacArthur reluctantly prepared for the second and third portions of his Southwest Pacific offensive, dubbed Operation Cartwheel. The U.S. Navy, having isolated itself from U.S. Army support, relied solely on naval means to carry out King's plan. The incursion into the Solomon Islands had so few resources that planners humorously dubbed it Operation Shoestring. King used Gen. A. A. Vandegrift's hastily formed 1st Marine Division to seize the island. Vandegrift, who had actually been promised several more months to organize his division before entering combat but was now given less than two, stoically carried out the task. The Marines initially had little trouble seizing Guadalcanal, but the U.S. Navy suffered from a surprise attack to its surface forces near Savo Island, resulting in the second-largest U.S. Navy defeat in history. Fearing that he was overextended, Admiral Ghormley withdrew his carriers, forcing the rest of

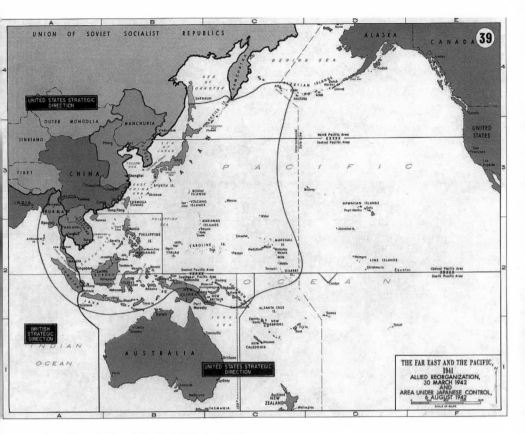

Army/Navy division of the Pacific Theater, 1942

the Pacific Fleet—including the ground force's partially unloaded supply ships—to leave as well. While the Marines survived on captured rations and scrounged equipment, the Japanese subjected them to a series of counter-attacks on land, air, and sea. The situation was tenuous.

Since the Marines' only lifeline at this point consisted of an airfield, Nimitz scrambled to assist them with air support, but MacArthur controlled the majority of land-based aircraft. Consequently, King asked Marshall to reallocate bombers and fighters to Nimitz's command. This was carried out to a limited extent, but Nimitz expressed the need for more planes while MacArthur pronounced frustration over the partition of his Army Air Forces. MacArthur was understandably aggravated with the Navy for diverting his assets to support the Marines on Guadalcanal, an island originally within his theater. After tallying the number of U.S. planes in the Pacific, General Marshall informed Admiral King that more than enough air power resided in the Pacific already if MacArthur and Nimitz simply pooled their resources.[20]

Marshall then related these same terms to MacArthur, telling him to work more closely with Nimitz.[21] Ironically, communiqués from Washington berated Nimitz and MacArthur for not solving the problems of dual command, a system the Joint Chiefs of Staff had created.

Eventually, both the Army and Navy sent air support to assist the besieged Marines. The product of absolute necessity, this was one of the few joint fighter operations in the Pacific War, colorfully dubbed the Cactus Air Force. Tenacity and ingenuity allowed the 1st Marine Division to repel repeated Japanese assaults, which, fortunately for the Marines, the Japanese carried out haphazardly. Regrettably, however, the Joint Chiefs did not fix the underlying cause of the situation. Instead of recognizing the problems of dual commands in the Pacific, King and Marshall simply reprimanded Nimitz and MacArthur for not making the system work.[22] Conflicts continued between the two Pacific commanders as they competed for limited resources, generating a legendary adversarial relationship between Nimitz and MacArthur. Such friction should have been expected. The root of the problem, and the huge rivalry that developed between the Army and Navy commands stemmed from the competing service interests of the Joint Chiefs of Staff. Lower echelons merely reflected Washington's own lack of unity.

After Guadalcanal, the Joint Chiefs of Staff found an urgent need for a comprehensive war plan that addressed the needs of both Pacific commands. Consequently, it approved a new strategic outline.[23] The principal scheme of maneuver, a northwestern route from Australia to the Philippines, favored MacArthur as the main effort. However, the plan called for Nimitz to secure Central Pacific islands in order to shorten lines of supply and communication from Hawaii to Australia. To King's dismay, and contrary to decades of prewar naval planning, the Navy had been assigned a supporting role in the Army's advance.[24]

Both the Army and Navy made ready to carry out their separate offensives through the summer of 1943.[25] Admiral Nimitz prepared to secure the Marshall Islands, which lay in a direct path between Hawaii and Australia.[26] He desired to undertake the operation as soon as possible, but General MacArthur needed the Pacific Fleet to support his Operation Cartwheel in the South Pacific. The Navy would not have the naval means to seize the Marshall Islands until after the Army had completed its campaign in the northern Solomons.[27] In an attempt to exert control over all naval assets immediately, King renewed the discussion over unified command. King suggested that Nimitz should control the timing and coordination of all Pacific operations.[28] His proposal essentially made Nimitz the supreme commander of the entire Pacific, but it was the only way the Navy could move forward with the Marshalls operation without delay.

The U.S. Navy had assumed control over the first American offensive against the southern Solomon Island of Guadalcanal. Now King wanted to delay Operation Cartwheel in the northern Solomons and Bismarck Archipelago so that the Navy could conduct another operation in the Central Pacific. This infuriated MacArthur, whose statement that "probably no commander in American history has been so poorly supported" was indicative of his frustration.[29] Despite King's attempt to give Admiral Nimitz overall Pacific authority, General Marshall refused to consent to a course of action that subordinated the Army. The chain of command remained unchanged. Admiral Nimitz was forced to honor the previous arrangement to support Operation Cartwheel, and the attack on the Marshall Islands would have to wait.

The Joint Chiefs of Staff had previously considered the idea of seizing an airfield in the Gilbert Islands in support of an advance into the Marshalls. Even so, the Joint Staff Planners had recommended that if the necessary forces could be made available without serious interruption to MacArthur's Cartwheel Operation, the "best course of action" would entail the direct seizure of the Marshalls.[30] However, standing by as General MacArthur advanced with his naval assets, Admiral Nimitz decided to seize the Gilbert Islands in the meantime in order to follow up on the Marshalls later. To spare enough manpower, support, and shipping to carry out both the Army's and Navy's drives nearly simultaneously, the two commands made alternating attacks. MacArthur seized portions of the Solomon Islands beginning in June and completed his campaign with an assault on the Admiralties in February. Nimitz squeezed the attack on the Gilbert Islands between MacArthur's assaults. The Gilberts operation took place in November 1943.

Scholars differ as to why the Navy chose to seize the Gilberts. Historian Louis Morton argued that Nimitz wanted to keep his forces on the offensive rather than wait on MacArthur to finish in the Solomons.[31] Nimitz maintained the necessity of the Gilbert operation as a precursor to an assault on the Marshalls, justifying the operation for one fundamental reason: the airfield seized in the Gilberts allowed B-24 Liberators to conduct photo-reconnaissance of the Marshall Islands.[32] Nimitz stated that carrier aircraft had not yet been adequately adapted for this task, which made an airfield within reach of the Marshalls an essential prerequisite for their seizure.

After the war, Marine Gen. Holland M. Smith bitterly argued that the Navy simply used the Gilberts to demonstrate its amphibious capabilities.[33] Despite the generalization by Nimitz to the contrary, the Navy did have the capability to photograph islands from the air and, ironically, did so extensively in preparation for the Gilberts. The difference between carrier- and land-based aerial photoreconnaissance derived from vertical and oblique photographic capabilities, the latter of which B-24s provided. The combination of the two angles proved extremely accurate in the Gilberts, pinpointing on some islands an "estimated ninety percent of the enemy's defensive installations."[34] However, the Navy seized other islands in the Gilberts based on vertical photographic intelligence alone.[35] Whatever the relevance of technical arguments about aerial photographic capabilities, one fact cannot be overlooked: the Navy originally planned to seize the Marshalls directly without the Gilberts until such time as MacArthur's advance in the Solomons delayed that action. Historian Louis Morton appears to have determined the primary impetus for the Gilberts operation: Nimitz decided to stay on the offensive rather than wait for MacArthur to release the rest of his naval forces.

Admiral Spruance commanded the Gilberts operation. Part of Spruance's reluctance in prosecuting Operation Detachment likely derived from his unhappy experiences in the Gilberts—specifically, the seizure of Tarawa Atoll. On Tarawa's primary island of Betio, the Japanese had constructed elaborate defenses, perhaps surpassed only by those on Peleliu in 1944 and Iwo Jima in 1945. The operation went awry for various reasons. Poor hydrographic intelligence, lack of proper landing craft, inadequate coordination, and inaccurate preparatory bombardment all contributed to heavy casualties.[36] In the opinion of the senior Marine in the Pacific, Holland M. Smith, the Navy had chosen the wrong objective since Betio had no strategic value.[37] After hearing of the casualties (1,027 dead, 2,292 wounded) MacArthur wrote directly to the Secretary of War concerning what he described as the Navy's "pride of position and ignorance."[38] In the Army general's opinion, as one who had experienced frontal assaults firsthand in World War I, "these frontal attacks by the Navy, as at Tarawa, are a tragic and unnecessary massacre of American lives."[39] On the home front, angry editorials demanded a congressional inquiry into the "Tarawa fiasco."[40] Tarawa not only cost the Marine Corps manpower, it also became a public relations debacle for the Navy.

As a test case, Tarawa did offer important examples (both positive and negative) on the proper employment of amphibious assault. However, historians who support the reasoning that the lessons learned at Tarawa justified its cost never fully address the fact that the Navy and Marine Corps overemphasized the application of some of those "lessons" at later assaults on Peleliu, Iwo Jima, and Okinawa—to negative effect. The Corps' more immediate success in the Marshall Islands a few months after the Gilberts

THE UNTOLD TRUTH

Campaign had more to do with unprepared and ill-defended islands in the inner Japanese defensive perimeter than with the lessons of Tarawa. In essence, when the Japanese finally made the transition from a fortified beachhead to a static inland defense in 1944, Americans remained fixated on the Tarawa scenario by improving frontal assaults from the sea when the fight was no longer at the shoreline.[41]

One man who would later play a key role in the planning of Iwo Jima, Gen. Holland M. Smith, came away from Tarawa especially resentful. His round face and the soft eyes behind round spectacles belied the general's notorious temper. Smith's fuming reputation had earned him the nickname "Howlin' Mad Smith" by those who worked with him. However, Smith often reserved his most vehement anger for Army and Navy officers, and played the part of a patriarchal figure to his Marines. Smith was one of the most experienced Marine officers in amphibious war. He had had a key role in the evolution of Marine amphibious doctrine from the 1930s onward. He also pushed for the development of Marine amphibious landing craft, specifically the LCVP (landing craft, vehicle and personnel), more commonly called the Higgins boat. The assault of Tarawa served as an excellent test case for amphibious assault, but he never accepted the necessity of the objective. Further, Smith held the Navy responsible for the thousands of casualties incurred during the operation, due to what he believed was inadequate naval bombardment.[42]

Both Guadalcanal and Tarawa revealed an inherent weakness in America's strategic decision-making process in the Pacific. First, the Joint Chiefs of Staff committee system in Washington was too far removed from the operations taking place to efficiently dictate the course of the war. Yet the Joint Chiefs refused to delegate responsibility for Pacific operations to a single commander. Second, the division of U.S. resources due to service interests endangered the success of operations by not concentrating the available assets at the proper time and place. Third, the cost in lives and resources of some operations exceeded the benefits. The attack on Tarawa is a case in point. The Gilbert Islands became of interest to the Navy only when it realized that the resources needed to seize the Marshall Islands would not be readily available. Competition between the Army and Navy fueled the increased pace of their dual drives. Keeping up offensive momentum, no doubt, was an admirable military aim, which Admiral Nimitz preferred, but the Navy had simply failed to appropriately evaluate whether costs justified the strategic gains. Regrettably, the limitations of the Joint Chiefs of Staff committee system would have even larger influence on strategy over the next two years, as U.S. offensives in the Pacific accelerated.

Bonin Islands Planning, 1943–44

The Bonin Islands extend several hundred miles directly south of the main island of Japan (Honshu) and include the islands of Chichi Jima and Iwo Jima. During the planning for war with Japan in the 1920s and 1930s (a series of plans called War Plan Orange), the Bonin Islands received scant notice. After Pearl Harbor, however, the U.S. Navy contemplated the use of an operating base in the Bonins, and the islands received regular re-examination from 1942 onward. Nonetheless, the Navy had little interest in Iwo Jima because of its complete lack of harbors. King's staff produced a study that focused on the seizure of the island of Chichi Jima, which, in the Navy's opinion, offered the best options as a combined fighter base, bomber base, and port facility.[43] With its airfield, excellent harbor, and fresh water, Chichi Jima (meaning "father island") was the cornerstone of the Japanese military garrison in the Bonin Islands. Keeping an eye open for future island campaigns, the Navy recognized the need to evaluate Chichi Jima's usefulness. Yet distracted by more immediate problems in the South Pacific, the Joint Staff Planners did not complete the first detailed war plan to secure the Bonin Islands until October 1943.[44]

After examining the Bonin Islands, the Joint War Plans Committee concluded that "while the Bonins occupy an important strategic position in the Central Pacific area, their potential value as an offensive base is limited."[45] Based on the slender information available at the time, planners considered Chichi Jima and its smaller neighbor Iwo Jima as the best choices for in-

Diagram of Relationships Between JCS Planning Organizations

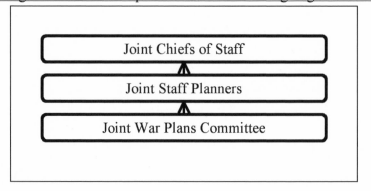

Hierarchy of JCS planning organizations

vasion. U.S. intelligence estimated a Japanese defense force of 3,000 men throughout the entire Bonin chain. The Joint War Plans Committee neatly summed up the study with these words: "the one outstanding advantage to be gained from the execution of these operations lies in the denial of the use of the Bonins to the Japanese . . . this advantage is more apparent than real, since repeated aerial and surface bombardments should cancel the effectiveness of these islands as enemy bases, thus obviating the necessity for their capture."[46] Ominously, the Joint War Plans Committee further predicted that "operations planned herein are likely to entail heavy losses, and to divert forces out of all proportion to the anticipated value of these islands to us."[47] In accordance with the planners' recommendation, the Joint Chiefs of Staff shelved the Bonin Islands plan.

Four months later, in March 1944, the fragmented command in the Pacific underwent yet another division.[48] The Joint Chiefs of Staff agreed that they would exert direct control over "very long-range bombing forces." This was the code name for the enormously expensive and technologically sophisticated B-29 Superfortress. The long-anticipated bomber was just rolling off the assembly lines after years of research and development. Desiring to keep direct control over this resource from Washington, the Joint Chiefs of Staff approved the activation of the Twentieth Air Force. They appointed their own member, Chief of Staff of the Army Air Corps Gen. Henry Arnold, as Commanding General in April.[49]

The newly established Twentieth Air Force opened up an entirely new theater of operation in the Pacific. The Commander-in-Chief of the Southwest Pacific, Gen. Douglas MacArthur, the Commander-in-Chief of Pacific Ocean Areas, Adm. Chester Nimitz, and, now, Army Air Forces Gen. Henry Arnold all competed for manpower and resources as they conducted independent operations against Japan. Even Arnold realized the Joint Chiefs of Staff's failings on the issue of strategy and command. Concerning his appointment as Commanding General of the Twentieth Air Force, he stated that it "was something I did not want to do," and that "there was nothing else I could do, with no unity of command in the Pacific."[50] Rationally, Arnold opposed the Joint Chiefs' division of Pacific resources. But in the contentious environment that already existed, he wanted neither MacArthur nor Nimitz to control the operations of the B-29. What Arnold desperately sought, however, was the establishment of an independent air force. Arnold realized his command in the Pacific could facilitate that ambition, and he eagerly anticipated the fruits of his labor.

Although a minor player in the Joint Chiefs of Staff until 1944, Arnold

Joint Chiefs of Staff Pacific strategy, March 1944

eventually became the dominant decision-maker in the resolution to launch Operation Detachment. His prominence requires some elaboration. Arnold graduated from West Point in 1907 in the middle of his class and made a start as an infantry officer. Ambitious, and seeking accelerated promotions within the limited opportunities of the peacetime service, he volunteered for the fledgling Army flight program in 1911. Trained by the Wright brothers, Arnold was the second Army officer to graduate flight training, a highly regarded status that likely contributed to his maverick image.

Arnold's flight career as a company and field grade officer, specifically in the ranks of lieutenant through major, included some adverse fitness reports—reprimands that shed light on his personality. In 1916 Arnold initiated a search for a downed aircrew against orders from his commanding officer to wait. In response, his superior evaluated him as disloyal, unwilling to cooperate, and a troublemaker.[51] Perhaps this one instance of overzealous behavior, based on honorable intentions, could be overlooked. However, once again in 1918, after numerous attempts to somehow find his way into combat in World War I, Arnold was labeled by his wartime superior as "inferior in judgment and common sense, inclined to be disloyal to his superiors and prone to intrigue for his own advantage."[52]

After World War I, Arnold strongly supported war hero Billy Mitchell's controversial proposals for an independent air force. The Army court-martialed Mitchell for making his opinions public. Subsequently, Arnold surreptitiously forwarded to certain congressmen further information in support of restructuring the Army for the purposes of giving the air component more autonomy.[53] An investigation revealed Arnold's efforts, and the major was reassigned from Washington, receiving yet another adverse fitness report that declared his "judgment and common sense fell below average," and "I should now hesitate to entrust to him any important mission."[54] The positive publicity Arnold received during the controversy may actually have helped him a decade later when the public generally considered both Arnold and Mitchell as martyrs with innovative ideas.

As a senior officer, Arnold demonstrated a polished ability to garner support for himself and his programs. In the early 1930s he commanded March Air Force Base in California and used demonstrations of air power, along with broadcasts on radio stations, to gain public appreciation for his cause.[55] In 1934 Arnold commanded lengthy assessment flights of B-10s to Alaska, receiving good press coverage and personal recognition from the President.[56] Throughout the 1930s, Arnold made several appearances at congressional hearings concerning the state of America's Air Corps, and generally attempted to fill the void left by Billy Mitchell. His visible leadership, effective social skills, and commendable level of operational experience earned Arnold the rank of general and eventually a job back in Washington as Assistant Chief of the Army Air Corps in 1936.

During the next few years, Arnold became well recognized as the foremost spokesman for the Army Air Corps on issues of air power and for an independent air force in the United States. He collaborated in the publication of essays and books that argued the importance of airpower to national defense, and from his new position in Washington, he rubbed elbows with senior government executives and military commanders. America's fascination with flying and technology, as well as the perceived threats from Germany and Japan, encouraged an enlarged role for the Army Air Corps in military defense. However, this situation also caused numerous conflicts between the Army Air Corps and the Army and Navy, whose budgets at the time were meager. The Army Air Corps insisted that the coasts could be effectively defended with air power, and the Navy emphatically denied that the airplane could replace the role of the battleship. Army Air Corps demonstrations that sank naval vessels must have amused General Arnold, but due to the limited funding available, both the Army and Navy stifled increases to the Army Air Corps' role. Air power was effectively harnessed in tactical support of ground and sea action, rather than the theoretical idea of strategic offense against enemy infrastructure, the vision that Arnold strongly espoused.[57]

After the tragic death of the Chief of the Army Air Corps, Gen. Oscar Westover, in 1938, Arnold assumed command of the Army Air Corps and industriously began planning for the war on the horizon. In tandem with the desires of President Roosevelt, he planned and supervised a massive build-up of American air power, unparalleled in aviation history. Throughout the prewar years, Arnold devoted his time and efforts entirely to air matters with little regard for land or naval topics, about which he had little knowledge or concern.[58] By the time the United States entered the war in 1941, the Army Air Forces had finally switched emphasis to strategic bombing through the platform of the B-17 Flying Fortress. As a member of the Joint Chiefs of Staff, Arnold sought to improve B-17 performance to meet the expectations prophesied for decades—the ability to destroy the enemy's capacity to wage war from long distances with high-altitude precision bombing.

Until the production of the B-29 Superfortress, Arnold primarily concerned himself with aircraft production and the destruction of German infrastructure through the strategic air campaign in Europe. The Joint Chiefs of Staff parceled out the air assets sent to the Pacific to either Admiral Nimitz or General MacArthur, leaving Arnold almost no say in their employment. However, he did offer opinions concerning the management of the Pacific war, stating that it "becomes more and more apparent that until there is one command, one plan, one thinking head, we will continuously misuse and hold idle our Air Force and our Army . . . No area in [the] Pacific can operate against Japs without it having a direct effect upon all other areas."[59] Although acknowledging the failures of dual command in the Pacific, Arnold refused to allow the Army Air Forces to be subordinated to the Navy, especially since it already struggled for parity within the Army.

In 1944, in anticipation of bomber bases in the Marianas, the Joint Chiefs of Staff created Arnold's new air command, the Twentieth Air Force.[60] Once the Navy seized the Marianas, Arnold could finally fulfill his dream of demonstrating effective strategic air power with the greatest bomber yet devised, relatively free of Army and Navy obstructions. The Navy's decision to seize island bases that the Army Air Forces could operate from signaled greater cooperation between these two organizations in the Pacific. Indeed, it shifted the dynamics of the two Army officers versus two Navy officers in the Joint Chiefs of Staff.[61] Arnold became dependent on the Navy to seize islands for his airfields and to ship the ordnance he needed for bombing operations. Once a spectator on Pacific operations, Arnold became an active player, and ironically, his most valuable teammate was his rival Admiral King.

Arnold designated the main arm of the Twentieth Air Force the Twenty-First Bomber Command—its weapon the B-29. Arnold had finally won autonomy, but he greatly feared losing control. In the highly competitive atmosphere of the Pacific, Arnold needed to clearly demonstrate the value of strategic bombing in a hurry. When informed in the summer of 1944 of the independent Twenty-First Bomber Command, Admiral Nimitz had "strong disagreements" and believed that he should control B-29s stationed in his theater.[62] Arnold's fear of losing autonomous control of his Superfortresses lasted until the end of the war. An entry in his diary in April 1945 stated that "MacArthur and Nimitz both want the Twentieth Air Force."[63] Admiral Nimitz continued his objections over the improper use of the Army Air Forces in the Pacific.[64] For Arnold, maintaining control of the B-29 Superfortress was essential. According to one historian, Arnold's "main goal was to make the largest possible contribution to winning the war and ensure that the AAF received credit for it through proper publicity."[65] If so, the B-29 presented him with his best opportunity to make that ambition a reality. Because of the huge expense of the Superfortress, which had cost billions of dollars to develop, Arnold needed to demonstrate its value quickly and decisively.

The Superfortress represented over twenty years of work in the development of strategic air power that had begun after World War I. Theoretical planning for the B-29 Superfortress began in 1939, and by early 1944 the aircraft was in full production. This marvel of industrial technology exceeded the capabilities of any bomber produced before it. The largest combat plane in the world, it was fitted with four rotary engines that could carry a gross weight of up to 140,000 pounds.[66] On a single tank of gas, the plane could drop full payloads at distances over 3,000 miles round trip. For defensive purposes, the Army Air Forces incorporated twelve .50 caliber machine guns and one 20-mm cannon.[67] Communication systems and bombing sights surpassed any existing system. Additionally, a pressurized and heated cabin allowed crewmen to fly long distances in relative comfort at high altitudes without the need for oxygen masks or heavy suits.

As the Navy finalized its plans for seizing the Marianas Islands, the Twenty-First Bomber Command set its sights on a location to launch fighter escorts for Marianas-based B-29s in an area called the Nanpo Shoto (a series of islands between Saipan and Japan). Fighter escorts had proved pivotal in bomber operations in the European theater, and the Army Air Forces searched for a way to provide them in the Pacific, too. Given increased interest in the Nanpo Shoto, the Navy launched a photoreconnaissance mission over the Bonin Islands.[68] Carrier planes obtained photos of the islands on various days from mid- to late June 1944.

This photographic evidence indicated that the Japanese had not yet fortified Iwo Jima to any great extent. The island's traditional Japanese beach defense consisted of trench fortifications around the outer edge of the island, especially the beaches accessible for amphibious landing. A Japanese officer described the state of the defenses: "The fact that Iwo Jima was not invaded in the summer of 1944 surprised us all. The island was barely able to defend itself! A fraction of the force which took Saipan could have stormed Iwo's beaches and crushed the token resistance which our skeleton forces then on the island could have mustered . . . Yet no invasion came. We considered this turn of events nothing less than a miracle."[69] Unknown to this Japanese officer, contemplating his fate on a miserable island of rock, the United States had not yet determined that the seizure of the Bonin Islands necessary and was currently focused on the task of seizing the Marianas Islands.

As General Arnold waited anxiously for his B-29 bomber bases, Central Pacific forces assaulted the Marianas Islands in mid-June 1944. In support of the landings, Admiral Spruance effectively neutralized Japanese land-based air forces in the Central Pacific with extensive carrier air attacks. These included strikes against the airfields of Chichi Jima and Iwo Jima on 15 and 16 June. Chichi Jima, which had remained the foremost option for a Bonin Islands invasion from 1942 through early 1944, continued to entice the Navy.[70] King's staff devised a plan to seize the island, code named Operation Farragut, that same month.[71]

Without the use of land-based aircraft, the Japanese Navy attacked the Pacific Fleet virtually on its own with little support from its army air forces. The collision of the Japanese and U.S. navies resulted in the largest carrier battle in history at the Philippine Sea on 19 and 20 June. The Americans effectively used radar to anticipate the Japanese attack, and lying in wait, veteran U.S. aviators swarmed down on the mostly inexperienced Japanese pilots. According to the returning U.S. pilots, shooting down Japanese planes was as easy as shooting turkeys. Historians have since dubbed this one-sided victory the Marianas Turkey Shoot. As U.S. Navy submarines finished off a number of Japanese carriers, Army and Marine Corps ground forces continued the seizure of Saipan, Tinian, and Guam. In connection with occupation of the Marianas Islands, Spruance initiated another series of raids against the Bonin Islands. The carriers *Hornet, Yorktown, Bataan,* and *Belleau Wood* launched aerial assaults on the airfields of Iwo Jima on 25 June.[72]

As Spruance carried out the invasion of Saipan, one of the planning teams from the Joint War Plans Committee in Washington proposed the immediate seizure of Iwo Jima for use as a bomber base for B-24 Liberators.[73] Taking advantage of the depleted Japanese carrier strength as a result of the victory at Philippine Sea, planners proposed "the immediate occupation of Iwo Jima with the forces set up for occupation of Guam."[74] Essentially, the planning team wanted to swap Guam for Iwo Jima, and follow up on the U.S. protectorate later. After an invasion by one reinforced Marine division, the planning team proposed stationing two fighter groups and two bomber groups on the island. The Joint War Plans Committee correctly considered the island and its 5,000 defenders poorly organized, as the Navy would later surmise: "At the time Saipan was invaded, only AA [antiaircraft] defenses, hasty fire trenches, and preliminary beach defenses had been prepared at Iwo Jima."[75] Nevertheless, the leadership of the Joint War Plans Committee, a joint secretariat made up of one Army and one Navy officer, disagreed with the proposal. They reasoned that the logistics involved in maintaining a bomber base on Iwo Jima would pose great difficulties. Even the team that proposed the invasion stated, "Iwo Jima is, due to total lack of harbors, a difficult place to supply." More important, the change in operations would throw months of planning out of sequence. The joint secretariat stated it was "improbable that plans and current operations could be altered in time to take advantage of it." [76] The Army Air Forces continued to support the idea of seizing Iwo Jima for use as an airbase of some sort, while the Army and Navy continued to hedge on the idea.

While the Marine Corps and the Army undertook the task of seizing the Marianas, the Army Air Forces turned to the problem of providing fighter escort. In distant Washington, D.C., on 29 June, Twentieth Air Force Headquarters ordered a study of the feasibility of providing B-29 fighter escort from Iwo Jima.[77] The most urgent question the report needed to answer was whether a U.S. fighter could successfully operate against mainland Japan. B-29 targets on the main island of Honshu were roughly 750 miles away from Iwo Jima, so flying there and back could require a range of 1,500 miles round trip. Based on the current capabilities, the distance was generally considered too far to provide effective fighter support.

Even the latest prototype and proposed fighter for basing on Iwo Jima, the P-51D "Mustang," had a range of 1,000 miles. In theory, the exterior fuel tanks provided the P-51D with a reach of up to 2,000 miles, but in actuality the maximum range of the P-51 varied according to the speed of travel and wind velocity encountered, not to mention the fuel expenditure needed for dog-fighting over Japan. The ostensible purpose of the Twentieth Air Force's inquiry was to look into the "feasibility" of using airfields on Iwo Jima, but the tone of the directive ensured that the Army Air Forces' suggested fighter escort would be seen as practical. This is shown, for example, by the deadline, which was set less than six hours after the study was ordered. The same afternoon of 29 June, the Army Air Forces decided that fighter planes could indeed fly the lengthy distance to mainland Japan. Little concern was expressed for the P-51's mediocre navigation equipment, which consisted only of compass, air speed indicator, and a map. There was no mention of the notoriously high winds often encountered at higher elevations over Japan. Accordingly, the Twentieth Air Force prepared a paper for the Joint Chiefs of Staff on its desire to seize Iwo Jima for use as a fighter base.[78]

As the Army and Marine Corps cleaned up resistance in the Mariana Islands, Spruance conducted a massive air raid and photoreconnaissance mission over the Bonin Islands from 30 June through 5 July. Of all the Bonin Islands, the Navy had by now decided to focus on Chichi Jima and Iwo Jima. Both were considered the most common staging areas for Japanese airplanes.[79] From 30 June through 9 August, the carriers *Hornet, Yorktown, Franklin, Bataan, Cabot,* and *Santa Fe* strafed the airfields on both islands with over a hundred planes.[80] On 4 July the cruisers *Mobile* and *Denver,* along with the destroyers

Brown and *Cowell*, celebrated Independence Day by bombarding the airfields on Iwo Jima with 5-inch and 6-inch shells.[81] The combined damage of the aerial and surface bombardment damaged or destroyed dozens of aircraft as well as ammunition dumps, gasoline storage facilities, and buildings. The Carrier Task Force concluded that Iwo Jima would provide a good base for American planes and that the Japanese defenses there were severely lacking.

Although Admiral Spruance was being swayed by Army Air Forces arguments to seize Iwo Jima, King's staff in Washington remained unconvinced. As the Central Pacific drive neared Honshu, the Bonin Islands received more scrutiny. In late June and early July the Joint Chiefs of Staff considered islands in the Nanpo Shoto as possible options for future seizure.[82] As they had in 1943, the Joint Staff Planners still regarded the Bonin Islands as being of limited use to U.S. offensive strategy. However, should the Joint Chiefs of Staff decide to move forward there, the island they found most useful to U.S. war aims was Chichi Jima. In addition to the lucrative port facility, the Joint Staff Planners stated, "fighters based in Chichi Jima can provide escort over Tokyo." They acknowledged that six islands in the Bonins could sustain airfields: Haha Jima, Chichi Jima, Iwo Jima, O Shima, Hachijo Jima, and Nii Jima. Contrary to the recommendations of the Twentieth Air Force, the Joint Staff Planners did not believe fighters could use Iwo Jima for B-29 escort. They specifically stated that the "distance to Tokyo for present fighters is too great."[83]

In response to the renewed interest in the Bonins, U.S. intelligence released a report on the islands' defenses. The Joint Intelligence Committee estimated that the Japanese had stationed no more than 35,000 troops on all five islands and that the defenders on Iwo Jima numbered 10,000 or less. Intelligence incorrectly alleged that Iwo Jima could not sustain a larger garrison force (a determination likely made due to the island's lack of fresh water). Although minor fortifications currently existed, intelligence predicted that the islands would be "rapidly strengthened and augmented" over the next several months, an ominous prediction of events to come.[84]

Collision's Progeny, 1944–45

With three theater commands in the Pacific, the United States launched operations against Japan from three directions on a collision course north of the Philippines. The Joint War Plans Committee and Joint Staff Planners began to revise Pacific strategy in the summer of 1944 in an effort to hasten Japan's defeat.[85] There was a shortened amount of time between the proposals of theater commanders, the decisions made by the Joint Chiefs of Staff, and the implementation of those assigned missions. Unfortunately, decisions began to be made with less planning, preparation, and coordination. Rapid operations against Japan kept the enemy off balance, but the accelerated process also made hasty decisions possible.

Operating from India and China, the B-29 had fallen far short of performance expectations. The Commanding General of the Twentieth Bombing Command, Gen. Curtis LeMay, wrote to Arnold in July that he was "having a great deal of difficulty with repair and maintenance." Some of his equipment would not stand up to prolonged operations over twenty-four hours. LeMay was well aware that the performance of strategic bombing against Japan "affects the entire B-29 program" for which Arnold needed to demonstrate results.[86]

Arnold made no attempt to disguise his agenda to use the B-29 to facilitate service independence. He wrote to General LeMay that "the B-29 project is important to me because I am convinced that it is vital to the future of the Army Air Forces."[87] General Arnold feared his assets would be parceled out to Nimitz or MacArthur for tactical support if he did not make successful strategic bombing runs on Japan by the close of 1944.[88] During the summer of 1944 Arnold's staff in Washington debated B-29 maintenance problems, bombing accuracy reports, and the need for fighter escort in the Marianas—all concurrently.[89] Arnold began to consolidate his B-29s from the Twentieth Bomber Command in India into the Twenty-First Bomber Command in the Marianas Islands during the fall of 1944. Before a single Marianas-based mission had been launched, the Twentieth Air Force wanted to ensure its future success by securing an intermediate air base for fighters. For that reason, the Army Air Forces had pushed hard for the inclusion of an attack on the Bonins in future operations. Arnold set his sights on Iwo Jima, which he claimed could provide fighter escorts for B-29s as well as a staging area for B-24 Liberators.[90]

U.S. Navy carriers continued to raid the Bonin Islands, hitting Iwo Jima twice and Chichi Jima three times on 4 August.[91] Appeasing Army Air Forces requests, the Joint War Plans Committee completed a plan to seize Iwo Jima on 12 August. General Arnold personally intervened in the planning process to reverse some of the planners' previous conclusions, which they had stated just one month earlier. Arnold wrote a memorandum on 14 July arguing the usefulness of Iwo Jima as a fighter base. Despite such serious pressure, the Joint War Plans Committee still hesitated to endorse the feasibility of using Iwo Jima for such purposes. The committee referenced

Arnold rather than taking responsibility for the idea. Specifically, they stated, "The feasibility of such escort missions has been determined by the Commanding General, 20th Air Force." The committee went so far as to insert a quote from Arnold, in which he squelched doubts concerning the lengthy distance between Iwo Jima and Japan. Arnold maintained that P-51s could cover the entire distance and have an additional twenty minutes of fighting ability before returning to Iwo Jima. [92] Using the latest intelligence, planners predicted that an amphibious force could capture the island in just five days with one reinforced division. Due to the island's soft and flat terrain (or so they thought), the planners claimed the Army Air Forces could easily soften the defenses on Iwo Jima through aerial bombardment.

The Army Air Forces was now fixated on Iwo Jima, but the U.S. Navy remained unconvinced that it should be the target of a future Bonins operation. The Navy conducted a study on seizing an advanced base in the Bonin Islands and concluded that only Chichi Jima and Haha Jima offered "sufficient size and import to warrant consideration for advance base development."[93] The Pacific Fleet launched yet another raid on Chichi Jima on 2 September.[94] Two cruisers and four destroyers approached from the northwest and bombarded the airfield and radar facilities.

While Army Air Forces' plans to secure Iwo Jima gained momentum, MacArthur stepped up his timetable to secure the Philippines. The Joint Chiefs of Staff approved Adm. William "Bull" Halsey's recommendation to bypass the previous objectives of Mindanao and the Palau Islands. Such a proposal enabled MacArthur to rapidly catch up with Admiral Nimitz in the Central Pacific by seizing Leyte Island in the central Philippines. However, the pace of operations now outstripped the Joint Chiefs of Staff's ability to make careful decisions, as shown by the almost forgotten battle for Peleliu that took place in September 1944.

Although he agreed with bypassing Mindanao, Nimitz insisted that the Navy still secure the Palau Islands before MacArthur's invasion of the Leyte. Nimitz did so even though the plan to seize the Palau Islands had been approved based on the support the island's airstrip could provide to the Mindanao invasion—and the Mindanao invasion had now been scrapped. Due to the dated strategic considerations examined months earlier, as well as the tremendous amount of time and resources that had already been invested, Nimitz could not bring himself to cancel the Palau operation so close to its execution. In his own words, he did not believe it "feasible" to reorient the plans for the employment of forces.[95] Reinforcing Nimitz's judgment, the commander of the Marine forces, Gen. William Rupertus, confidently predicted that he could subdue Peleliu in two or three days. Rupertus believed it would be a quickie, rough but fast. Yet, tragically, not only did the assault on Peleliu Island take sixty-eight days longer than expected, but the cost of the battle (1,529 dead and 6,282 wounded) greatly exceeded the island's value to subsequent operations.

Since the Japanese had little offensive capability in the form of naval or air power by late 1944, Peleliu posed little threat to the United States. Additionally, Peleliu's distant airfield had little relevance to subsequent operations, and it could easily have been bypassed. In the words of one historian, "the war in the Pacific moved on too quickly; enemy [strategic] capabilities were far less than assumed; Peleliu became a backwater almost before it was invaded." Historian Ronald Spector stated that the island had only marginal strategic significance and that "Nimitz would have done well to cancel the Palau operation along with all the others." Historian Russell Weigley put it more bluntly: "Proceeding with the Peleliu invasion was probably a mistake."[96]

As the Army and Navy advanced northward in the Pacific and neared the boundary dividing their two main theaters of operation, the service rivalry concerning who would dominate a single and unified command from that point onward caused controversy and delay in Washington. The Pacific Fleet had nearly completed the seizure of the Marianas and still had no approved plan from the Joint Chiefs of Staff for subsequent operations. Based on disagreement over who would command, Admiral King and General Marshall continued to debate the timetable for the planned invasion of Formosa. King wanted Nimitz to command the combined Army and Navy forces required for the operation—the largest amphibious invasion of the war. Further, King continued to debate the merits of retaking the Philippines. He insisted it would only delay the Pacific Fleet's seizure of Formosa. Instead, King wanted to bypass Manila. In contrast, Marshall wanted to delay the Formosa operation until after the invasion of the Philippines. Following the recapture of the Luzon, Marshall believed MacArthur should command the invasion of Formosa. Neither Marshall nor King would budge on their choice of the Formosa commander, and the direction of future operations remained in flux.

With his Pacific Fleet standing by, Nimitz exhibited increasing frustration over Washington's delay of his advance. He wrote to King in late August that the lack of direction on future operations was "proving to be a serious handicap to sound decisions on current problems." Nimitz requested immediate approval of the Formosa operation. He stated, "In order that the pressure and momentum of our operations in the Pacific may be maintained I urge that a directive be issued now."[97] At an impasse, the Joint Chiefs of

Staff responded by telling Nimitz and MacArthur to plan for both Formosa and the Philippines simultaneously—a nearly impossible task.[98] Once again, the Joint Chiefs of Staff asked Nimitz and MacArthur to solve problems created by the JCS's inability to rectify service interests.

In an attempt to break the deadlock, King proposed leaving the Army out of the Formosa invasion altogether. He suggested that with all six Marine divisions, the Navy could seize the southern portion of the island without the Army. He requested only two Army divisions as follow-on forces for garrison troops.[99] Proposing that the large and heavily defended island of Formosa could be seized with a mere six divisions indicated the dangerous risks King willingly accepted in order to circumvent Army influence over the Navy's advance northward. Essentially, as he had done previously at Guadalcanal in 1942, King proposed another "Operation Shoestring."

With Washington's delay inhibiting the momentum of his Pacific Fleet, Admiral Nimitz decided to offer an alternative strategy himself. In early September he asked his senior admirals for advice. Resourcefully, Admiral Spruance told Nimitz that he disagreed with King's plan to seize Formosa. Gen. Millard Harmon, Commanding General of the Army Air Forces, Pacific Ocean Areas, had been advocating a move into Bonin and Ryukyu Islands.[100] Spruance said he preferred this idea of "taking Iwo Jima and Okinawa instead."[101] Frustrated by delays in Washington, Nimitz continued planning his Pacific Fleet's advance. He suggested to King that Iwo Jima might be seized one month later, in October.[102] This option, however, did not receive enough attention or support to carry out, and Nimitz continued to wait for a plan of advance.

As the arduous battle for Peleliu raged on through September 1944, the debate over who would command future operations in the Pacific reached a crescendo. The Joint Chiefs had given MacArthur the option of seizing either Formosa or Luzon, and this did not satisfy Admiral King. General MacArthur certainly favored the capture of Luzon over Formosa. Meanwhile, Admiral Nimitz's competing drive toward Japan remained at a standstill.[103] Therefore, King urged the capture of both Luzon and Formosa simultaneously. In contrast, General Marshall believed the Joint Chiefs should wait until MacArthur secured Luzon. Afterward, MacArthur could command the Formosa operation as well.[104]

With the Pacific Fleet waiting in the Marianas Islands and the Army making ready to seize the Philippines, the dual drives in the Pacific had finally collided. It appeared that only one commander could assume overall control of a single advance from this point onward. A Nimitz-led operation against

Formosa, using the combination of the entire Pacific Fleet and a large number of Army divisions, would likely have assured his command over future joint operations toward Japan, an idea strengthened by MacArthur having reached the northern boundary of his theater. However, the huge island of Formosa called for extensive ground operations, and the Army wanted control over the task of seizing it.

Time was running short, and tensions began to mount between Marshall and King. With the decision for supreme commander at a critical juncture, General Marshall requested that the Joint Chiefs of Staff issue a new directive. Since present directives covered only the operations scheduled for MacArthur's invasion of Leyte, Marshall pointed out that "there is an obvious need for early issuance of a directive for future operations in the Pacific." He went on to clarify the central issue that had caused months of delay in Washington: "As we reach the Formosa-Luzon area, we begin a period of major land campaigns, and the combat zones of the two theaters are fused." He stated that "in order to assure the maximum effective use of the limited Army resources we have, the best thing to do is to make them all available to one commander, and give him a specific directive with the responsibility for getting done the tasks required." In order to make maximum use of the joint Navy and Army operations, he demanded that all ground forces, logistics, and cargo shipping in the Pacific be consolidated under MacArthur immediately. Furthermore, he called on the Joint Chiefs to grant MacArthur control of both the Luzon and Formosa operations.[105]

Admiral King responded to General Marshall's proposition with a fiery rebuttal that took direct affront at Marshall's proposal. In his opinion, the Navy should command Pacific operations from that time forward. Specifically, this included the Formosa operation, the establishment of bases on the China coast, *and* the invasion of Japan. All these operations would take place in Nimitz's theater, and King had no intention of dividing command responsibilities there. He made clear that no proposed action could go forward without substantial naval forces, which made those operations inherently amphibious. King argued for Admiral Nimitz to command the consolidated forces of the Army and Navy in future Pacific operations.[106]

The Joint Chiefs of Staff had arrived at a turning point. There appeared little other option but to finally choose between MacArthur and Nimitz. However, the Army and Navy had not reached a consensus. Far from it: over the preceding two years the command structure fractured into three separate theaters of operation. The Joint Chiefs could not set aside self-interest, and neither King nor Marshall would support the other's choice. If the

Joint Chiefs wanted to decide the future direction of the 1945 offensive, the window of opportunity was quickly closing. Due to debate over command, planning remained gridlocked through the month of September under a thick cloud of tension.

With the Joint Chiefs of Staff at an impasse, Nimitz continued to pressure King with another choice, an option that would break the deadlock in Washington and preserve the Navy's leading role in the drive toward Japan. Rather than sending more communiqués, he arranged to meet King face to face. On 29 September an outnumbered King met with Admirals Nimitz, Spruance, and Forrest Sherman (Nimitz's Deputy Chief of Staff) in San Francisco.[107] Nimitz recommended that the Navy bypass Formosa and seize Okinawa instead. A switch from Formosa to Okinawa disregarded years of planning to establish a link with America's Chinese allies on the Asian coast. However, Okinawa still achieved many similar objectives to Formosa by further blockading sea routes to Japan and providing a staging area for the invasion of Kyushu and Honshu. The most important factor in breaking the Washington deadlock, however, was the admirals' belief that the invasion of Okinawa would not require large support from the Army, which allowed Admiral Nimitz to retain command over the operation.

Meanwhile, the Army Air Forces had been recommending the capture of Iwo Jima. While the Navy prepared to seize Okinawa, it could quickly secure Iwo Jima for the Army Air Forces. The combination of the two objectives ensured that Gen. Henry Arnold would support the change in strategy. King, however, questioned the necessity of taking Iwo Jima, which he regarded as a liability. Specifically, King described the island as a "sink hole in the hands of whoever held it."[108] Sherman responded that the Army Air Forces wanted the island's airstrips in order to provide fighter escort for B-29s.[109] Spruance, who had originally suggested Iwo Jima to Nimitz one month earlier, was unusually sheepish during the meeting—his silence perhaps indicative that he was not quite comfortable being responsible for the Iwo Jima decision. Since all those present respected his opinion, Nimitz prodded Spruance to speak up—at which point he simply told King that he agreed with Nimitz and Sherman. With their combined influence, the three admirals finally convinced the reluctant King to endorse the two new objectives.[110]

On October 2 King recommended to the Joint Chiefs of Staff that the Navy capture Okinawa. The proposed Okinawa operation envisioned the use of all six Marine divisions and one Army division. One month before Okinawa, Nimitz would quickly occupy Iwo Jima for the sole stated purpose of providing "fighter air support for B-29s operating from the Marianas."[111]

Since King proposed that Nimitz could use three of the same Marine divisions against Okinawa just forty days after the landings on Iwo Jima, he obviously did not believe Operation Detachment would cause significant losses.[112] In actuality, the epic contest on Iwo Jima would make it impossible for the same three divisions to fight on Okinawa.

Leahy endorsed King's proposal to seize Okinawa, and the addition of Iwo Jima ensured Arnold's endorsement. Essentially, the combined objectives provided enough benefits to the majority of the Joint Chiefs of Staff to ensure approval. King's proposal also postponed, once again, the need to decide on a supreme Pacific commander for larger operations planned to invade the Japanese main islands. Since the other members of the Joint Chiefs approved, Marshall could find little reason to oppose the plan. He typically agreed with a proposition if both Arnold and King supported it.[113] The Joint Chiefs of Staff accepted King's proposal the next day.[114]

Five days later, on 7 October 1944, Nimitz issued a directive to the Pacific Fleet to seize Iwo Jima. The plan made clear that an attack in the Bonin Islands directly supported Army Air Forces' operations in the Marianas. It stated only one reason for the necessity of Operation Detachment: "long range bombers should be provided with fighter support at the earliest practicable time" and Iwo Jima "is admirably situated as a fighter base for supporting long range bombers."[115] Notably, King and Nimitz emphasized the need to seize Iwo Jima for the sole purpose of providing fighter escort. Yet later, when the huge death toll had been counted and when fighter operations proved infeasible, both men would use entirely different reasons to justify the operation.[116]

In late October, when the Navy finally attained up-to-date photoreconnaissance of the island, the photos stunned their audience. The Japanese had been busy constructing elaborate defensive positions since June. The extent of the fortifications surprised both Nimitz and Spruance. At the time the two admirals proposed Iwo Jima to King, neither one believed the operation would be difficult.[117] After viewing the photos, however, Marine Gen. Holland M. Smith told Spruance that the island would cost an enormous number of lives and that he could see no purpose in taking it.[118] Smith's comments had a profound impact on Spruance, who later stated that "this left certain doubts in my head as to whether Iwo Jima would be worth what it cost us."[119] In the words of his biographer, Spruance "began to doubt whether the costs of taking the island would be worth the gains, and the uncertainty troubled him throughout the three-month planning period from October through December."[120]

THE UNTOLD TRUTH

In hindsight, June photoreconnaissance should have been updated before the Joint Chiefs of Staff decided on Iwo Jima in October.[121] It might also have been prudent to obtain the opinion of the Marine Corps before authorizing the operation. It appears that neither action was taken. Unfortunately, the time for debate was over. The Navy called on the Marine Corps to carry out the assigned mission, while its commanders had no input into the choice of objectives. The Joint Chiefs of Staff ignored doubts expressed by planners since 1943 regarding the necessity of capturing the island. They also overlooked reservations concerning the distances U.S. fighters would need to fly between Iwo Jima and Japan. The urgency of the Army Air Forces to improve the poor performance of B-29 strategic bombing had prevailed.

As the paths of Nimitz, MacArthur, and Arnold converged, the conflicting service interests produced a hurried decision. American decision-makers had not adequately accounted for Japanese agency. Admirals Spruance, Nimitz, and King made the decision based on outdated photographs, but the determination also derived from overconfidence in America's technological and military superiority without regard for Japanese opposition.[122] The Americans had not anticipated that a shrewd and calculating soldier, Tadamichi Kuribayashi, had rapidly turned the object of U.S. strategic compromise into one of the strongest island fortresses designed in modern warfare.

War is one endless train of personal tragedies and squan-
dered human talent, to say nothing of the human suffering.
This is the sort of reality of war which I think so very many
military historians don't understand in the least. The many
I have met (except those rare cases of men who have been
in fierce combat) rarely seem to realize that war is a human
tragedy and not some great complex adventure for them to
analyze.

EUGENE SLEDGE, *22 October 1993*

No one who was at Iwo can analyze the battle objectively.
The carnage was so horrifying that the blood and agony of
the struggle saturated one's mind, dismally coloring all
thought. Iwo was unlike any war I had ever seen. It was a
fight to the finish with no man asking for quarter until he
was dead . . . There is such a thing as dying decently, but not
on Iwo . . . Veterans of two and three years of war in the Pa-
cific were sickened.

EDGAR L. JONES, *April 1945*

CHAPTER 3   *Struggle for Sulfur Island*

T he winter days of 1945 were cold on the lonely isle. Life for the
residents on the rock could generally be described as a combination
of methodical discomfort, stark discipline, and endless duty. Before
the sun rose, the island bustled with activity. In a small underground shelter,
the island's guardian rose from his sleep. Under the constant threat of naval
and aerial bombardment, he declined to remove his uniform at night.[1]

Most days, the defense leader's routine was predictable. An orderly brought
in a cup of water, and the general would wash the dust from his eyes.[2] Hot

sulfur springs on the island gave up brackish water that proved too foul for human use. Since no wells existed on the island, fresh water could be obtained only from rainfall, which the garrison collected in large cement cisterns placed underground to protect them from aerial bombardment. These also remained locked so that officers could ensure proper distribution of the water they contained. The island's two airfields were also constructed in such a way as to allow rain water to drain off the runways into reservoirs.[3] Water remained an extremely precious commodity, and in the absence of a shower or bath, the general's single luxurious act of cleaning his face may have been the most agreeable portion of his day. As the old soldier performed a few exercises, the orderly quietly removed the basin. A junior officer, followed by the orderly, conserved water supplies by reusing the same basin to wash. Whatever remained of the water, the orderly returned in a small can for the general's hygiene.[4]

After breakfast, the general straightened his uniform and began a routine tour of the island's defenses.[5] Many of the troops he inspected were excavating fortifications by hand into the belly of a volcano. The volcano was inactive, but at least twenty major vents and fissures on the island emitted steam and sulfurous vapor.[6] The nature of the assignment forced the men to wear gas masks while they worked, to protect themselves from sulfur fumes.[7] The underground toil was sweltering. The men did most of the work with picks and shovels, while hundreds more stood in line to hand-relay buckets of mud and sand.[8] When men rested topside between excavations, they were consumed by an army of insects that thrived around the countless hot sulfur springs.[9] Despite the apparent dreariness of their situation, the men worked at a steady pace. Perhaps their motivation derived less from a sense of responsibility than from an awareness of the impending conflict. The soldiers had their own song to keep them focused:[10]

In the lonely mid-Pacific,
Our sweat a fortress will prepare.
If the enemy attack us
Let him come, we will not care.
Until the hated Anglo-Saxons
Lie before us in the dust
Officers and men together
Work and struggle, strive and trust.

After he inspected the busy troops, the island's general held staff meetings in the afternoons. He might then inspect the mortar, rocket, and artillery positions, or supervise unit maneuvers. American bombers from the islands to the south sometimes interrupted his schedule with torrents of exploding bombs. When the attackers winged away, the undeterred Japanese emerged from their catacombs and continued preparations. In the evenings, the general wrote letters to his family or composed poetry.[11] One of his favorites became a smash hit in Japan:

> For many a month since we left the homeland
> We have marched across mountains and rivers
> With this beloved horse with whom I share life and death
> The horse and I are comrades blooded through the rein.[12]

He wrote to his wife that most of his officers and men had come down with sickness and disease on this miserable isle.[13] On any given day, about one-fifth of his defense force suffered from illnesses such as malnutrition or paratyphus.[14] Fortunately for him, the commandant remained in excellent health. Tadamichi Kuribayashi needed all his vigor to transform Sulfur Island into a virtually impenetrable deathtrap.

Face of the Enemy

Americans faced the most dangerous of opponents in Gen. Tadamichi Kuribayashi. Commissioned from the Military Academy in 1914, he graduated at the top of his Army Cavalry School class in 1916 and second from Staff College in 1920.[15] His later assignments provided more extensive training. From 1928 through 1930 he served as a military attaché in Washington D.C. While in America, he also trained with the U.S. Army.[16] He genuinely liked America and its people and held serious reservations about war with the United States. He told his wife that it was "the last country in the world that Japan may fight. Its industrial potentiality is huge and fabulous, and people energetic and versatile. One must never underestimate the American's fighting ability."[17] Kuribayashi went on to serve as military attaché in Canada for the next three years. His six years abroad in North America gave him a solid understanding of how Western nations conducted war.[18]

After 1937, during the war with China, Kuribayashi held numerous command and staff positions with the Japanese Army in Manchuria. He commanded a cavalry regiment during the "China Incident" of 1937, and was Chief of Staff of 26th Army Corps in South China from 1941 to 1943. The fighting in China and Indochina unleashed vicious destruction against military personnel and civilian alike. Notably, Kuribayashi provided prominent leadership in both these horrific arenas where Japanese brutality was the norm. Nevertheless, the distinction of the general's combat performance landed him the prestigious position of Commanding General of the emperor's Tokyo Division in 1943, placing him in command of the most elite Japanese forces. Without a doubt, Kuribayashi represented the highest caliber of leadership in the Japanese Army.

When U.S. forces seized the Marianas in the summer of 1944, Japanese intelligence became concerned that Americans would assault the Bonin Islands in the future.[19] The Japanese high command decided to send one of its finest officers to halt the enemy's advance. In late June 1944 the Japanese high command ordered the fifty-three-year-old Kuribayashi to Chichi Jima to head the newly organized 109th Infantry Division. The emperor himself cajoled him by saying "Only you among all generals is qualified and capable of holding this post. The entire Army and nation will depend on you."[20]

The U.S. decision to attack the Bonin Islands came as no surprise to Kuribayashi. Yet when initially assigned to defend the region, he believed he needed only to hold it long enough for the Japanese Navy to arrive. Kuribayashi had believed false Tokyo propaganda about recent victories at sea. Not until one of his subordinates, Maj. Yoshitaka Horie, who ran the radio transmitting facility on Chichi Jima, made him aware of the many Japanese naval defeats did the general truly understand the gravity of his situation. The realization that the Japanese Navy no longer had any real offensive power came as a great shock, and Kuribayashi's face grew pale at the news. Afterward, his letters home incorporated a resignation to a doomed fate, and he often gave his wife instructions on what to do upon his death.[21]

By August 1944 Kuribayashi became convinced that the Americans would attempt to seize Iwo Jima rather than Chichi Jima, the island the United States believed he would spend a good portion of his strength defending.[22] Kuribayashi's calculated predictions about future U.S. strategy predated by two months (August–September) America's own decision to initiate Operation Detachment and by six months (August–January) the Japanese high command's recognition of the upcoming invasion.[23] As time went on, the hundreds of American B-24 Liberator sorties sent from the Marianas Islands to bombard Iwo Jima's airfields certainly reinforced the correctness of his foresight.

Kuribayashi knew that with little air or sea support from home, he and his men would have to face alone the full power and technological might of the U.S. forces. He harbored little hope of surviving such a battle.[24] In characteristic fashion of a Japanese military culture entrenched in an ancient code of *bushido* ("way of the warrior"), Kuribayashi responded to the difficult situation with determination. The general denied his men the diversion of imported sex-slaves, evacuated Iwo Jima's civilian population to the mainland, and tore down existing buildings to reuse the materials for defense construction.[25] Kuribayashi planned to obstruct the American advance using every means at his disposal. If he lacked the offensive firepower to destroy the enemy, then he would exact the highest possible cost from his assailants.

Kuribayashi had assembled the majority of his 109th Division by September 1944.[26] His defense force was a diverse assortment of military units. His best force was the 145th Infantry Regiment, made up of recruits from the southern Japanese island of Kyushu, which, historically, had a strong military tradition. Like much of his force, the 145th had been diverted to Iwo Jima after the fall of the Marianas in June 1944.

Olympic gold medalist Baron Takeichi Nishi arrived in July with the 26th Tank Regiment.[27] Nishi, an excellent equestrian, set a world record for a horse jump by hurdling a 2.1-meter-high bar in 1930.[28] He also won a gold medal in the individual jumping event of the 1932 Olympics. Nishi reportedly liked to live life on the edge, and was attracted to speed, gambling, and fighting. Because the baron was regularly seen in the company of Hollywood film stars, some considered him the "playboy of the Western world." Although only half of Nishi's equipment (twenty-eight tanks) got past U.S. submarines, his arrival gave Kuribayashi some medium-sized guns as well as a favorite subordinate. As cavalry men, the two had much in common.

The rest of Kuribayashi's force was largely composed of the 2d Mixed Brigade, 17th Independent Mixed Regiment, the Brigade Artillery Group (consisting of all indirect fire units), and a sizable land-based naval support unit of approximately 7,500 sailors. When Kuribayashi instituted the change in emphasis from Chichi Jima to the defense of Iwo Jima, he transferred most of the 109th Division to Sulfur Island.[29]

The Imperial Army's career forces had all but vanished by 1945.[30] With the exception of the 145th Regiment, which consisted of about 2,700 men, most of the Japanese soldiers on Iwo Jima consisted of conscripts, a stark contrast to the opposing Marines, many of whom were volunteers. Although the majority of the Japanese sailors had probably volunteered, many had not yet completed a primary school, and they ranged in age from thirty to forty years old.[31] In general, most of those in Kuribayashi's command had inferior training, and evidence indicates their spirits and discipline were substandard. As early as 1939 the Japanese military became increasingly concerned with the poor morale and inferior obedience in their units. Courts-martial and other punishments for disobedience increased noticeably during the war.[32] These soldiers and sailors on Iwo Jima hated the island and despised Kuribayashi's harsh discipline.[33] Kuribayashi himself stated that his soldiers were untrained recruits whose officers were "superannuated scarecrows."[34] He also complained that his staff reacted "slowly to everything, and I can't restrain my impatience."[35]

Some Japanese officers reciprocated with animosity toward the general. One of the subordinates described Kuribayashi as a man who "had the mind of a squad leader" and who was overly obsessed with details.[36] Another officer stated that Kuribayashi was "sternly disciplined and very strict with subordinates . . . the troops dislike the general possibly because of these very attributes."[37] Slightly more complimentary, another described him as "not a soft-spoken man . . . he was sharp and caustic-tongued, working around the clock with inexhaustible energy . . . few other Japanese generals in the war worked as hard as Kuribayashi did by inspecting every platoon at every nook and corner every day. He respected reason, yes Western reason, and despised Oriental despotism."[38]

Although the common soldiers who defended Iwo Jima did not boast superior training or have much experience, the militaristic Japanese government had conditioned them for most of their lives. Indoctrination took place mainly through the educational system. After 1904 the government produced or approved all elementary school textbooks, and at a very young age, children were taught to honor the emperor by engaging regularly in patriotic customs.[39] In relation to the other industrialized nations of that period, such as much of Europe and the United States, nationalistic education was the norm. However, after the Russo-Japanese War, Japanese schools progressively incorporated militarism, strict obedience, and emperor worship. Curricula began to include military training in 1917, and active-duty military officers were assigned to every male middle school and high school after 1925.[40] When the Pacific war took on a more global nature in the late 1930s, the Japanese propaganda machine intensified themes of heroism and sacrifice. Education even included regular prayer to photographs of the emperor. Although the samurai class had virtually disappeared by the twentieth century, the modern Army and Navy became obsessed with the samurai history, myths, and legends. They crafted a new twisted version of the *bushido* code and made it applicable to everyone, eventually forcing even civilians to adhere to some of its extreme standards of sacrifice, self-discipline, and courage.[41] Consequently, when Japanese citizens were conscripted and sent to Pacific islands, they had already been "overdosed with submissiveness to authority and glorification of war."[42] This social conditioning proved quite valuable to Kuribayashi.

Kuribayashi planned Iwo Jima's defenses untraditionally. For instance, he forbade the use of *banzai* charges and counterattacks.[43] The traditional *banzai* charge had a long history in Japan dating back to the medieval period. On command, a Japanese lord's samurai would heroically sprint forward into danger shouting, "*Banzai!*" Literally translated, *banzai* means "may you live ten thousand years." The Japanese military continued to utilize this dated tactic in desperate circumstances on numerous occasions in the Pacific. Though it often produced confusion and fear in the enemy, it frequently ended in tactical defeat for the Japanese. According to historian Ronald Spector, "the Japanese army had never experienced at first hand the full power of modern weaponry of the sort used on the European fronts of World War I" and continued to focus on offensive traits of aggressiveness and fighting spirit as preferable to the defense.[44]

Americans, of course, tended to view the *banzai* charge as alien and suicidal. Then again, an interesting comparison can be made to the Western Front of World War I, when Germans, British, French, and Americans slaughtered each other by charging headlong against enemy machine gun and indirect fire. Inspired by chivalrous ideals, European and American officers upheld their honor by leading their men into impossible odds and sure death. The romanticism of glory and bravery, as well as the risk of being labeled a coward, ensured that soldiers followed. The resulting massacres sacrificed millions of young European men. The difference in the Pacific war was that the Japanese had not yet fully experienced the lessons of romanticism versus modern technology. But by 1945 Kuribayashi clearly understood the historical consequences of cultural idealism and harnessed his soldiers to more practical standards.

General Kuribayashi encountered considerable resistance from senior Army and Navy officials, including most of his staff, in endorsing an un-conventional defense plan. The stiffest opposition to Kuribayashi's plan came from Navy officers, specifically his highest ranking subordinate, Adm. Toshinosuke Ichimaru. Some of this animosity derived from the intense rivalry between the Japanese Army and Navy. Technically, because the two services refused subordination to each other, Kuribayashi had no direct authority over Admiral Ichimaru. This unproductive schism between the Army and Navy was typical and adversely affected nearly every Japanese campaign.

Both a dedicated warrior and a poet, Ichimaru ecstatically embraced his assignment to Iwo Jima. Arriving on Sulfur Island about a month after Kuribayashi, he composed the following *haiku* to celebrate the occasion:[45]

> Let me fall like the flower petals scatter
> May enemy bombs aim at me, and enemy shells
> Mark me as their target

A traditional man, both in spirit and mind, Ichimaru objected to the idea of foregoing the beach defense. Instead, he wanted to defend the beachhead by attacking the enemy ships with his naval cannons as prescribed by Navy doctrine.[46] Ichimaru's desires contradicted Kuribayashi's plan. To ensure Ichimaru's cooperation, Kuribayashi was finally forced to concede. He gave the admiral material for a beach defense—items that could have been used to better effect inland. Around 80 of the 135 pillboxes armed with 25-millimeter machine guns that Ichimaru built at the water's edge could not be employed during the battle because they did not face the advancing Marines.[47]

But to Ichimaru's way of thinking, maintaining Kuribayashi's inland defense could not lead to victory. Consequently, he saw no logical reason to pursue such a strategy. And Ichimaru was exactly right. The defenders could only defeat an American invasion by preventing the enemy from establishing a foothold on the island, launching a successful counterattack, or waiting for relief by the Japanese Navy. Additionally, the plan to establish the primary defense line on the Motoyama Plateau gave up access to the only airfield long enough for bombers. This course of action made it impossible to resupply during the battle. The combination of permitting the Americans to control both the air and sea routes, allowing them to land unopposed, and fighting from defensive positions preordained defeat. Kuribayashi's staff and subordinate commanders did not know, however, that the U.S. Pacific Fleet had destroyed the preponderance of the Japanese Navy, and the general decided it would be unwise to inform them—presumably to maintain morale.

Opposed to wasting resources on impossible victory strategies, Kuribayashi made the horrifying decision to cause the maximum possible amount of damage to the enemy. Because beach defenses had failed to adequately defend islands like Tarawa from the colossal might of the U.S. naval arms, he resolved to allow the attackers to reach the shores with relative ease. Once the enemy arrived, preregistered indirect fire would plummet onto the beachhead.[48] The discharge would come from the Brigade Artillery Group, which was made up of all the indirect fire assets on Iwo Jima. This included 75-millimeter artillery pieces, light mortars, naval guns, enormous 320-millimeter mortars, and rocket-propelled projectiles (some weighing over 700 pounds). One of the most effective Japanese mortars, the "spigot mortar," stood about 5 feet high and caused significant damage even when shells missed their target.[49] As the enemy advanced, the Japanese planned to defend the island in sectors from mostly static positions with interlocking fields of fire. With this in mind, Kuribayashi had his men bury light and medium tanks in immobile positions for use as direct fire assets.

In general, Kuribayashi's plan did not allow for much consolidation or withdrawal from primary defense positions. Instead, it focused on employing "the maximum number of weapons of all calibers fired continuously from well-concealed and protected positions until they were destroyed, reduced, or captured."[50] The general ordered the majority of soldiers to fight to the death from their prescribed locations.[51]

Despite the likelihood of defeat, Kuribayashi ordered his troops to fight under the most adverse circumstances and without hope of survival. He stated, "We are here to defend this island to the limit of our strength. We must devote ourselves to that task entirely. Each of your shots must kill many Americans. We cannot allow ourselves to be captured by the enemy. If positions are overrun, we will take bombs and grenades and throw ourselves under the tanks to destroy them. We will infiltrate the enemy's lines to exterminate him. No man must die until he has killed at least ten Americans. We will harass the enemy with guerilla actions until the last of us has perished. *Tenno banzai* [may the emperor live ten thousand years]!"[52]

Heavily outmatched in industrial output throughout the Pacific war, Japan relied upon human spirit to make up for material inferiority. Kuribayashi was counting on the elevation of self-denial to a virtue to act as a force-multiplier.[53] Beyond the forfeiture of common comforts, the ultimate expression of Japanese devotion to country could be achieved through the sacrifice of one's own life for the greater good of the nation. Such concepts had a long history in Japan (and in many other cultures as well, including the United States), but in the latter stages of the Pacific war, the sacrifice of large numbers of Japanese became a form of collective purification, a euphemistic endorsement of *gyokusai* (shattered jewels). Essentially, death in battle ensured that Japanese society remained unpolluted by destroying the

46

invading *gaijin* (foreign barbarian) at any cost through *yamato damashii* (Japanese spirit). The scale of self-sacrifice was perhaps unparalleled in modern history.[54] The defenders of Iwo Jima likely perceived heroic death as an act of purity and transcendence, to be looked upon with glory and honor.[55] Kuribayashi encouraged this cultural conviction to fight against difficult or even impossible odds. He made special badges for select volunteer soldiers who strapped themselves with explosives and charged enemy tanks as human projectiles.[56]

The taboo against surrender made it dishonorable to even contemplate the possibility. Discussion of surrender led to public humiliation or retribution that could affect one's family. Japanese propaganda further ensured that the majority would choose death over surrender. Most soldiers believed Americans massacred and tortured prisoners. In particular, the Japanese were taught to despise Marines, who purportedly had to murder their own parents to qualify for enlistment.[57]

Many times in the Pacific war Americans had witnessed the determined will of Japanese soldiers and sailors to make "Alamo-like stands." What made Iwo Jima's defenses most extraordinary was the intricate design of its fortifications. Kuribayashi brought in engineers from Japan to draw up a series of blueprints for underground fortifications.[58] The extensive planning and subsequent excavation allowed for the island's entire garrison to live, work, eat, and fight out of caves, bunkers, and pillboxes. While Suribachi Yama ("cone-shaped mountain") had over one thousand caves and pill boxes, the rest of the island was honeycombed with as many as fifteen thousand such installations, some of which were both massive and intricate.[59] Caves on Suribachi Yama had vast galleries for supplies, steam, water, and electricity. Some of the walls were even plastered.[60] The defenders constructed one underground defense system on the Motoyama Plateau that was 32 feet deep and 540 yards long, with shelter for 300 men. It had 17 entrances, a kitchen, an assembly room, and a medical facility.[61] Other complexes were even larger. The 109th Division Headquarters was 75 feet deep, had a dozen entrances, and the capacity to house over 2,000 men.[62] After the battle, Marine engineers described how the Japanese made clever use of these fortifications: "The underground defenses were such a maze of intercommunicating passageways and tunnels that enemy infantry, when driven into one cave, would reappear above ground, fighting from another cave."[63]

When the defenders built fortifications aboveground, they made them out of heavy sections of concrete and steel. Some had 50-foot piles of sand around the walls for additional protection. Some of the reinforced concrete walls on fortified pillboxes measured 4 feet thick and were impervious to nearly anything but a direct hit from a battleship.[64] Yet Japanese ground defenses protruded only a few feet from the surface, making them difficult targets for naval gunfire. Reporter Robert Sherrod described a typical Japanese blockhouse: "Its outer walls were of reinforced concrete, 40 inches thick. The vent did not open toward the sea, but slantwise toward the upper beaches: the 120mm gun inside could fire on the beaches and some of our ships, but could not be hit except from a particular angle. There was no sign that it had been touched by anything but a flame-thrower. Beside it lay the bodies of eight marines—the apparent cost of taking what was only one of several hundred similar positions, nearly all of which have to be knocked out by men on foot with explosive charges or flame-throwers."[65] According to historians Isely and Crowl, observers who examined German fortified areas in both World War I and World War II testified that they had never witnessed a location so thoroughly defended as Iwo Jima.[66] Another historian stated, "Iwo was one solid, coordinated defense, the density of which has never been exceeded in any objective taken by American arms."[67]

Despite his remarkable efforts to fortify Iwo Jima, Kuribayashi had great difficulty acquiring the necessary materials to complete construction. In the context of this naval situation, Kuribayashi had a twofold problem in getting supplies to Iwo Jima. First, Iwo Jima had no port facility and could not receive most ammunition, troops, materials, or equipment directly from Japanese ships. Consequently, the general was forced to use the port at Chichi Jima, offload the goods, and then transport them to Iwo Jima via shallow-draft vessels.[68] Ships bound for Chichi Jima had to navigate through the U.S. submarine net with little protection. No fewer than 1,500 Japanese troops drowned in the Nanpo Shoto attempting to reach the Bonin Islands.[69] At least half of Kuribayashi's tanks and an untold amount of equipment and supplies failed to reach Chichi Jima because of U.S. submarine operations. By the time Japan recognized the threat of the upcoming invasion in 1945, its high command was "deeply concerned" about the lack of defensive materials reaching Iwo Jima.[70] The Japanese were forced to use planes from the 60th and 120th Air Regiments of the 6th Army Air Forces to move 30 tons of material from Yokosuka Naval Base on mainland Japan to Iwo Jima. This was accomplished the week of 4–12 February in one last attempt to reinforce the defenses.[71] By the time the battle commenced, the defenders had ammunition supplies around "60% of the standard issue . . . sufficient for one engagement" and "approximately four months' rations and forage."[72] Despite splendid U.S. submarine operations, a considerable amount of supplies made it to the Bonin Islands before the invasion.

THE UNTOLD TRUTH

In addition to the well-planned fortifications, another factor that aided Kuribayashi's defense was the terrain on Iwo Jima. The island has been commonly referred to as resembling a pork chop from an aerial perspective. The narrow beaches on the southern portion of the island, the only place where amphibious assault forces could land, contained steep banks of volcanic ash. The Japanese made abundant use of antipersonnel and antitank mines in this area.[73] South of these beaches rose the tallest point on the island, Suribachi Yama, a steep-sided, funnel-shaped mountain with a crater in the middle. The Japanese honeycombed the face of this volcano with direct fire positions overlooking the landing area. Nevertheless, Suribachi was not the cornerstone of Kuribayashi's defense plan, as many American histories have inferred. The prominence of the mountain ensured that the enemy would focus its colossal firepower on it, yet Suribachi housed only 7 percent of the Japanese fighting force, about 1,600 soldiers.[74]

The central and broadest portion of the island angled gently upward to the two airfields. It was here that Kuribayashi established his main line of resistance. The relative flatness of this region allowed for first-rate fields of fire. Beyond the landing strips rose a series of steep folds generally perpendicular to the attacker's axis of advance. Such terrain forced the invader to fight uphill against an entrenched enemy, then move down the reverse slope under enemy fire, before again attacking the positions on the subsequent ridge. From the landing area to the last pocket of resistance, Kuribayashi ensured that the predictable scheme of the Americans' advance would be terribly slow. After the battle, Marine intelligence would state that the "defensive organization of Iwo Jima was the most intelligent and complete yet encountered."[75] In the words of historians Isely and Crowl, "Comparisons are difficult, but it is probable that no other given area in the history of modern war has been so skillfully fortified by nature and man."[76]

Operation Detachment

While General Kuribayashi and his troops prepared to defend Iwo Jima, Adm. Chester Nimitz assembled a large naval armada to seize it. Despite the vast resources of his Pacific Fleet, Nimitz had difficulty gathering the requisite vessels for Operation Detachment.[77] A significant factor in this dilemma was the prioritization of the Philippine invasion and Okinawa operation over Iwo Jima within a tight timetable that did not allow for maximum reallocation of available resources. From late 1944 through early 1945, MacArthur used an abundant amount of naval shipping for the invasion of the Philippines.

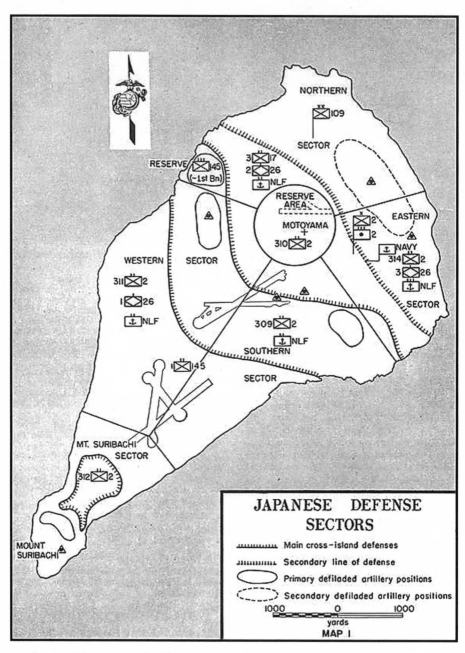

Japanese defense sectors on Iwo Jima

Nimitz soon discovered that the thirty-day interval scheduled between the Luzon operation and Operation Detachment was insufficient to reacquire the desired shipping back from the U.S. Army. As the battle for Luzon became prolonged, MacArthur retained his naval support, and the Navy postponed the D-Day for Iwo Jima to mid-February. Postponing Operation Detachment, however, pushed it closer to the Okinawa operation, which the Joint Chiefs of Staff had scheduled to begin on 1 April. As had happened on several occasions in the Pacific, the partition of U.S. forces between the Army and the Navy in competing drives adversely affected preparation for Iwo Jima.

Admiral Nimitz assigned command of the Fifth Fleet to his talented subordinate, Raymond A. Spruance, who then divided it further into several task organizations. Spruance himself would accompany Task Force 58 on a diversionary attack on mainland Japan. A Joint Expeditionary Force of Navy and Marines, designated Task Force 51, would carry out the assault on Iwo Jima. Spruance gave overall command of this Joint Expeditionary Force to Vice Adm. Richmond K. Turner. Lt. Gen. Holland M. Smith headed the Marine component, Task Force 56. Actual command of the V Amphibious Corps, assigned to seize Iwo Jima with the 3d, 4th, and 5th Marine Divisions, belonged to Gen. Harry Schmidt.

Following the debacle of Holland Smith firing Army Gen. Ralph Smith on Saipan in June 1944, General Marshall reportedly flew into a rage during a Joint Chiefs of Staff meeting, declaring that he would never allow Marines to command Army units again.[78] Army generals maintained that Marines like Holland Smith did not have the proper training or experience to command operations larger than a division. Marines, of course, considered this criticism as reflecting jealous rivalry. Although the Navy officially supported Holland Smith, the Army's heated animosity toward him pressured Nimitz to deny Smith future command positions.[79] Smith was fired through promotion, by means of the creation of a new position, Commanding General Fleet Marine Force Pacific. From this station, Smith could act as an intermediary between the Marines on the ground and the Navy at sea but could not command the forces ashore. Such treatment of Smith bordered on patronizing, and at war's end he was not invited to the surrender ceremonies in Japan, which added to his postwar bitterness.

With Admiral Spruance, Admiral Turner, General Smith, and General Schmidt now assigned to their respective command positions for Operation Detachment, naval forces conducted both bombardment and photography of Iwo Jima repeatedly from November 1944 through January 1945. Surface bombardment by carrier air power, cruisers, and destroyers inflicted little substantial damage, but aerial photographs proved extremely valuable to the amphibious forces planning to assault the island. The deep water surrounding most of Iwo Jima made it a suitable target for submarine photography. Approaching the island undetected in November, the USS *Spearfish* lay a couple of hundred yards offshore near Mount Suribachi, where for hours it took pictures of Japanese defense positions near the shoreline at periscope depth.[80]

Iwo Jima's elaborate defenses surprised Nimitz and Spruance in October 1944. Unfortunately, Navy and Marine Corps dismay at the prospect had only just begun. Aerial photographs taken from December through mid-February confirmed that Kuribayashi continued to increase the island's fortifications.[81] The defenders' spirit seemed undaunted. One U.S. aerial photograph showed a Japanese soldier brazenly holding a Rising Sun flag above his head for the plane's camera to see.[82] Because the entrenched positions of Iwo Jima resembled and even surpassed those encountered at Tarawa, Gen. Holland Smith became primarily concerned over the amount of preparatory bombardment the island needed before the invasion. In August 1944, Joint Staff Planners had boasted that Iwo Jima could be easily softened with air power. Reality would prove otherwise.

Despite repeated attempts by the Army Air Forces to pulverize Iwo Jima with heavy bombers, Japanese defenses steadily improved. Bombing raids from the Marianas appeared to have the reverse of the intended effect. From August 1944 through February 1945, the Army Air Forces flew 2,807 B-24 Liberator sorties over Iwo Jima.[83] But as D-Day approached, the Navy concluded that the surface destruction served only to motivate the defenders to dig deeper. Both Spruance and Nimitz urged the Army Air Forces to carry out bombing runs at lower altitudes to improve accuracy, but the majority of B-24s continued to bomb from over 15,000 feet.[84] The Army Air Forces used napalm attacks on Iwo Jima as well, dropping a couple of tons of it in February, but to no appreciable effect.[85] Spruance and Nimitz further requested that the Army Air Forces target Japanese ships that supplied the island with construction material and provisions.[86] The Twentieth Air Force refused, stating that its pilots were not trained for antishipping missions.[87] B-24s continued to bomb Iwo Jima at high altitudes even though regular cloud cover over the island made such methods largely ineffective. In the final assessment, aerial bombardment "had no appreciable effect in the reduction of the enemy's well-prepared and heavily fortified defensive installations."[88]

That enemy positions appeared undamaged should not have been surprising. B-24s dropped nearly all their ordnance on the island's airfields and not on the defenses. The Army Air Forces acknowledged the lack of success by launching an investigation into the matter two months after the battle.[89] One Army Air Forces report explained that Navy men's negative view of airmen was "further enhanced by the lack of desired results produced by the Seventh Air Force."[90]

The work undertaken by the Twentieth Air Force to prepare the island for assault was simply inadequate. The Army Air Forces sent B-24 bombers from the Seventh Air Force to soften up the airfields and defenses while utilizing the B-29, the aircraft that might have made the most impact with its massive payloads, on other missions. The Army Air Forces' Superfortress continued to give a poor performance against mainland Japan.[91] Arnold ensured that Gen. Haywood Hansell, Commanding General of the Twenty First Bomber Command, felt responsible for not getting the B-29 to live up to expectations. He wrote to Hansell in November, "You realize as well as anyone the important part that you and the Twenty-First Bomber Command will play in the Twentieth Air Force program, and consequently, in the program of the entire Army Air Forces."[92] According to Hansell, the Twentieth Air Force was under "extreme pressure to perform."[93] Nevertheless, by mid-January 1945, B-29s "had not destroyed a single target in Japan" and "looked more and more like an expensive and embarrassing failure."[94] In response to the poor performance, Arnold relieved Hansell of command. LeMay took over the Twenty-First Bomber Command in January.[95]

The necessity of proving the effectiveness of strategic bombing of Japan overshadowed the more immediate need of suppressing defenses on Iwo Jima. Consequently, LeMay remained reluctant to use the Superfortress in tactical support of ground objectives. The Army Air Forces relegated Iwo Jima to "shakedown and training missions."[96] The Twenty-First Bomber Command made only six B-29 Superfortress raids against Iwo Jima, and nearly every mission aimed to neutralize the airfields, not the island's defenses. Only one mission of twenty-one B-29s targeted the fortifications on Iwo Jima before the landing.[97] In their history of the battle, Isely and Crowl stated that "the performance of army airmen in softening up Iwo Jima was disappointing."[98]

With the full failure of the aerial attacks, the preliminary fires of naval guns became all the more important. Admiral Nimitz originally planned for eight days of offshore bombardment, discharged from Task Force 51 with the use of fifteen "large-gunned vessels."[99] General Smith protested that the Navy's plan was inadequate and repeatedly requested an increase in the number of days for preliminary fires. Unfortunately, the Marines would actually receive much less than the eight days and fifteen large-gun ships originally planned for.

Three factors made the effectiveness of naval bombardment difficult: the quantity of ammunition, the duration of fires, and the number of warships. Rectifying this conundrum was the responsibility of the Joint Expeditionary Force Commander, Adm. Richmond Turner. The Chief of Naval Operations described Turner as "brilliant, caustic, arrogant, and tactless"—the perfect man for the job.[100] Turner carried out the amphibious support duties of the majority of Pacific landings. By the time of Operation Detachment, no other Navy officer had such a wealth of knowledge on either naval bombardment or amphibious shipping. This experience combined with his natural intelligence made for an exceptional naval officer. Nevertheless, Turner received an inordinate amount of subsequent criticism concerning deficient naval bombardment on Iwo Jima.

Admiral Turner conserved the ammunition allocated for Iwo Jima in order to provide a much larger bombardment on Okinawa, which turned out to be wasted since the Japanese left Okinawa's landing areas undefended. The extensive coastal areas of Okinawa ensured that the Japanese could not possibly have defended the entire shoreline. From this perspective, criticism of Turner has merit. Still, the Navy's prioritization of Okinawa over Iwo Jima, with regard to shell allocation, derived from faulty U.S. intelligence and underestimation of the enemy. Turner had little control over assessments of Japanese defenses. Shortage of available time and gun-ships limited the amount of ammunition to be fired more than any other factor. Turner would not have been able to increase ammunition supplies for Iwo Jima without altering one or both of these constraints.[101]

The rigid schedule placed on Pacific operations did the most to inhibit effective naval bombardment. The Joint Chiefs of Staff tightly squeezed Operation Detachment between two major campaigns. A mere four weeks separated the invasion of Luzon and the assault on Iwo Jima. After D-Day on Iwo Jima, the Navy had only six weeks to finalize preparations for Okinawa. According to Admiral Spruance, "the planning for and the actual execution for the Iwo Jima operation were affected to a considerable extent by the operations in the Philippines which immediately preceded it, and by the necessity of preparing for the Okinawa operation which was to follow it."[102] In order to begin the invasion of Okinawa on schedule, Admiral Turner denied Holland Smith's request for a full ten days of preparatory bombardment.[103]

Any extension to Operation Detachment would set back the Okinawa campaign, and Okinawa was the Navy's priority. To make matters worse, General MacArthur's operations on Luzon ran behind schedule and tied up shipping required for Iwo Jima. Out of necessity, the Navy set back the landing on Iwo Jima by a full month from 20 January to 19 February.[104] Concurrently, the Navy shortened the planned eight days of preliminary bombardment to just three days.[105] Howling mad at this point, General Smith repeatedly objected, arguing that the majority of targets on the island would not be destroyed. But the Navy refused to budge, and in the end, the Marines received only three days of fire.

The number of warships available for Operation Detachment also influenced the effectiveness of the preparatory bombardment. General MacArthur's operations in the Philippines used significant portions of the Pacific Fleet. In mid-January, Admiral Nimitz asked MacArthur to release the battleships and destroyers used for the Luzon invasion. With a history of struggle for naval support, MacArthur planned to retain these assets to secure the rest of the Philippines. He insisted on keeping six battleships and twenty-six destroyers. Although Nimitz sought a compromise, MacArthur released none of the ships in time to participate in Operation Detachment.[106]

One should not place all the blame for the shortage of battleships and cruisers on the U.S. Army. Admiral Nimitz further divided his own assets available for Operation Detachment in order to launch a surprise attack on Tokyo. The original Bonin Islands plan called for naval aircraft to carry out raids up and down the coast of mainland Japan as a distraction from the main assault on Iwo Jima. Spruance assigned this diversion mission to Task Force 58, which was made up primarily of the Fifth Fleet's aircraft carriers. He insisted, however, on taking an additional *twenty-three* battleships and cruisers along, primarily as anti-aircraft platforms.

In his memoirs, Holland M. Smith criticized Spruance's division of the Pacific Fleet's resources. "To me, naval insistence upon the priority of the strike against Japan at the cost of fire support for our assault on Iwo Jima was incomprehensible. To take the better part of the fleet away ignored the principal aims of our mission. It simply weakened the power we could use at Iwo Jima. To my way of thinking—and I am sure that I was right—the operation was planned for the capture of Iwo Jima, but Spruance permitted the attack on Japan to overshadow the real objective."[107]

Unfortunately, Marine Corps frustration with Navy priorities did not end there. Just before D-Day, Spruance "yanked" an additional two battleships, which were already loaded with off-shore-bombardment ammunition, away from Task Force 51.[108] The loss of these two vessels left only eleven large-gunned ships available to fire on the defenses of Iwo Jima: *Tennessee, Idaho, Texas, New York, Nevada, Arkansas, Chester, Salt Lake City, Tuscaloosa, Pensacola,* and *Vicksburg.*

The invasion force had less than half the battleships and cruisers allocated for preparatory bombardment (11) that the Navy used for the Tokyo raid (23). At this point, Admiral Turner even joined General Smith in protest, but Spruance insisted that the Navy could not jeopardize the strike on mainland Japan.

General Smith's Chief of Staff, Col. Dudly Brown, responded to the loss of the two battleships in the following personal correspondence: "In view of the fact that the ships . . . are not available for the pre-D-day support of the landing force, it is the opinion of the undersigned that the naval gunfire support has been so weakened as to jeopardize the success of the operation. Certainly, under the present plan of support, assuming the initial landings are successful, the cost in Marines killed will be far greater than under the plan agreed upon before our departure from Pearl Harbor."[109]

Gen. Holland Smith became so gravely concerned with the insufficient preparatory bombardment that he wrote a personal letter to the Commandant of the Marine Corps, Gen. A. A. Vandegrift: "As you know, I have nothing to do with strategy in the Pacific, and only express myself when called upon for a statement. I believe that the operation is not worth the casualties we will suffer. On two separate occasions, I protested that naval gunfire is insufficient, with the result that it has been increased to some extent, but not enough, in my opinion, to suffice. I can only go so far. We have done all we could do to get ready . . . and I believe it will be successful, but the thought of the probable casualties causes me extreme unhappiness . . . would to God that something might happen to cancel the operation altogether."[110]

Although many naval commanders remained convinced that the operation would be quick, Gen. Holland Smith, who routinely demonstrated an uncanny ability to correctly assess intelligence information, believed just the opposite—that the battle would be bloody and long.[111] Unquestionably, the Navy did not take Smith's misgivings seriously enough.

In February, as the Fifth Fleet closed on the Bonins, Spruance launched his naval air assault on mainland Japan. Adverse weather conditions hampered the operation, and official reports conflict over how much damage the Navy caused.[112] However, Spruance did successfully divert a small portion of Japanese resources. If nothing else, Task Force 58 may have sidetracked more than fifty Japanese planes from the landing force (Task Force 51) that were sent to the carrier force (Task Force 58) instead.[113]

Notwithstanding this small success, Task Force 58 did not make satisfactory use of its twenty-three large-gunned vessels. The overemphasis placed on the carrier attacks may have derived from a desire to avenge Pearl Harbor. In his dramatically staged press announcement of the Tokyo raids, Admiral

Nimitz stated that the "operation has long been planned and the opportunity to accomplish it fulfills the deeply cherished desire of every officer and man in the Pacific Fleet."[114] Surely, it would have been proper for the Commander of the Fifth Fleet to accompany the main effort, but Admiral Spruance went with Task Force 58—a further illustration that the Tokyo raid overshadowed the Iwo Jima invasion.

As with previous matters, a primary reason for the Navy's emphasis on the Tokyo carrier raid was service rivalry. In November 1944, Spruance stated, "We [the Navy] should stop fighting the products of the Jap aircraft factories on the perimeter and take our carrier air in to the center to knock out the factories themselves. We cannot afford to await the outcome of bombing 'with precision instruments' from 30,000 feet."[115] In the words of historian Craig Symonds, Spruance "may have been eager to prove that carrier strikes could be more effective in destroying Japan's industrial infrastructure than high-altitude B-29 raids."[116]

The carrier attacks certainly captivated the public interest, garnering headlines in major American newspapers. The *San Francisco Examiner* boasted that the Navy had carried out the "biggest air assault" ever conducted against Japan.[117] Considering the poor performance of the B-29 up to that point, such public display of naval air power clashed with an Army Air Forces agenda of demonstrating the effectiveness of strategic bombing. The raids left little doubt that Admiral Nimitz commanded the Central Pacific in spite of General Arnold's Superforts based within his theater. Whether the motivation for the raids derived from revenge against the Japanese or competition with the Army Air Forces, Holland Smith voiced valid criticism over the inappropriate proportion of battleships allocated to the Tokyo raid instead of the invasion.

The Navy and Marine Corps anticipated the same predictable defense at Iwo Jima that they had encountered in earlier battles. As at Tarawa, the Japanese would defend the shoreline, but they could not possibly stand up to the combined fleet's offshore bombardment. After the Navy pulverized the Japanese coastal defenses, the Marines would seize the beachhead. Once Marines were ashore, the Japanese would launch desperate *banzai* attacks, facilitating their deaths quickly.[118] As a result, plans estimated the seizure of Iwo Jima could take as little as three or four days.

Not all American intelligence agreed with the view that the Japanese on Iwo Jima would defend the beach or conduct *banzai* attacks. One report in January stated, "Above all it is to be noted that the Japanese are learning how to fight defensively and how to get away from the rigid perimeter defense that they had so fixedly adhered to until recently. They are beginning to understand the advantages of an active, fluid defense and the uselessness of beating against our well established beachheads. In consequence it may be expected that if their plans for counterattack fail to dislodge a landing, the remnants will fall back into the high ground in the center of the island and carry out the 'cornered rat' defense encountered on Peleliu."[119] Although some officers better recognized the dangers of the upcoming invasion than others, it proved difficult to change popular preconceptions of the Japanese.

Despite the stated deficiencies mentioned in the planning and organization for Operation Detachment, the enormous naval amphibious force finally employed to seize Iwo Jima consisted of tens of thousands of America's finest sailors and Marines. Most of their equipment was superior to that of their Japanese opponents, and regardless of the anxiety of impending combat, the enthusiastic confidence onboard the warships was intoxicating.[120] Only the intricate fortifications and dedicated Japanese soldiers on Sulfur Island stood between the Americans and victory: the final decision was imminent.

Ground Warfare in Dante's Inferno

The 3d, 4th, and 5th Marine Divisions assigned to seize Iwo Jima consisted of 68,000 sailors and Marines, backed by 14,000 V Amphibious Corps support troops, whose duties ranged from 155-millimeter howitzer battalions to engineering units.[121] Gen. Harry Schmidt commanded the V Amphibious Corps. Gen. Graves Erskine commanded the 3d Marine Division, Gen. Clifton Cates commanded the 4th Marine Division, and Gen. Keller Rockey headed the newly created 5th Marine Division. By and large, these divisions probably offered the finest infantry capability in the world.

Over the course of the war, the Marine Corps had developed a unique fighting doctrine. Each division emphasized the firepower and responsibility of squads, platoons, companies, and battalions to destroy enemy fortifications within respective zones of action. It was expected that the Marine rifle squad, broken up into three fireteams, would do most of the fighting at the small unit level. Most of the burden for attacks on dug-in fortifications was placed on the assault demolition squad, consisting of automatic rifles, bazookas, bangalore torpedoes, heavy explosives, and flame throwers. These assets were dispersed to platoons and rifle squads for use as each saw fit. Leavened with the leftovers from the disbanded raider and parachute battalions (most especially the 5th Marine Division), the V Amphibious Corps was a formidable force.

On 16 February Admiral Turner commenced preliminary fires on Iwo Jima. The limited visibility over the next three days prevented proper assessment of the results, but the simple tonnage of bombardment exceeded anything previously carried out in the Pacific.[122] Battleships, cruisers, and destroyers concentrated fire in their prescribed zones, targeting as many visible positions as possible. The Navy did not realize that the restrictions placed on ammunition and time meant that the majority of defense installations were not destroyed.

Fortunately for the Americans, the defenders made an error on 17 February. Despite General Kuribayashi's instructions to the contrary, Admiral Ichimaru decided to open fire.[123] As underwater demolition teams approached the landing area, Ichimaru attacked prematurely, thinking that this was the first wave of the assault. The Japanese fired direct fire weapons on the destroyer transports, thereby revealing their positions. Reacting quickly, the U.S. Navy gunners concentrated their counter-fire, destroying numerous Japanese coastal defenses overlooking the landing area. Had the Japanese held their fire, these guns would likely have taken a heavy toll on the assault force.

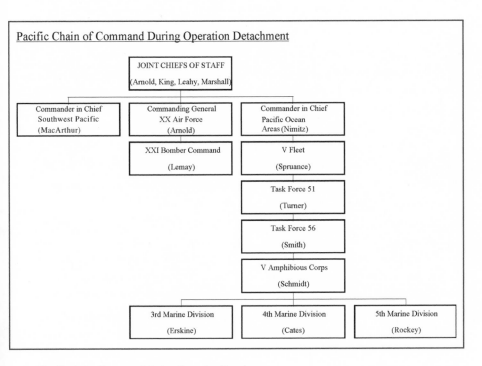

Pacific chain of command during Operation Detachment

The first waves of LCVPs (landing craft vehicle, personnel) circle the waters in anticipation of the final naval bombardment.

As the defenders struggled for safety under the unprecedentedly heavy naval bombardment, General Kuribayashi attempted a meager counterattack. On Airfield Number Two on Motoyama Plateau, he constructed a concrete shelter to conceal two Japanese Zero fighters. Armed with 60-kilogram bombs, the planes had been set aside to ram U.S. warships.[124] One of the two designated pilots refused to carry out Kuribayashi's orders, but another aviator was found to volunteer. The two planes managed to take off and gained enough altitude to fly over the crest of Suribachi, but were quickly targeted by ships offshore and crashed into the sea. The bombardment of Iwo Jima continued without interruption.

After finishing their traditional pre-assault breakfast of steak and eggs, the 4th and 5th Divisions made ready for the initial landing. The 3d Marine Division remained in reserve offshore. The carrier task force (Task Force 58) had returned from Tokyo to offer up two more battleships and eleven cruisers for bombardment. On 19 February, the final day of preparation, the combined naval forces in Task Force 51 leveled the entire firepower of their armada for a final and magnificent barrage on the landing area. The first waves of the

THE UNTOLD TRUTH

Third and fourth waves head toward the beach. Naval bombardment has obscured the landing area.

landing forces streamed in columns toward the designated beaches, which Kuribayashi had left nearly vacant, to land on the sands of Iwo Jima.

To their surprise, the invasion force encountered scant signs of Japanese resistance near the shoreline. Instead, the debarking troops quickly discovered three adverse environmental conditions. First, although soil samples had indicated sand, the beach actually consisted of a black volcanic ash and dust that proved extremely difficult to traverse, even by foot. Second, intelligence had calculated a 4-foot high terrace from sea level to the first plateau. Instead, the terrace generally exceeded 8 feet and in some places rose to 15 feet.[125] Due to the combination of steep terrain and weak soil, wheeled vehicles could not make it up the terrace and even tracked vehicles had difficulty getting off the beach. Third, the heavy surf proved too violent for many of the amphibious landing craft, which were overwhelmed while they attempted to offload. The tide soon became cluttered with the wreckage of V Amphibious Corps logistics train.[126] The wrecked hulks of landing craft surging back and forth in the waves created terrible obstacles for follow-on forces, and hampered offload efforts.[127]

Due to the lack of initial resistance, the Marines from the 4th and 5th Divisions generally felt confident that most of the Japanese defenders had been annihilated by preliminary bombardment.[128] Then, fifteen minutes after men and supplies began stacking up on the beaches, Kuribayashi unleashed his mortars and artillery.[129] The strong concentration of American forces meant that the Japanese had little difficulty engaging targets. Veteran Thomas Lyons explained the situation upon debarking: "When we hit the beach, it was, of course, black sand, and there was a steep embankment right out of the water. For the first several yards, the Japs couldn't even see you because we were down behind the embankment. One of the boats got hit after they were done unloading, killing everyone. We got off the beach. As we were moving toward the runway, [one of the men] got completely emasculated. A shell exploded right in front of him, right under his feet. He was begging people to shoot him . . . He was a very close friend of mine."[130]

Indirect fire continued to rain on the disembarking Marines. The easily manipulated volcanic sand at least proved beneficial for sandbags to cushion shrapnel bursts.[131] Nevertheless, the extent of the destruction from indirect fire surpassed anything the Marines had ever faced and left ghastly injuries.

The 5th Division hits the beach on D-Day, 19 February 1945. The dead and living mingle.

Minutes after the landing, the initial assault force crosses over the beach and moves inland.

Time and *Life* correspondent Robert Sherrod, who had accompanied many Marine landing in the Central Pacific, stated: "It was sickening to watch the Jap mortar shells crash into the men . . . These huge explosive charges—'floating ash cans' we called them—would crash among the thin lines of marines or among the boats bringing reinforcements to the beach, throwing sand, water, and even pieces of human flesh 100 feet into the air."[132] Sherrod went on to say that "along the beach . . . lay many dead. About them, whether American or Jap, there was one thing in common. They died with the greatest possible violence. Nowhere in the Pacific war have I seen such badly mangled bodies. Many were cut squarely in half. Legs and arms lay 50 ft. away from any body. Only the legs were easy to identify—Japanese if wrapped in khaki puttees; American if covered by canvas leggings. In one spot on the sand, far from the nearest clusters of dead men, I saw a string of guts 15 feet long."[133] One Marine veteran emotionally described his most vivid memory on Iwo Jima of a fellow Marine who repeatedly, but unsuccessfully, tried to fold his own entrails back into his abdomen. Dazed, desperate, confused, the Marine slipped on his own innards and fell down in the process.[134] Contrary to romantic portrayals, the nightmare on Iwo Jima was remorseless, repulsive, and extremely violent. And it had just begun.

Although the Navy had learned from debacles on Tarawa and Peleliu not to give official predictions, planners certainly expected the seizure of Iwo Jima to last no more than three or four days.[135] Due to the ease of the landing on the first day, Admiral Turner reported to Admiral Nimitz that he would secure the island as anticipated in four days.[136] However, Turner's overconfidence derived from his unawareness of the true nature of the Japanese defenses. He failed to realize that Kuribayashi had intentionally lured the Marines onto the beaches. While the Navy reveled over the events of D-Day, the Marines began to feel the severity of the actual situation. As the progress of Marine ground units slowed against stiff enemy resistance, indirect fire poured onto the beachhead.

The strength of the Japanese opposition shocked Marine ground forces. U.S. intelligence had reported in early January that the island's garrison consisted of fewer than 14,000 men.[137] Days after the Marines landed, those estimates nearly doubled, to over 20,000 enemy troops.[138] To make matters worse, preliminary fires had left 88 percent of the enemy's fortifications undamaged.[139] Tragically, 82,000 Marines had been left to excavate 21,000 well-prepared Japanese defenders with hand grenades and bayonets. Over the next thirty-five days, an island of sulfur and rock became eight square miles of unadulterated hell.

The first hours found most Marines clustered around the landing area— but for Marines, hunkering down did not last long. The 4th and 5th Divisions rapidly and fervently punched an opening across the breadth of the island to the opposite shore and effectively cut Iwo Jima in half. As illustrated by war hero John Basilone's experience, many courageous veterans paid the ultimate sacrifice for leading the younger men forward.[140] Basilone had won the Medal of Honor three years earlier at Guadalcanal, where he had successfully defended American machine gun positions against the relentless assault of the Sendai Division (*sendai* meaning "second" in Japanese). He may have personally killed over three dozen enemy soldiers. For his tenacity, Basilone got a free ticket home and the opportunity to become an officer, but he turned it all down in order to join the V Amphibious Corps in the assault on Iwo Jima. Younger Marines found Gunnery Sergeant Basilone a larger-than-life figure, an image that certainly assisted him in leading his platoon over the terrace and onto the plateau. He attempted to set up a machine gun position, but his courage only bought him two hours of glory on the sands of Iwo Jima before a mortar shell mortally wounded him and four other Marines in one gigantic burst. Inspiring men to move forward at the cost of one's own life quickly became commonplace on Sulfur Island.

Marines who had experienced horrors elsewhere in the Pacific despaired on Iwo Jima. One recalled, "At Tarawa, Saipan, and Tinian, I saw Marines killed and wounded in a shocking manner . . . But not like the ghastliness that hung over the Iwo beachhead. Nothing any of us had ever known could compare with the utter anguish, frustration, and constant inner battle to maintain some semblance of sanity, clarity of mind, and power of speech . . . None of us would concede that death would have been a merciful *coup de grace.* Everybody was seized with an insensate lust to live."[141]

The hundreds of wounded were sent back to the landing area, where they quickly stacked up on the beach. Their horror and agony had just begun, as indirect fire continued to land among them. The violent stress of war pressured some casualties past their mental breaking point. Veteran T. Grady Gallant vividly remembered one Marine on a stretcher sitting up and shrieking for what seemed like an eternity as the mortar rounds peppered the landing area. The man finally died, to the relief of

The carnage near the surf was due to both enemy indirect fire and fierce waves.

Struggle for Sulfur Island

Wrecked vehicles, ships, and tractors churn in the surf.

many of the disturbed onlookers. Gallant wrote, "He was quiet and still and the battle was no longer his battle. Others had died with him, but he had screamed for them all. The others had died quietly, but he had protested; he had been their advocate. He had argued their cause, and had protested the injustice, the cruelty, and the helplessness of the trial they had undergone."[142]

As night fell, the two divisions set into defensive positions supported by artillery in preparation for the *banzai* attack that never came.[143] A correspondent described his first night with the Marines: "Iwo Jima can only be described as a nightmare in hell. It was partly the weather—Iwo is as cold as Ohio at this season . . . All through this bitter night the Japs rained heavy mortars and rockets and artillery on the entire area between the beach and the airfield. Twice they hit casualty stations on the beach. Many men who had been only wounded were killed."[144]

On the morning of 20 February the 4th and 5th Divisions wheeled right to begin the long and torturous northern offensive. Meanwhile, a portion of the 4th Division, the 28th Regiment, turned south to finish the task of seizing Suribachi Yama. The hundreds of pillboxes on the mountain mostly stood around the base, with intricately designed caves along the slopes.[145] But hundreds of yards stretched between the Marines' current positions and the mountain—every inch containing imminent death and despair. Facing such difficult circumstances, the 28th Marines dutifully employed the assault tactics that had made them so famous in the Pacific.

One of the Marines of the 28th Regiment, Richard Wheeler, struggled forward with his friends toward the base of the volcano. On the morning of 21 February, looking out over the last 200 yards of open terrain, Wheeler contemplated the final reckless charge, some of his friends fixing bayonets: "Though we'd all joined the Marines expecting tough assignments, the thing we were about to do seemed suicidal."[146] Yet despite the fear that gripped him, Wheeler charged forward in the face of enemy rifle, machine gun, and mortar fire. He later explained, "There probably wasn't a man among us who didn't wish to God he was moving in the opposite direction. But we had been ordered to attack, so we would attack. And our obedience involved more than just a resignation to discipline. Our training had imbued us with a fierce pride in our outfit, and this pride helped now to keep us from faltering. Few of us would have admitted that we were bound by the old-fashioned principle of 'death before dishonor,' but it was probably this, above all else, that kept us pressing forward."[147] Wheeler made it only halfway across the killing fields before shrapnel in his face halted his advance. Others would suffer more horrible fates as Marines and Japanese defenders, two forces of similar spirit, brothers in the macabre dance of mutual destruction, finally collided at the base of Suribachi Yama, engaging in fierce grenade fighting and close combat.

After three days of intense combat, the 28th Marines completed the conquest of Suribachi and scaled the summit. Historians Isley and Crowl deftly summarized the mountain's usefulness: "Capture of Suribachi was expected to improve terrestrial observation, but by the time it was done the northeastern front had moved up to the jumbled terrain, and this fact plus poor maps and smoke and haze characteristic of the island hindered vision."[148] Essentially, despite myth to the contrary, seizing Suribachi had modest positive tactical effect on the rest of the battle. And unfortunately for the Marines, Suribachi would prove far easier to capture than objectives of later struggles, such as "the Quarry," "the Amphitheater," and "the Meat Grinder."[149]

As Twenty-Eighth Regiment struggled to seize Suribachi Yama, the Japanese Navy launched a successful air strike on the Joint Expeditionary Force offshore with a special attack unit, more commonly known as *kamikaze*. On 21 February 32 Japanese planes, consisting of 20 bombers and 12 fighters, took off from Hitoria air base in Honshu and refueled on the Bonin Island of Hachijo Jima.[150] On Hachijo Jima the pilots likely held a ceremony consisting of drinking *sake* (rice wine) and wrapping *hachimaki* (white cloths) around their heads, just as legendary samurai had done before fighting to the death. Subsequently, the special attack unit initiated devastating strikes on the Pacific Fleet anchored off Iwo Jima. The escort carrier USS *Bismarck Sea* sank, and a handful of other ships were also damaged. The light carrier USS *Saratoga* was so badly mauled that its repairs took over three months to complete. The majority of the Navy's nearly 1,800 casualties resulted from these *kamikaze* attacks, and 21 February proved a mournful day indeed.

While the U.S. Navy fought off *kamikaze* attacks, the 4th and 5th Divisions wheeled north against the main Japanese defense line, 4th Division on the right and 5th Division on the left. The units resorted to tactics that can only be described as a relentless frontal assault, beginning at the first airfield and continuing onto the Motoyama Plateau. The Japanese often inflicted terrible casualties with traversing fire, then withdrew northward to secondary positions at the last possible moment, leaving the Marines to discover only empty pillboxes. After fighting across the level region around the first airfield, the two divisions encountered the first series of folds that funneled out from the central ridgeline of the Motoyama Plateau like an intricate spider web. These chains of elevated crests proved extremely difficult to assail directly. Furthermore, the Marines found it nearly impossible to flank the enemy positions on the jagged outcroppings from the shorelines, a situation complicated by the Japanese having trained many of their guns diagonally to cover the width of the ravines. Offensive momentum necessitated the dissection of the Japanese defenses right down the middle. On 22 February General Schmidt brought in his reserve, the 3d Marine Division, to crack the center.

Once Marines took the fight to the Motoyama Plateau, the environmental conditions changed drastically, from terrible to even worse. Isely and Crowl describe it best:

The volcanic ash characteristic of the waist of the island gave way to a solid lava as the ground rose. This lava was andesitic, soft and seemingly pliable to the hands; and even the plateau was strewn with debris and full of hidden crevices, jagged edges of stone, dangling ledges, and caves carved by nature as well as by the Japanese. Fissures of steam spewed from cracks in the ground and evil-smelling sulphur fumes vied with the repulsive odor of decomposing bodies. Everywhere were Japanese defenses, grottoes, bunkers, blockhouses, pillboxes, deep caves, antitank ditches and walls, minefields, and a profusion of flat-trajectory antitank guns, dual purpose automatic antiaircraft weapons, and small arms, all backed by lethal mortars and rockets firing from reverse slopes.[151]

Concerning the same area, historian Whitman S. Bartley stated, "In many places the ground is hot. Steam hangs in ghostly veils over the gray-brown sulpher vents that emit their characteristic fumes."[152] Unable to explain the horrors of the landscape adequately to their readers at home, correspondents most often referred to illustrations of Dante's *Inferno.*

Logistics teams at the shoreline, consisting primarily of manual labor, unload supplies.

The effects of Japanese mortars and artillery on the rear area can be seen, as even amphibious tractors are violently tossed around.

As the fighters moved inland to rocky and difficult terrain, the logistics train continued to battle the heavy surf in the landing areas. The waves hit the beaches at angles, repositioning the boats sideways, and then overturning them on subsequent strikes. Seabees and Marine beach parties attached cables from the ramps of the boats to bulldozers ashore and the rear to tugs in the water. The process kept the landing craft stable long enough for men to swarm the crafts and unload supplies. Working parties dodged mortars and artillery fire as well as the surf. Beach masters with loudspeakers stood on high ground in half a dozen places, shouting directions. Once offloaded, craft returned to transport vessels with "litter-loads of pain-crazed bodies; not really men, just bodies, which were salted down as the heavy seas broke over the bows of the lurching landing craft, jarred into sickening consciousness as the waves hurled the boats against the high walls."[153] The vicious combat for the wounded was over, but for 3d Division, the relentless terror had just begun.

The Marines in 3d Division moved up from the beach to the airfield, placing themselves in a position between the 4th and 5th Divisions to smash the enemy's strongly fortified center. The 3d Division had the privilege of

THE UNTOLD TRUTH

leadership provided by Gen. Graves B. Erskine, one of the most experienced and intelligent Marine officers in the Pacific. As Holland M. Smith's former Chief of Staff of V Amphibious Corps, Erskine had been intimately involved with the planning of Central Pacific operations from 1943 through 1945. In regard to tactics on Iwo Jima, Erskine believed in maneuver warfare concepts, including massing available firepower in support of a singular unit advance within his entire area of responsibility (usually of battalion size). Erskine also desired to maintain a forward momentum up a narrow front and envelop the bypassed enemy positions from the rear rather than utilize frontal assault up his entire zone of action.[154] These ideas were a distinct departure from assault doctrine used in most previous Marine campaigns.

Despite the advantages of his tactical approach, General Erskine had tremendous difficulty breaking the main Japanese defensive line. For one thing, he never had the full use of his division. Although Erskine and General Schmidt both requested the 3d Marine Regiment (held in reserve offshore) for use against the center, Gen. Holland Smith refused to release it—a contentious aspect of Operation Detachment still not fully understood today. The real issue at stake in the release of the 3d Marines was not just having more bodies ashore. Instead, it was the proficiency this intact regiment could provide in lieu of the miserable system of replacing wounded from the pool of inexperienced Marines, which left combat units less effective and further prone to casualties. According to General Erskine, General Smith believed there were enough Marines on the island already. When Erskine protested, Smith replied, "You keep quiet, we've made the decision."[155] To make things worse, although Schmidt assigned the 3d Marine Division the difficult task of cracking the center, he failed to allocate Erskine enough artillery support, preferring instead to divide it among the three divisions almost equally. Erskine had the fewest tanks, so he made every attempt to get his own artillery and tanks ashore. It took two and half days before the 3d Marine Division had enough fire support to make forward progress.

Finally on 27 February Erskine planned and instituted a rolling barrage made up of mortars, artillery, naval guns, and air support, followed by infantry assault. This ultimately brought the 3d Marine Division some forward momentum. On 28 February the center of the main defensive line finally broke, and the division advanced beyond the second airfield into the high ground around the abandoned Motoyama Village.

Despite the static design of Iwo Jima's defenses, General Kuribayashi employed some dynamic and imaginative counterattack schemes as V Amphibious Corps advanced. The defenders remained in the relative security of their fortified positions during daylight hours. But at night, the Japanese frequently redeployed forces or conducted raids on the Marines' rear areas. One such practice particularly frustrated Marine engineers. The numerous crippled and destroyed tanks that littered the landscape of the interior testified to the unprecedented number of landmines the Japanese employed on Iwo Jima. To keep support and supplies moving forward, Marine engineers worked feverishly to remove landmines from high-traffic areas, clearing 2,000 of the deadly devices from 5th Division's area alone. Yet as the Marines slept, Japanese would boldly infiltrate front lines and lay mines on roads that the engineers had previously cleared. Consequently, Marines were forced to guard the roads at night.[156]

In another case, Kuribayashi practiced an amphibious assault of his own. Under cover of darkness, he loaded a barge with soldiers and disembarked them onto 5th Division's landing beaches.[157] His surprise attack in the rear area caused havoc and mayhem, but the outnumbered Japanese were eventually overwhelmed. Much more frequently, Kuribayashi used small-scale

Demonstrating perhaps the most effective weapon in the infantryman's arsenal, Marines use flame-throwers on a Japanese pillbox.

THE UNTOLD TRUTH

infiltration attacks, but despite recurrent nighttime operations, the Japanese never had enough resources to do more than harass the Marines, and when the sun came up, the Marines renewed their unrelenting offensive.

One of the most symbolically important events on Iwo Jima occurred on 9 March. A patrol from the 3d Division broke through the center of the island and reached the northern shore. The enthusiastic Marines filled a canteen full of salt water, labeled it "for Erskine's inspection," and brought it back to 3d Division Headquarters. This likely provided one of General Erskine's most memorable moments on Iwo Jima. Impressed with the symbolism, Erskine presented the grimy canteen full of sea water to General Schmidt with the label "for inspection, not consumption."[158] The men of the 3d Division had finished their primary mission of cracking the center, but the battle for territory on either side of their advance continued.

Although the Japanese defenses had finally been split down the middle, the task of killing the last of the defenders dragged on. The relentless conflict left an indelible mark on the combatants. One Marine in 3d Division sent a picture of himself home to his family, but could not believe his own strange appearance. He wrote, "Here's my picture, but there's something wrong with my eyes."[159] The Marine later clarified the experience in poetry:

A Marine Always dies,
Wounds are in his soul,
That only he can know,
And the scars that do not show,
Are showing in his eyes.[160]

While 3d Division cracked the center line, 4th Division doggedly cleared out the Quarry, the Amphitheater, and the Meat Grinder on Erskine's right flank—resulting in the toughest fights of the battle. General Cates tried to envelop from the high ground that 3d Marine Division had purchased on his left. However, the rugged terrain made the task exceedingly difficult and restricted the use of tanks. Additionally, the Japanese refused to withdraw farther north as they had done previously. The importance of the high ground in the area, especially Hill 382 (the Meat Grinder), obligated the Japanese to fight at all costs from their caves, pillboxes, foxholes, and trenches.[161] As a result, the 4th Marine Division did the most hand-to-hand fighting.

Despite the advantages of their defenses, the Japanese counterattacked on the night of 8 March. Having lost contact with General Kuribayashi or simply defying his orders, Navy Capt. Samaji Inouye led his sailors in one final *banzai* charge. Inouye, a naval artillery expert, was also a superlative swordsman and likely trained his men for hand-hand combat.[162] Now, he motivated his sailors with the ambitious goal of recapturing Suribachi Yama.[163] The *banzai* charge presented an alternative to waiting for certain death. It even offered Inouye and his troops a chance to survive (however meager that chance actually was) if they could defeat tens of thousands of Americans in hand-to-hand combat and force them back to the sea. Then again, perhaps the counterattack was the easier psychological choice since it either resulted in victory or brought a quick end to the misery.

Whatever the motivation leading up to the human assault wave, 4th Division repelled the attack through close combat and devastating presighted artillery. At noon the next day the body count of Japanese dead totaled nearly 800, the largest single-day enemy death toll recorded on Iwo Jima.[164] The eradication of so many defenders in the open made the 4th Division's continued advance northward much easier—exactly what Kuribayashi had wanted to prevent by employing a static defense. The 4th Marine Division eventually secured the beach areas of the northern sector two days later, around 10 March. On 12 March General Cates made a number of appeals for surviving defenders in his sector to surrender. Hearing of this, Kuribayashi radioed Tokyo: "The Americans advised us to surrender by loud-speaker, but we only laughed at their childish trick."[165]

The 5th Marine Division turned to the difficult task of overcoming the prepared defenses on the western portion of Sulfur Island. Like the 4th Marine Division, the 5th under General Rockey attempted to use the elevated property taken by the 3d Marine Division in the center to flank the enemy positions to his front. Instead of recognizable terrain features, Rockey faced a maze of interlocking pillboxes on wave upon wave of elevated folds. In spite of that, the terrain proved level enough (at least initially) for 5th Division to make effective use of tanks.

At times, the systematic aspects of killing by automated means, yet still within visible sight of targets, proved emotionally traumatizing for the operators. One Marine tank crewman remembered: "As our tank maneuvered around a large boulder we saw a Jap sitting down with no clothes on, he appears to be blind and crying. We fire a burst from the machine gun at him [and] just as we do our tank turns slightly to the right. The burst misses his chest and takes his left arm off at the elbow. His life's blood is now leaping [out] in great spurts and in rhythm with his heart beat. Our next burst hits him in the chest and his body slams back against the ground with a great invisible force."[166] Catching Japanese in the open was a rare occurrence on Iwo Jima, and this memory proved a painful one. Such was the reality of the Pacific war, not so glamorous but the essence of its prosecution nonetheless.

Regardless of the advantages of the 5th Division's mechanical assets, most of the work still fell to its infantry. As in the other divisions, the majority of officers in Rockey's battalions suffered injury during the torturous weeks of fighting. Yet amazingly, the division continued to function admirably at the company level, a tribute to the Marine Corps philosophy and emphasis on small unit leadership.

Despite the material advantages and technological superiority of 5th Division in relation to the enemy, the aggressive use of rifle companies to seize defensive installations over a prolonged period left unparalleled numbers of casualties. Navy corpsmen bore the horrifying responsibility of treating the terrible wounds of an almost endless supply of patients. Even more than audacious Marines, corpsmen were forced to expose themselves routinely to deadly fire during the conduct of their duties.

The Marines' ethos as the world's greatest and most dedicated infantrymen pressured their corpsmen to go one step further in taking risks. One corpsman, George Wahlen, landed with the 5th Marine Division on 19 February and performed his medical duties throughout operations across the two Motoyama Airfields and onto the Motoyama Plateau. As his company pushed through the rocky crags of the plateau on 26 February, Wahlen was painfully wounded but remained on the battlefield. He pressed forward of the front lines, and evacuated a wounded Marine under concentrated Japanese fire. After attending to the injured Marines in his own unit, he offered assistance to at least fourteen Marines in the adjacent company, braving deadly Japanese mortar, machine gun, and rifle fire in the process. Wahlen suffered wounds a second time during a rapid attack on 2 March, but refused evacuation in order to render aid to other members of his platoon brought down by enemy fire. While treating the many wounded, Wahlen suffered a third wound so grievous that he could not walk. Undeterred, he crawled at least 50 meters to render aid to another Marine. Although corpsmen like Wahlen made up only about 3 percent of the fighting forces on Iwo Jima (an average of one corpsman for every forty-man platoon), they were later awarded four of the twenty-seven Medals of Honor, or 15 percent. In effect, however great the risk to infantry was in any given situation, the risk to corpsmen was even greater. Seven hundred corpsmen became casualties, and those that did not bore the mental imprint of hellish mutilations for the rest of their lives.[167]

While judging Japanese tactics like *kamikaze* and *banzai* charges as alien and suicidal, the Marines simultaneously adopted and applauded similar approaches of sacrifice in their own desperate conduct of battle. As in Japan, many of America's most idealistic youths carried out such practices. The actions of 5th Marine Division's Jacklyn Lucas, who had turned seventeen less than a week before the landing, typified this courage. While on patrol, Lucas's squad traversed a narrow ravine. The enemy threw a hand grenade into the rift, which landed in close proximity to a number of Marines. Recognizing the danger to his friends, Lucas threw his own body over the deadly explosive in order to protect them from harm. As Lucas awaited his death, a second Japanese hand grenade fell into the area. Lucas reached out, scooped up this other device, placed both hand grenades under himself, and absorbed the impact of the explosions. Amazingly, Lucas survived the event. Most Marines who carried out such acts of selflessness, however, paid for it with their lives. Adding to the 5th Division's combat effectiveness, the Marines' feeling of *esprit de corps* was instrumental in the difficult offensive north into what eventually encompassed the steepest terrain on the Motoyama Plateau. The 5th Division encountered the remainder of Kuribayashi's resistance and, consequently, would be the last to leave the despair of Sulfur Island.

Iwo Jima has often been described in terms of its black volcanic sands, sulfur fumes, lava crags, and labyrinthine caves. One particular expression used by American pioneers to describe the badlands of the Wild West seems appropriate: "hell with the fire out."[168] However, it is difficult to judge the combat setting on the island by merely acknowledging the lunar-like terrain, complete with rocks, craters, and charred vegetation. Certainly, the nature of the topography that one can readily identify in pictures does not adequately describe the surroundings in which the fighting took place, especially in its final week. The sight of dead bodies and the smell of rotting flesh was everywhere. One journalist described it this way:

> Somehow the sight and smell of the Japanese dead were bearable;
> mostly I think, because a dead Japanese does not look quite human.
> The yellow skin darkens and the bodies seem unusually small and
> characterless, like figures in a wax museum. One cannot look at them
> and be unmoved, but they lack the personal quality which grips the soul
> of an observer. The sight on Iwo which I could not force myself to see
> again was the section of the beach allotted for an American cemetery
> . . . The dead were brought in faster than they could be buried . . .
> there was half an acre of dead Marines stretched out so close together
> that they blanketed the beach for two hundred yards. The stench was

THE UNTOLD TRUTH

One of the many massive concrete fortifications on Iwo Jima

overpowering. There, in mangled lots, not laid in neat rows, was part
of the price paid for Iwo . . . The smell of one's countrymen rotting in
the sun is a lasting impression . . . The Marines fought with courage
and determination seemingly beyond human capabilities. They died the
hard way.[169]

In the fourth week of fighting, Marines and Japanese continued to die hard.
It was as if no amount of suffering, no matter how great and terrible, could
break their indomitable spirits.

Even after weeks ashore, Marine generals continued to debate over how
best to employ the remaining infantry. When General Schmidt asked General
Erskine to reinforce General Rockey's 5th Division at Kitano Point with his
3d Division, Erskine replied, "I'll be goddamned, I am not going to do it!"[170]
When Schmidt informed Erskine that the 5th Division had been trying to
seize Kitano Point for five days, Erskine responded, "Hell, I am talking about
the 3d Division, not the 5th."[171] Eventually Schmidt relented and allowed
Erskine to seize the northern shoreline of Kitano Point independently; his

northward advance moved laterally in front of the 5th Division. Erskine's scheme of maneuver left a gap between the two Marine divisions. But now isolated within the last major pocket of Japanese resistance, Kuribayashi was caught between the 3d Division, which rotated to drive south, and the 5th Division, continuing to advance north. With relentless will, the Marine vise crushed the remaining life out of the Japanese.

As the Marine divisions seized the bloody real estate around him, Gen. Tadamichi Kuribayashi tenaciously fought on, yet was forced to recognize his inevitable defeat.[172] He radioed his farewell address to Tokyo on 15 March, saying goodbye to his seniors and friends. Then, around midnight of 17 March, his staff changed clothes into enlisted uniforms to ensure that the Marines would not discover their true identity if killed. Kuribayashi left his command post with about 200 troops. During the movement, shell fragments wounded Kuribayashi in his right thigh, and his men assisted him to a new cave about 150 meters west of the original command post. Most of the survivors from the elite 145th Infantry Regiment gathered around Kuribayashi, about 450 total (150 were wounded). The 5th Marine Division

Marines use a hot pipe from a sulfur vent to heat up some coffee.

THE UNTOLD TRUTH

surrounded the cave shortly afterward and began bombarding it with indirect fire, and attempted to burn the Japanese out with flame-throwing tanks. The defenders had no food or water for five days and could only counterattack with rifle fire. Their situation became both miserable and desperate. Despite the horrible circumstances, General Kuribayashi relayed the following poem to Tokyo.[173]

Ada utade nobe ni wa kuchiji
ware wa mata natabi umarete hoko wo toramuzo
Foe unvanquished, I won't perish in the field;
I'll be born again, to take up the halberd seven more times!

As the speed of the costly advance slowed near the end of March, senior Marine officers made several appeals to the Japanese in their last strongholds to surrender. All three divisions tried to end the conflict without further destruction. Such was the case on 23 March, when the 5th Division began broadcasting via loudspeaker for the Japanese in Kuribayashi's cave to surrender. Kuribayashi approached the front of the cave himself and discussed the surrender of his troops in English with one of the Marine sentries, who had no idea whom he was actually speaking to.

Hearing of Kuribayashi's actions, Lt. Col. Nakane, a member of Kuribayashi's staff, had a particularly violent argument with the general. During the discussion, Kuribayashi argued that some Japanese needed to survive in order to provide a correct interpretation of the battle's history, but Nakane maintained that the honor of the combatants was more important. Nakane's line of reasoning eventually prevailed. Thoroughly exhausted, the general sat down to write a final note to the emperor. He stated his profound apologies that he had failed to defend Iwo Jima, and said that he would return in spirit to revive the Japanese Army.[174] Directly afterward, Kuribayashi committed *hara-kiri* (literally, "belly-cutting"), slicing his own abdomen open with a short sword while Nakane decapitated him from the rear. Because he had failed in his duty, Kuribayashi performed the ancient *bushido* custom to retain his honor through the painful exposure of his spirit (his intestines). By cutting off Kuribayashi's head, Nakane humanely ended the general's painful resolution. After Kuribayashi's death, his staff buried his body in the cave. Then, most of the surviving senior leadership on Iwo Jima, including Nakane, followed the example of Iwo Jima's guardian and carried out similar acts of suicide. The 5th Marine Division did not discover what happened to Kuribayashi, and his body was never recovered.[175]

Three days later, on the night of 26 March, the survivors of the Japanese 145th Infantry conducted a final counterattack. About 300 weary defenders, armed with both Japanese and U.S. weapons, infiltrated the rear areas near the beach in the southwest. The confused engagement that followed caused significant casualties to both sides, but American support personnel, including many black Marines in the segregated service units, vigorously fought off the counterattack. About 200 Japanese dead were found in the morning. It was the final major episode the Marines faced on Sulfur Island.

On 26 March the 147th Army Infantry Regiment officially took over garrison functions and patrolling operations. Conducting over 6,000 daylight patrols and night ambushes, the 147th continued to combat over 2,500 surviving Japanese defenders until the end of the war.[176] Two men, Yamakage and Matsudo, at last surrendered four years later, in 1949.[177]

Red Blood, Black Sand

The title of Charles W. Tatum's book *Iwo Jima: Red Blood, Black Sand, Pacific Apocalypse* (1995) directly implies the tragic price of seizing Sulfur Island.[178] Clearly, Operation Detachment cost the United States dearly, incurring considerably more casualties than planners expected. Medical personnel intended to evacuate 350 wounded personnel per week, yet during the battle, "[one] half or two thirds of the planned weekly evacuations were being carried out daily."[179] Over 17,000 wounded personnel were evacuated, which was more than three times the amount of bed space made available in the Marianas (1,500 beds in Saipan and 3,500 beds in Guam).[180] In many ways, the price paid surpassed that of other Pacific battles. However, sources continue to underestimate the actual ratio of American to Japanese losses.

While the U.S. government upheld a positive confidence about Iwo Jima in the press, the extensive casualties negatively influenced decision-makers, including the President. When Franklin D. Roosevelt returned from Yalta on 21 February, the Joint Chiefs of Staff informed him of the 4,500 casualties at that point, and stated that the Marines still had a long way to go to secure the island. The President was visibly shaken. According to one biographer, Jim Bishop, "It was the first time in the war, through bad news and good, that anyone had seen the President gasp in horror."[181] Journalist Tedd Thomey said that the President expressed displeasure with the Joint Chiefs of Staff. He reminded them that they had promised Operation Detachment would take only a handful of days and cost few casualties. In response, the Joint Chiefs attempted to explain the circumstances that had made the battle more difficult than expected.[182] Two days later, the President's appointed civilian supervisor on naval affairs, Secretary of the Navy James Forrestal, made a personal visit to the battlefront. As if to put to rest fears to the contrary, Forrestal prepared a radio address for the Pacific Theater on 25 February that claimed Marines were exacting a "4-to-1" death toll on the enemy.[183]

Political pressure and public condemnation may have influenced Nimitz's decision to prematurely declare the island secure.[184] His press release of 16 March stated that the "battle of Iwo Island has been won" and that "organized resistance on Iwo Island ceased at 1800 on 16 March."[185] This created initial confusion over the actual number of U.S. casualties. Astonishingly, and much to Gen. Harry Schmidt's surprise, Nimitz never consulted the Marine ground force Commander before making his announcement. Actually, heavy fighting continued for ten more days, and the early declaration minimized the casualty figures released in the press.[186] Consequently, official casualty figures following the battle indicated only 4,189 dead and 15,308 wounded, far fewer than the actual total the Marines suffered.[187]

While the premature figures released by Nimitz understated actual losses, Chief of Staff of the Army Air Forces Gen. Henry Arnold made even greater misrepresentations. Although he had access to much higher figures going all the way back to the battle reports of March 1945, Arnold appears to have used Nimitz's premature press release of 4,000 dead and then subtracted the number of sailors killed (roughly a thousand). Arnold then argued that the United States had secured Iwo Jima at the cost of 3,000 Marines.[188] Others have similarly attempted to justify Iwo Jima by understating the actual cost, but Arnold's use of statistics resulted in what is probably the smallest casualty number ever offered. He not only maintained such low figures in 1945 but published identical statistics four years later, in 1949.[189]

American casualty figures for Iwo Jima steadily rose over the decade following the battle. Estimates changed for various reasons. The military continued to identify the bodies of men classified as missing, and many casualties died of wounds. The main complicating factor was that it actually took Marines another ten days to pacify the island after Nimitz released the initial casualty figures. Later, the Marine Corps dubbed the period between Nimitz's declaration (16 March) and the last major Japanese encounter (26 March) the "capture and occupation phase." Over time, this period became incorporated into the legitimate timeline of the battle's events and thus expanded the number of recognized casualties.

Published in 1954, Whitman Bartley's official Marine Corps monograph continues to serve as the primary authority for U.S. casualties on Iwo Jima.[190]

Bartley based his data on casualty figures released by the Marine Corps in August 1952. He concluded that 6,821 Americans died as a result of Operation Detachment. The United States suffered an additional 19,217 wounded, and the Navy classified another 2,648 personnel with a debilitating neuropsychiatric condition known as "combat fatigue." To date, no one has disputed Bartley's figures, and they represent the most accurate tally.

Scholars have reached no consensus on the size of the defense force or the number of Japanese casualties. Kuribayashi proved to be the most security-conscious Japanese commander the Marine Corps encountered.[191] The general took every precaution not to compromise Japanese documents, especially tables of organization. In King's report to the Secretary of the Navy in March of 1945, he stated that the Navy had destroyed 20,000 Japanese troops. A mere three months later the Joint Chiefs of Staff compiled a report for the President that indicated 25,000 Japanese casualties.[192] Historians have claimed that the number of Japanese dead and wounded was as high as 23,000, but most adhere to the figure of 21,000.[193] Generally, scholars have overestimated Japanese losses.

To attain the most accurate number of defenders, prudence demands a return to the meticulous data accumulated by Bartley. For information on

Medical personnel disinfect American dead for insect and disease control.

THE UNTOLD TRUTH

Japanese forces, Bartley relied on a V Amphibious Corps intelligence report submitted in April.[194] This report, which in Bartley's judgment presented the most accurate tally, indicated that there were between 20,530 and 21,060 Japanese defenders. As to how many Japanese died during the battle, Bartley candidly stated that the number of casualties was unknown.[195] Bartley skillfully sidestepped the issue he surely knew to be true—that Japanese casualties during the battle numbered far less than commonly accepted.

One can estimate the damage sustained by the defenders during Operation Detachment by working backward. Amazingly, the Japanese continued fighting even after the Marines declared the island secure a second time in late March. After the Marines left, the island's Army garrison encountered Japanese resistance until at least the end of May. In a report released in June, the Army garrison established that it had taken 867 prisoners and had killed 1,602 Japanese.[196] Subtracting these numbers from the forces on the island in February shows that the number of Japanese casualties incurred during the battle likely numbered between 18,061 and 18,591. Table 1 shows the corrected breakdown of Operation Detachment's human cost.

The inflation of Japanese losses to 21,000 or 23,000 by previous historians diminished the horrific reality of Iwo Jima. The ratio of American to Japanese casualties tragically surpassed that of any other amphibious operation, with *three American casualties for every two Japanese*. Despite the Navy's and Marine Corps' overwhelming superiority in experience, training, firepower, technology, and numbers, Kuribayashi and his island of death inflicted horrible devastation on the attacking forces. Showing the enormity of American

TABLE 1
U.S. and Japanese Casualties from Operation Detachment (19 Feb – 26 March 1945)

Organization	Killed in Action Missing in Action	Wounded in Action	Combat Fatigue	Taken Prisoner	Total
U.S. Marines	5,931	17,272	2,648	0	25,851
U.S. Navy	890	1,945	0	0	2,835
U.S. Army	9	28	0	0	37
Total	6,821	19,217	2,648		28,696
Japanese Defense Force	(estimated) 17,845-18,375			216	(estimated) 18,061-18,591
Ratio of American/Japanese casualties					1 : 64

TABLE 2
Statistical Comparison of Island Battles in World War II

| Battle | United States | | | Japan | | | |
	KIA & MIA	WIA	Total	KIA & MIA	Taken Prisoner	Total	US/Japan Total Rat
Luzon	8,310	29,560	37,870	192,000	9,700	201,700	1:5.3
Tinian	389	1,816	2,205	9,162	N/A	9,162	1:4.2
Marshalls	711	2,339	3,050	11,087	361	11,448	1:3.8
Leyte	3,593	11,991	15,584	48,790	N/A	48,790	1:3.1
Okinawa	11,933	39,119	51,052	110,000	10,755	120,755	1:2.4
Saipan	3,452	13,160	16,612	27,000	2,000	29,000	1:1.7
Guam	1,435	5,648	7,083	10,000	N/A	10,000	1:1.4
Palaus	1,948	8,515	10,463	13,600	302	13,902	1:1.3
Gilberts	1,933	2,725	4,658	5,236	430	5,666	1:1.2
Iwo Jima	6,821	19,217	26,038	18,110	216	18,326	1:0.7

losses on Iwo Jima, Table 2 compares Operation Detachment with other island battles.[197]

Only in Operation Detachment did Americans suffer significantly more dead and wounded than the Japanese. The ratio of U.S. to Japanese casualties in Operation Detachment nearly doubled that of the bloody Gilbert Islands campaign. The U.S. losses for Iwo Jima also outweighed all but the principal battles for Luzon and Okinawa. Furthermore, the price of Iwo Jima's runway (26,038) surpassed that for all three B-29 bases on the considerably larger islands of Guam, Tinian, and Saipan combined (25,900).

Combining those prisoners taken by the Marine Corps (216) and Army (867), by June 1945 Americans had captured over 1,000 Japanese defenders. Yet these soldiers and sailors faced further humiliation when eventually returned home to a defeated nation. The civilian population quickly blamed the military for entering a losing contest. In general, the military became despised. Servicemen who had spent years pursuing a lost cause now faced public disgust for having done so. Historian John Dower aptly described them as "pariahs in their native land."[198] Veterans might find solace in each other's company, but that comfort did not fully extend to former prisoners of war. Their mere existence dishonored and made meaningless the sacrifices of those who had died. Iwo Jima survivors had "failed in their duty to the homeland."[199] Essentially, repatriated prisoners became outsiders in both military and social circles.

Some Japanese survivors could not live with the shame and despair. Yamakage was one of the last to surrender on Iwo Jima, in 1949—four years after the battle. He later returned to the island with a historian and journalist named Stuart Griffin. Yamakage had convinced Griffin that he had left a diary on the island with over five years of entries. Although the two men searched in Yamakage's last cave, they found nothing. Irritated, Griffin told Yamakage he did not believe his story about a diary, and Yamakage disappeared for the rest of the evening. He eventually returned the next morning with torn hands, presumably from searching for something he valued. Just before their plane was supposed to leave, the two men climbed Suribachi Yama to take some pictures. At the top, Yamakage "started trotting with eyes on the ground. He paused, turned, and slowly walked back. Then he again loped toward the edge of the cliff overlooking the sea. He picked up speed, threw both arms in the air, shouted something and jumped. Griffin ran to the edge of the cliff. There was a drop of twenty yards to a rocky ledge covered with sand, and he saw an indentation as if something had hit it. Out of sight, a hundred yards below on another ledge, lay the body of Yamakage."[200] Although an extreme case, Yamakage's example demonstrates the inner conflict felt by survivors.

On the American side, prolonged exposure to the horrors and stress of desperate combat drove some Marines past their mental breaking point. Over the thirty-day struggle, 2,600 Marines became so mentally incapacitated that they could no longer effectively function. Although the condition labeled "combat fatigue" had accompanied earlier battles in the Pacific, it became increasingly apparent during the later phases of the war, specifically at the Battles of Peleliu, Iwo Jima, and Okinawa. In 1942 and 1943 Marines usually faced the prospect of constant assault for no more than a few days before interruption in the fighting occurred or the battle ended. For instance, although Marines fought on Guadalcanal for three months, there were routine breaks in the fighting. The amphibious assaults in the Gilbert and Marshall Islands lasted only a few days. As battles lengthened into weeks, neuropsychiatric disorders became more prevalent.

Fervent infantry assault against zealous Japanese defenders had an increasingly negative effect on the Marines' mental capacity to carry out such aggressive methods consistently over time. Veteran Eugene Sledge described his condition after weeks of combat on Peleliu:

"The grinding stress of prolonged heavy combat, the loss of sleep because of nightly infiltration and raids, the vigorous physical demands forced on us by the rugged terrain, and the unrelenting, suffocating heat were enough to make us drop in our tracks. How we kept going and continued fighting I'll never know. I was so indescribably weary physically and emotionally that I became fatalistic, praying only for my fate to be painless. The million-dollar wound seemed more of a blessing with every weary hour that dragged by. It seemed the only escape other than death or maiming."[201]

In addition to the negative mental effect on individual soldiers, Sledge acknowledged that his entire unit became less effective over time, a fact the enemy also noticed. Captured Japanese documents described the Marines as "worn out."[202]

In comparison to Peleliu, combat on Iwo Jima had greater impact on the mental well-being of the assault forces. The unprecedented amount of artillery and mortar fire that Kuribayashi directed at the Americans had the most debilitating consequences on the spirit. Many Iwo Jima veterans remember men having mental breakdowns as a result of such indirect fire.[203] Again, Eugene Sledge vividly described the effect of indirect fire on the psyche:

> To be under a barrage or prolonged shelling simply magnified all the terrible physical and emotional effects of one shell. To me, artillery was an invention of hell. The onrushing whistle and scream of the big steel package of destruction was the pinnacle of violent fury and the embodiment of pent-up evil. It was the essence of violence and of man's inhumanity to man. I developed a passionate hatred for shells. To be killed by a bullet seemed so clean and surgical. But shells would not only tear and rip the body. They tortured one's mind almost beyond the brink of sanity. After each shell I was wrung out, limp and exhausted. During prolonged shelling, I often had to restrain myself and fight back a wild, inexorable urge to scream, to sob and to cry . . . I feared that if I ever lost control of myself under shell fire my mind would be shattered. I hated shells as much for their damage to my mind as to the body. To be under heavy shell fire was to me by far the most terrifying of combat experiences. Each time it left me feeling more forlorn and helpless, more fatalistic, and with less confidence that I could escape the dreadful law of averages that inexorably reduced our numbers . . . the terror and desperation endured under heavy shelling are by far the most unbearable."[204]

Compared to preceding engagements with the Japanese, a higher portion of those wounded on Iwo Jima were the result of Japanese mortar and artillery fire, resulting in extraordinarily ghastly wounds and an unusually high death rate.[205] The unprecedented amount of indirect fire leveled at the 3d, 4th, and 5th Marine Divisions had the greatest effect on the high number of combat fatigue victims.

THE UNTOLD TRUTH

Even under the shared adversity of war, it appears that little empathy was shown for neuropsychiatric disorders. For instance, Gen. Clifton Cates candidly stated that "battle fatigue cases were the ones that were just yellow."[206] Many Marines viewed combat fatigue victims as quitters who had obviously failed to uphold the masculine ideal to tough it out.[207] After the battle, most reports ignored the existence of the mental condition altogether. Except in a one-sentence footnote, the Marine Corps official history failed to mention combat fatigue, even though it constituted 10 percent of the casualties and had a very negative effect on the fighting.[208] More important, the mental scars of those who continued to fight also went unaddressed and left unresolved questions concerning veterans' combat effectiveness if they had been placed under similar circumstances again—such as an invasion of the Japanese mainland.

One of the greatest costs of Operation Detachment was in the quality of manpower that the Marine Corps sacrificed. In 1939 the Marine Corps consisted of over 27,000 personnel, of whom only 800 were officers.[209] By March 1945 the Corps strength rapidly increased to nearly 500,000 and the officer corps to 37,000—a factor of forty-six growth in numbers in a five-year

A group of dead Japanese in the open.

A rifle and helmet combination mark the spot of a fallen friend.

period.[210] Necessity dictated a thin distribution of trained and experienced officers, and Operation Detachment put some of this irreplaceable leadership to the most horrific test imaginable. Many of the officers and senior enlisted met the challenge before them the only way they could—by making the ultimate sacrifice.

The casualties incurred by 3d Battalion 9th Marines (3/9) reveal the harsh reality of combat leadership on Iwo Jima. A typical battalion consisted of about 48 officers and 800 men. As Marines died or were wounded, replacements were allocated from a reserve pool. By the end of the ordeal, the battalion had suffered 54 officer casualties (112 percent). Of those, 32 were killed in action, 3 died of injuries, and 19 were wounded. The officer casualty rate of 3/9 exceeded that of any other unit, affecting well over 100 percent of its landing-force strength.

The wounded and fatalities sustained by 3/9 were no anomaly. Nine other battalions suffered over 30 officer casualties (62 percent), and 25 battalions sustained more than 20 dead or wounded officers. The loss of leadership certainly increased the number of other casualties on Iwo Jima because

Separated only by a few yards, white Marines (in the forefront) and black Marines (in the rear) work to bury dead in a large trench.

it reduced the combat efficiency of the assault forces.[211] According to one medical study, of 17,677 men wounded on Iwo Jima only 1,674 were ever returned to duty (less than 9 percent), and over 16,000 sustained wounds serious enough for the men to be evacuated from theater.[212] Iwo Jima's tens of thousands of dead and wounded could not lead in future operations against more critical targets. Functioning with such a limited prewar career force and running short on volunteers by 1945, the Marine Corps could ill afford to sustain such heavy damage without harming combat proficiency.

Beyond some simple arithmetic formula, the unprecedented numbers of Marine careerists and veterans killed and wounded on Iwo Jima endangered the 3d, 4th, and 5th Divisions' uniqueness as elite forces. In a similar comparison, Craig Cameron effectively argued the negative effects losses had on the 1st Marine Division after its epic struggle for Peleliu: "In losing the cream of its veteran infantry, the division also lost its essential distinctiveness from the Army. A flood of replacements fleshed out the depleted regiments long before the Okinawa landings, but there was to be in that campaign little

A Marine helps his wounded comrade toward the rear for medical treatment.

to distinguish the division from the veteran Army divisions alongside which it fought. The new men did not have the same attitudes that had animated the division earlier in the war, and although they claimed for themselves the same qualities that had distinguished their predecessors, their performance never fully bore them out."[213]

The Marine Corps maintained its image as an all-volunteer force and could not simply substitute newly recruited conscripts to replace the extensive loss of veterans on Iwo Jima. Over 78 percent of the 247,000 Marines recruited in 1943 and 1944 had been drafted from selective service, and by 1945 they constituted the mainstay of replacements in the Pacific.[214] The presence of "old breed" Marines and volunteers leavened the ranks of the

THE UNTOLD TRUTH

3d, 4th, and 5th Divisions. But once they disappeared, the distinctive flavor that made the Marine Corps exceptional could not be easily sustained.

Several months after the meat grinder of Sulfur Island, the Joint Chiefs of Staff expected the 3d, 4th, and 5th Marine Divisions to take part in the seizure of the southern Japanese home island of Kyushu and eventually to participate in the invasion of Honshu itself. Such operations were fundamental in accomplishing America's national war aims for unconditional surrender. Yet after the damaging impact of the horrendous casualties incurred in the Bonin Islands, it is doubtful that these three divisions would have conducted subsequent campaigns with the same proficiency or fervor that made the seizure of Iwo Jima possible.

*Any positive American counter offensive based on blind
faith in mechanical and material strength is most welcome,
for it offers Nippon an opportunity to inflict huge and
devastating manpower losses in the enemy.*

GENERAL YAHAGI, *Tokyo speech, 6 July 1943*

*If the weapons only allow us to achieve costly successes
like those on Iwo Jima or Tarawa, then perhaps the Marine
Corps will not really have won at all, even if we do hold
the ground at the end of the battle.*

JON T. HOFFMAN, *"The Legacy and Lessons of Iwo Jima," February 1995*

CHAPTER 4   *Price of a Runway*

Fourteen costly days after the Marines landed on Iwo Jima, engineers
from the 2d Separate Engineer Battalion and the 62d Naval Construction Battalion busily worked to repair Airfield Number One. Japanese
and Americans still fought fiercely along the forward edge of the battle area,
and there remained a constant threat of indirect fire to the Marines on the
airstrip. A few observation planes had utilized Iwo Jima since late February.
Consequently, a short wooden control tower had been constructed on the
airfield just large enough to hoist a single Marine observer 20 feet above
the airfield. In the afternoon of 4 March, Airfield Number One received
an unanticipated message from one of the naval support ships. Apparently,
a B-29 had run short on fuel, was headed their way, and planned to land
on Iwo Jima.[1]

The predicament must have caused excitement among the ground crew on Airfield Number One. There was no time to coordinate a cease-fire of artillery or naval gunfire; the silhouette of the B-29 could be seen in a slow approach on the Pacific horizon. "Clear the airfield!" the shout may have gone out to construction crews. These veterans, accustomed to impromptu commands, likely scrambled to remove engineer equipment and personnel.[2] The massive Superfortress came onward at what must have seemed a snail's pace, attracting the attention of Japanese anti-aircraft and mortar fire. Yet it continued forward and finally touched down on the airstrip. Marines and sailors stopped and watched in amazement as the enormous flying battleship slowed to a stop.[3]

One Marine combat correspondent described what went through his mind as the B-29 landed. "Like a giant bird, it set down on Motoyama Airfield Number One . . . The B-29 landed on hallowed ground, volcanic ash surfaced with hard clay which recently had soaked in the blood of American Marines . . . These Leathernecks from your and my hometowns made it possible for the B-29 to land here. Now, those lads are buried in the shadow of Mount Suribachi, where Old Glory flies from the crest, proclaiming to all that American Marines conquered the Japs who held the formidable volcano fortress."[4]

When the first B-29 touched down on Iwo Jima, ground fighters could not contain their enthusiasm. They left their covered positions to surround the bomber *en masse*. This scene made for quite a famous photograph.[5] The Americans on Iwo Jima deemed much to celebrate in this seemingly trivial event. The men longed to understand the purpose behind the past two weeks of vicious combat, and amid the chaos of death and destruction, they believed it had suddenly landed directly in front of them. In the first days of the battle men argued whether the island would have any "lasting military significance," but the appearance of the B-29 quelled all that.[6] By the end of hostilities, thirty-six Superforts had made landings on Iwo Jima.[7] The euphoria surrounding these events had an immediate impact on the high commands of the Army Air Forces, Navy, and Marine Corps. The media also picked up on B-29 landings, giving rise to legends. As the flag-raising on Suribachi assumed heroic proportions, so did the romanticism justifying the need for Iwo Jima.

The Bonin Islands did have strategic relevance. They lay in a direct path of bombing raids to Tokyo. B-29 crews from the Marianas flew fourteen hours at a time without a friendly airfield between Tinian and Honshu. The confinement of American airstrips to Tinian, Guam, and Saipan somewhat

The first B-29 Superfortress landing on Iwo Jima. Exuberant Marines surround the plane.

restricted air rescue operations to the areas near the Marianas. In the chain of islands extending from the Marianas to mainland Japan (the Nanpo Shoto), the Japanese had already built airfields on several islands. The Bonin Islands offered one of the most suitable sites for construction of a forward air base.

Yet despite the benefits of having Iwo Jima in American hands, there were at least six other islands in the Nanpo Shoto under consideration by the Joint Chiefs of Staff. And by December 1944, it was becoming quite apparent that seizing Sulfur Island would prove difficult. In weighing the necessity of the battle, one must determine whether Operation Detachment accomplished its designed purpose, whether there were alternatives to accomplishing the same goals, and what Iwo Jima's impact was on future operations.

Multiplying Justifications

Part of the difficulty in probing the reasons given for Operation Detachment involves the inconsistency of sources. In the plan approved by the Joint War Planners, the justifications for the Bonin Islands operation read as follows:

a. Providing fighter cover for the application of our air effort against Japan.

b. Denying these strategic outposts to the enemy.

c. Furnishing air defense bases for our positions in the Marianas.

d. Providing fields for staging heavy bombers [B-24 Liberators] against Japan.

e. Precipitating a decisive naval engagement.[8]

After the battle, both King and Marshall continued to maintain that Iwo Jima provided essential fighter cover for Superforts, but they began shifting emphasis to the B-29 landings on Iwo Jima. In Marshall's report to the secretary of war, he stated, "Iwo fields saved hundreds of battle-damaged B-29s, unable to make the full return flight to their bases in the Marianas, 800 miles farther to the south."[9] King argued that significantly more B-29s would have been shot down over Japan "had Iwo Jima not been available for emergency landings." He estimated that "the lives lost at sea through this latter factor alone . . . exceeded the lives lost in the capture itself."[10]

Other sources have offered additional justifications for Iwo Jima. An Army Air Forces publication stated that air-sea rescue units based on the island critically promoted the rescue of downed aircrews.[11] Admiral Spruance pointed out that taking Iwo Jima removed a Japanese early-warning system for Superfortress bombing raids.[12] Gen. Haywood Hansell, Commanding General of the Twenty First Bomber Command until January 1945, stated that securing the island improved the morale of B-29 pilots.[13] The official Army Air Forces history claimed that B-29s needed to run a dog-leg course around the Bonins due to the threat of Japanese fighters stationed on Iwo Jima.[14] Over the years, scholarship has integrated many of these arguments as well.[15]

Table 3 compiles known justifications for Iwo Jima. Justifications 1–5 were made before the decision to initiate Operation Detachment. Others offered justifications 6–10 after the battle was over.[16]

The principal reason for seizing Iwo Jima originated from plans to use it as a fighter base for B-29 escort. Before the invasion, the Navy maintained this line of reasoning, both through the military chain of command and in the press. It was the only reason Admiral King mentioned in his proposal for the island's capture to the Joint Chiefs of Staff.[17] Accordingly, on 16 February, three days before the landing, Admiral Turner gave a press conference to the reporters stating that the primary reason for the capture of Iwo Jima was to provide "fighter cover for the operations of the B-29s which are based here

TABLE 3

Justifications Given for Operation Detachment

Justification	Approximate Date Released
1. Provide fighter escort for bombing raids over Japan	August 1945
2. Deny the Bonins' use to the enemy	August 1945
3. Reduce enemy air attacks on the Marianas.	August 1945
4. Provide airfields for staging heavy bombers against Japan	August 1945
5. Precipitate a decisive naval engagement	August 1945
6. Deprive the enemy of an early warning system	?
7. Improve the morale of B-29 pilots	September 1945
8. Provide for air-sea rescue operations	September 1945
9. To stop Japanese fighter interception of B-29 flights over Iwo Jima	?
10. To use as an emergency landing field	September 1945

in the Marianas."[18] Notably, neither King nor Turner made any mention of B-29s using Iwo Jima's airfields. After the invasion, the Army Air Forces rotated the 45th, 46th, 47th, 72nd, 78th, 531st, 548th, and 549th Fighter Squadrons from the VII Fighter Command onto the island; this included at any one time over one hundred P-51 Mustang fighters. The limited number of fighters in comparison to nearly a thousand B-29s in the Marianas made the escort of most bombing missions impossible in the face of rampant operations.

The limited number of fighters, however, was the least of the VII Fighter Command's problems, which primarily derived from long distance to objectives, mechanical limitations of the P-51, and harsh weather conditions over the Pacific Ocean. The single VHF radio had a range of 150 miles in line-of-sight circumstances.[19] The navigation systems on the P-51, consisting of a compass, an air speed indicator, and a clock, proved grossly inadequate for the 1,500-mile trips over the Pacific Ocean.[20] Ironically, the P-51s became dependent upon B-29s to escort them to and from targets. In March, when the VII Fighter Command attempted practice runs from Iwo Jima to Saipan, it quickly realized that the P-51 was not adequately designed for the long trip over the Pacific (unfortunately, the Army Air Force did not carry out these practice flights until after the island's capture).[21] The cramped, cold, and nonpressurized cockpit of the P-51 also made the nine-hour round trip over ocean waters difficult for pilots. Moreover, unlike the Superfortress, the P-51 did not fully withstand the harsh weather. As a result, storms caused many of the planes to crash.[22] The VII Fighter Command attempted to

THE UNTOLD TRUTH

escort Superforts in early April but soon realized the infeasibility of the task. The VII Fighter Command flew only three escort missions, on 7, 12, and 14 April, before terminating escort efforts.[23] The Army Air Forces did not use Iwo Jima for the purpose that had led to its capture.

What also needs consideration when discussing fighter operations is the duplication of effort. For instance, Okinawa had the capacity to provide dozens of airfields for land-based fighters, and did so. Limitations on range did not allow Okinawa-based fighters to travel as far north into mainland Japan, but VII Fighter Command had difficulty covering that distance from Iwo Jima as well. More important, carrier-based fighters routinely hit targets on the mainland. By the end of 1945 the United States had produced an unprecedented thirty aircraft carriers and eighty-two escort carriers for the U.S. Navy, the largest assembly of naval air power in world history.[24]

The versatility of the Pacific Fleet allowed for fighter escort for B-29s. Naval fighters could launch and recover at much shorter and safer distances than the 1,500-mile trip from Iwo Jima. In terms of numbers, one heavy carrier carried about as many planes as there were P-51s stationed on Iwo Jima, and it seems irrational to think that the airfields on Iwo Jima, with the poor logistical situation of having no port facility, could provide air support that carriers could not.

Initially, when B-29s began operations in November 1944, the Navy agreed to support the Army Air Forces with carrier-based fighter support.[25] Because Navy air power was tied up in other operations that month, the proposal eventually fell through. The Army Air Forces decided to go in alone rather than wait for Navy fighter support. The concept of joint aerial operations never again materialized. Increased cooperation between the Army Air Forces and Navy would have proven more beneficial than P-51s stationed on Iwo Jima.

Ironically, before the battle had reached its climax, the need for fighter escort had already become questionable. In early March Army Air Forces Gen. Curtis LeMay switched the B-29s' usual tactic of high-altitude precision daylight bombing to that of low-altitude firebombing raids at night. According to Army Air Forces General Hansell, this solution increased bomb loads since "in daylight the force had to fly in formation and operate at high altitude in order to defend itself against Japanese fighters," which restricted tonnage.[26] Conversely, Japanese night air defenses offered feeble and ineffective resistance. Damage from friendly fires concerned LeMay more than Japanese air defenses. Consequently, LeMay stripped the B-29s of anti-aircraft guns and gunners to make room for larger payloads.[27] The general only later reinstalled a portion of the B-29s' defensive systems for purposes of morale. Meanwhile, bombardiers more easily hit targets at lower altitudes than at 30,000 feet. Initially, LeMay worried that bombing runs at 5,000 feet would increase Superfort losses, but the results surpassed his expectations. Not only did firebombing destroy the desired targets, but the devastation gutted large portions of Japanese cities in the process, killing thousands of people. With the new bombing tactics, the argument for fighter cover stationed out of Iwo Jima became largely irrelevant, even before the epic battle for Iwo Jima had ended.

Although fighter escort from Iwo Jima proved both unsuccessful and unnecessary, P-51s stationed there did serve in other capacities. B-29s guided fighters to Japanese airfields in Nagoya, Osaka, Kobe, and Tokyo from April through August 1945. Most of these missions took place in June and July, when weather conditions were favorable. But by the time VII Fighter Command's operations picked up, the Americans had already crushed Japanese air power. The Commanding General of VII Fighter Command, Gen. Ernest Moore, "lamented the lack of opposition" and stated, "I hope they [Japanese fighters] will at least give us a little competition, because it is not very encouraging to fly that far in hopes of combat, and not get it."[28] During early operations from April through June, P-51s flew 832 sorties, but the Army Air Force considered only 374 as successful.[29] The VII Fighter Command claimed that it destroyed 74 enemy planes and damaged another 180 on the ground. The results were meager at best. In the words of the Army Air Forces history, "the total P-51 effort was not very fruitful."[30] Another, more recent Air Force study found the contributions of the VII Fighter Command "superfluous."[31]

Denying the Bonin Islands to the Japanese was another reason given for Operation Detachment. In military terms, such an enterprise could be described as "neutralization." In 1945 the airfields on Iwo Jima constituted a threat, but U.S. forces bypassed many islands with contained airfields as they moved toward Japan. The foremost example of bypassed enemy strongholds was the island of Truk in the Caroline Archipelago. Truk boasted major Japanese air and naval bases. Initially, the Joint Chiefs of Staff designated Truk as a primary U.S. objective.[32] However, after consideration, the Joint Chiefs determined that the cost of seizing Truk outweighed its usefulness (or perhaps there were not enough forces available to pursue that course of action). Consequently, the Army Air Forces and Navy successfully neutralized the island with frequent aerial bombardments and a naval blockade.[33] In a similar manner, the Joint Staff Planners determined in 1943 that the

Bonin Islands could be neutralized and were not worth the cost of seizing.[34] Neutralization of the Bonins did not require the seizure of Iwo Jima.

Military strategists also sought to reduce the threat of enemy air attacks on the Marianas. The Japanese had launched several air attacks on Saipan, using planes that probably refueled in the Bonin Islands. The attacks came infrequently and were only marginally effective. From early November 1944 through early January 1945, the Japanese launched a total of seven attacks. They destroyed 11 B-29s and did substantial damage to another 8. The Americans destroyed 37 Japanese fighters in the process.[35] When the Twenty-First Bomber Command stepped up bombing missions on Iwo Jima in January, the attacks ceased altogether.[36] Essentially, the damage caused to the airfields and related facilities through aerial and surface bombardment, combined with the growing shortage of Japanese planes, pilots, and fuel, ensured that airstrips on Iwo Jima had little offensive usefulness to Japan.

Considering the circumstances, the Japanese could not afford sustained losses in fuel, planes, and pilots against long-range targets in the Marianas. They would only risk a handful for flights to Iwo Jima. Army Air Forces records indicate the average number of enemy planes sighted on the island from January through early February was only 13, and those planes were likely running last-minute supplies to Kuribayashi's ground forces.[37]

Even if the Japanese could have continued attacks against Saipan or Tinian by refueling at Iwo Jima, further attempts likely would not have proven successful. Daylight raids gave the Americans easy warning, and the Japanese fighters had poor night-fighting capability. As had been the case at Pearl Harbor, air attacks on the Marianas demonstrated the Japanese ability to utilize daring and surprise against an overconfident enemy. Once the Japanese lost this element of surprise, further raids became inconsequential. In a letter to Arnold in November, Hansell stated that the Japanese preferred to attack under a full moon, and that is exactly what the Japanese continued to do through early January.[38] Not only did he predict the periods of attack, but Hansell also understood Japan's current tactics and prepared the Twenty-First Bomber Command to meet the threat. Even the Army Air Forces history surmised: "Japanese raids against B-29 bases, though troublesome, were not important enough alone to have justified the cost of capturing Iwo Jima."[39]

By 1945 Iwo Jima had little offensive relevance to the Japanese. In the words of Japanese officers, "our first line Army and Naval air forces had been exhausted in the recent Philippines Operation. The anticipation to restore our air forces, bringing their combined number to 3,000 planes, could materialize only by March or April and even then, mainly because the types of airplanes and their performance proved to be impracticable for operations extending beyond 550 miles radius, we could not use them for operations in the Bonin Islands area."[40] The Japanese wanted to defend Sulfur Island in order to deny its use to the Americans. General Kuribayashi considered destroying the island through demolitions in order to sink it into the sea or cut the central portion in half to severely damage the airfields.[41] Although Kuribayashi's idea about destroying Iwo Jima may have been whimsical, he considered the island more of a liability than an asset. When the continued maintenance of Motoyama airfields detracted from his defense construction efforts, an irritated Kuribayashi sent the following communiqué to Tokyo: "We must avoid constructing hopeless airfield."[42]

In American hands, Iwo Jima did provide an intermediate airfield for staging bombing missions against Japan. B-29s could extend their range and slightly increase their payloads by refueling there. However, the vast majority of Marianas-based B-29s did not use Iwo Jima for these purposes.[43] Quite simply, the B-29s could hit nearly every desired target within the range already provided by bases in the Marianas Islands. Furthermore, utilizing Iwo Jima to slightly increase payloads was not pivotal. The Twenty-First Bomber Command dropped so many bombs under LeMay's direction that it ran short of incineration ordnance. The Army Air Forces had little need to increase payloads with a time-consuming stop at Iwo Jima.[44] Additionally, the size of many sorties—over 500 planes at times—made a stopover on Iwo Jima difficult, if not impossible. To complicate matters, all unloading of supplies and material had to be done without a port facility, which made getting fuel and ammunition onto Sulfur Island dangerous and unproductive.[45] Some missions used the island as a staging area, and doing so improved bombing efficiency, but the staging area did not prove critical to the war effort.

U.S. planners further anticipated that an assault on the Bonins could force the Japanese Navy out of hiding and precipitate the decisive naval engagement, long desired by the U.S. Navy. However, the naval situation changed during the planning for Operation Detachment. In late October 1944, the Japanese and American navies clashed at the Battle for Leyte Gulf.[46] The series of engagements that followed destroyed the majority of Japanese capital ships. Precipitating a decisive naval engagement by attacking the Bonins became a moot point.

Admiral Spruance reasoned that the U.S. capture of Iwo Jima deprived the enemy of an early-warning system. But Iwo Jima was only one of several islands in the Nanpo Shoto that could radio the mainland with news of incoming air raids. Seizing one island did not negate the warning capabilities of the others. Lying roughly midway between Guam and Tinian, the Japanese-held island of Rota provided an excellent example of the Japanese early-warning system. At a distance of less than 50 miles from either island, the garrison on Rota actively collected and transmitted intelligence information on U.S. bombing missions. The Joint Chiefs of Staff knew of these capabilities yet never found it necessary to invade Rota.[47]

Admiral Spruance's 1945 after-action report to Nimitz and King stated only one requisite for Operation Detachment: "to operate with greatest effectiveness and with minimum attrition, fighter cover for the long range bombers was required at the earliest practicable time."[48] Yet when interviewed for his 1974 biography, Spruance argued that the battle was necessary to stop Iwo Jima's advance-warning system—specifically, its radar facility.[49] Regardless of how he arrived at this conclusion, Iwo Jima's radar facility, with its range of around 60 miles, did not impede B-29 operations.[50]

The most effective means available to the Japanese of predicting a U.S. raid did not come from radar but through interception of American radio messages. This widely practiced method gave Japan four to five hours' advance notice of an impending attack, about two to three hours *faster* than radar on Iwo Jima.[51] One historian succinctly stated the ineffectiveness of such countermeasures: "For the Japanese, even this margin [five hours] was not of much help—partly because the information, though timely, was too general. Unless the target of a raid could be pinpointed, the fighter commanders were reluctant to send their planes aloft; for one thing, fuel was in such short supply that every drop was precious. Confirmation from radar and other elements of the system was necessary to complete the warning cycle and justify scrambling planes. As the B-29 raiders bore down on the islands, however, the limitations of Japanese communications facilities combined with geography to put the defense seriously behind schedule."[52]

Even if the primitive radar on distant Iwo Jima alerted Japan of incoming raids, the garrison could not pinpoint the American targets. Consequently, the Japanese failed to intercept the majority of these missions. The radar on Iwo Jima became even less significant in March, when the weakness of Japanese night air defenses prompted LeMay to take the drastic measure of stripping anti-aircraft guns from B-29s to increase the weight of their payloads. With air defenses so ineffective, the radar facility on Iwo Jima did not warrant invasion.

Army Air Forces General Hansell claimed that one of the primary benefits of Operation Detachment was to improve the morale of B-29 pilots. When crews from the Twenty-First Bomber Command began their first flights in November, they did so in planes in which they had little experience. Pilots flew over 3,000 miles round-trip in some of the harshest weather conditions on the globe. Aircrews attempted precision bombing at high altitudes over cloud cover. The results were not very successful. Arnold worried that continued failures would jeopardize his autonomous command.[53] Consequently, he exerted tremendous pressure on the Twenty-First Bomber Command to perform, sacking the Commanding General, Haywood S. Hansell Jr., in January 1945. Though morale in the Marianas was probably low in February, it must have picked up again in March after LeMay changed to more successful tactics and began fixing maintenance problems with the aircraft. Securing an intermediate air base at Iwo Jima certainly improved confidence even further—how much, is uncertain—but even so, a marginal improvement in aircrews' morale does not justify the thousands of lives lost at Iwo Jima.

One unquestionable benefit of Iwo Jima's airfields was their direct contribution to air-sea rescue efforts, but this affected only a very small number of aircrews. With 1,400 miles between the Marianas and mainland Japan, the use of an island within the Bonins cut that distance in half. Consequently, the Army Air Forces stationed an air-sea rescue unit as one of the first detachments on Iwo Jima. Table 4 details the American rescue operations.[54]

The average rescue rate from November through February was around 34 percent. After the capture of Iwo Jima, this rate rose to 61 percent. Air rescue units stationed on Iwo Jima were only minor players in the rescue of B-29 crews. Although the Army Air Forces established an additional air rescue base on Okinawa in July, it was naval efforts in the Nanpo Shoto—"its Dumbos, its surface craft, and its submarines"—that played the biggest role.[55] Applying the average rescue rate before Iwo Jima's capture through the entire period, air-sea rescue operations saved an additional 223 airmen over the previous rate. Iwo Jima was not solely responsible for this increase. The VII Fighter Command's air-sea rescue unit on Iwo Jima saved 57 airmen during the entire war.[56] Although Operation Detachment increased the performance of rescue operations, the number of American lives saved pales in comparison to the number lost in the island's capture. Additionally, the Bonin chain offered more islands than Iwo Jima to serve as an air rescue base.

In his report to the Secretary of the Navy, King maintained that Iwo Jima was the *only* island in the Bonins that "lends itself to the construction of airfields."[57] In the official Marine Corps history, Whitman S. Bartley carefully sidestepped this issue by stating that Iwo Jima "was the only island

THE UNTOLD TRUTH

TABLE 4

Air-Sea Rescue Operations, 1944-1945

Month	Year	Total Crewmen Down at Sea	Total Crewmen Rescued	Percentage Rescued
November	1944	36	14	39
December	1944	179	63	35
January	1945	155	20	13
February	1945	136	65	48
March	1945	107	79	74
April	1945	167	55	33
May	1945	230	183	80
June	1945	180	102	57
July	1945	120	73	61
Total		1,310	654	50

that could support a large number of fighter aircraft."[58] These statements failed to acknowledge that Iwo Jima was not the only island in the Bonins that provided landing facilities. Both Chichi Jima and Haha Jima had sizeable airfields already built—a fact that has not received enough historical scrutiny.

Although the unevenness of Haha Jima's airfield limited its employment, the island of Chichi Jima had an excellent port facility and fresh water, and was 150 miles closer to Japan (Chichi Jima was 510 miles from Tokyo and Iwo Jima was 660 miles). Chichi Jima literally means "father island," and until Kuribayashi transferred his headquarters to Iwo Jima, the Japanese considered Chichi Jima the cornerstone of the Bonin Islands in terms of both utility and defense. The mountainous terrain, steep cliffs, and limited landing areas surrounding Chichi Jima made it a difficult target for amphibious assault. American intelligence incorrectly assumed that most of the 109th Infantry Division was still stationed there. In reality, Kuribayashi had transferred the majority of his manpower and material to Iwo Jima. Chichi Jima acted mainly as a communication and logistics facility in support of Iwo Jima and other Bonin Islands.[59]

Chichi Jima provided a valid and useful base to support both land and sea operations. The mountainous island had heavy naval guns surrounding the port, bristled with anti-aircraft guns, and had few landing beaches. Although it is difficult to imagine a defense more thoroughly impregnable than Iwo Jima, the defenses on Chichi Jima were certainly formidable. However, perhaps due to confidence in the island's geography, the 15,000 Japanese defenders of Chichi Jima (6,000 less than on Iwo Jima) did not start seriously organizing the defenses for the purposes of repelling an invasion until July 1945, four months after the assault on Iwo Jima.[60]

Chichi Jima proved enticing to the U.S. Navy, and planners devised a plan to seize the island, code named Operation Farragut, in June 1944.[61] The largest airfield at Iwo Jima before its capture was approximately 4,245 x 425 feet, while the one at Chichi Jima was 2,900 x 900 feet with water at both ends of the runway.[62] This airstrip actually consisted of landfill placed in the water between two rocky outcroppings of the island, which accounts for its unusually broad width. Fighters like the P-51 required less than 1,000 feet to take off or land, but the B-29s typically used over 8,000 feet of runway. Planners estimated that it would take 2 construction battalions 55 days for each 500-foot extension to Chichi Jima's runway. The Navy formulated a plan to create an advanced naval base on the island in August 1944, which included a 4,000-foot fighter strip and an alternative plan for a 6,000-foot medium bomber airfield (B-29s made emergency landings on Iwo Jima on shorter runways).[63] Capturing the island would have satisfied several U.S. objectives, including fighter support and air-to-sea rescue, but making the airfields suitable for B-29s in a timely fashion would have proven a difficult task. It is hard to speculate on the available options in hindsight, but to deny that there were other landing facilities in the Bonin Islands misrepresents the choices available.

One common argument contends that Japanese fighters on Iwo Jima threatened B-29 flights over the Bonins.[64] This line of reasoning has two major weaknesses. First, the Japanese did not permanently station fighters on Iwo Jima. The lack of a port facility on the island made logistics arduous, which relegated the airfields to staging and refueling purposes. The Japanese primarily used Iwo Jima's airfields before June 1944 as a waypoint between Honshu and the Marianas Islands.[65] After the United States seized the Marianas in June 1944, Iwo Jima's usefulness to the Japanese greatly diminished, and it had little relevance to defending Japan from B-29 attacks.

Iwo Jima lies about 700 miles from the mainland, which made it impossible, given the time constraints, to get fighters from Honshu to Iwo Jima and intercept B-29s, even with several hours' advance notice. Under the circumstances, it just was not possible for Zeros to simply "react" to unanticipated flights over the Bonins. Likewise, the supposed "dog-leg course" that some historians have maintained had a negative effect on bomber operations has little credibility. Bombers simply flew in formation to a point opposite Iwo

THE UNTOLD TRUTH

Jima and then proceeded on an individual basis to the Marianas from that point onward.[66] While not flying directly over Iwo Jima was prudent, it did not prove a hindrance to operations.

Even if the Japanese did attempt to predict a B-29 mission and send a few fighters to Iwo Jima for an ambush, those Zeros would be highly susceptible to bomber attack from the Marianas. The airfields on Iwo Jima could be (and were by January of 1945) effectively neutralized by repeated aerial bombardment. Most important, it does not appear that harassment of B-29s over Iwo Jima was ever a significant threat. From August 1944 through February 1945, 2,800 B-24 Liberator sorties flew *directly* over Iwo Jima to bomb the airfields, and only 9 were shot down by either enemy fighter or anti-aircraft fire.[67] Considering that defenses on Iwo Jima could incapacitate less than half a percent of planes that attacked it, simply flying past the island at 30,000 feet posed little danger. The official Army Air Forces history failed to mention even a single instance of a B-29 shot down near the island. Its authors declared that "the idea of seizing the island derived less from its menace while in Japanese hands than from its potential value as an advanced base for the Twentieth Air Force."[68]

After Iwo Jima had failed to fulfill its purpose as a fighter escort base, the military presented several other justifications for Operation Detachment. Some of these reasons have more validity than others; none outweighs the tremendous cost incurred by the island's capture. Initially, at least, there was public criticism about the need for Iwo Jima. Writing in *Newsweek*, Adm. William V. Pratt, a retired Chief of Naval Operations, summarized the situation on the home front: "There has been a certain amount of public criticism over this expenditure of manpower to acquire a small, God-forsaken island, useless to the Army as a staging base and useless to the Navy as a fleet base. The public wants to know if the occupation of Iwo Jima was a military necessity and wonders if the same sort of airbase could not have been reached by acquiring other strategic localities at lower cost."[69]

The landing of the first B-29 on Iwo Jima in March 1944 prompted Admiral Spruance to immediately write to Admiral Nimitz that "we are paying, and shall pay, a very high price" for Iwo Jima, and its "potentialities must be fully exploited." By this Spruance meant that the missions of fighter escort and air-sea rescue did not clearly justify the cost of the operation and that attention should instead be given to "B-29 emergency use."[70] Spruance realized that the initial reasons provided for seizing Iwo Jima did not justify the terrible losses incurred in the process, and he sought additional justifications that would more visibly demonstrate the island's usefulness. The admiral recognized the media frenzy over the B-29 landing and actively sought to use that new line of reasoning, in hindsight, to justify the invasion.

Spruance was not the only commander who harbored doubts about Iwo Jima's necessity. Popular military journals revealed the prevalence of these concerns by forcefully attempting to contest them. In articles entitled "Motoyama Airfield No. 1," "P-51 Escort from Iwo," and "Iwo Pays Off," the Marine Corps, Army Air Forces, and Navy attempted to reinforce the island's importance to the bombing campaign. These articles used similar lines of reasoning to show that "Iwo Jima's airstrip already is paying for itself."[71] At least one public statement about Iwo Jima's importance bordered on distraction. The Navy released a press bulletin in May implying that Iwo Jima played a vital "part in Japanese agriculture economy."[72] As the rationale for the island became less certain, the U.S. military increasingly began to focus on the only reason that might substantiate Iwo Jima's value: emergency landings.

Validation in Hindsight

The primary justification for the casualties incurred in the seizure of Iwo Jima resulted from a statistic produced in 1945 by the Army Air Forces. *Impact* was an Army Air Forces journal published during the war from early 1943 to late 1945. Members of all services read the periodical, but the target audience consisted of airmen. The Army Air Forces entitled the last issue *Air Victory over Japan*, attributing Japan's surrender as a result of air operations. An article dedicated to Iwo Jima stated that "from 4 March, when the first crippled B-29 landed there, to the end of the war, 2,251 Superforts landed at Iwo. A large number of these would have been lost if Iwo had not been available. Each of the B-29's carried 11 crewmen, a total of 24,761 men. It cost 4,800 dead, 15,800 wounded, and 400 missing to take the island . . . but . . . every man who served with the 20th Air Force . . . is eternally grateful."[73] Note that 2,251 is stated as the number of B-29s that landed on Iwo Jima, *not* the number that made emergency landings.

Some Pacific war historians have questioned the emergency landing theory, but none has taken more than parting shots at it. As early as 1951, Jeter Isely and Philip Crowl at Princeton University questioned whether Iwo Jima's airfields saved 20,000 airmen. Isely wrote to Col. Gordon Gayle at the History Division of the Marine Corps concerning his doubts. After weighing Gayle's response, Isely estimated that "roughly one-fourth of these flyers would have been lost if the island had not been in American hands."[74] More recently, Ronald Spector stated, "By the end of the war the bomb-

THE UNTOLD TRUTH

ers had made about 2,400 emergency landings on Iwo Jima, leading some writers to claim that taking into account the eleven-man crews, the island airstrips saved about 20,000 airmen. Of course, such a figure assumes that none of the bombers in distress would have reached the Marianas and that if forced down at sea, the crews would not have been rescued—an obvious exaggeration."[75] Yet these historians did not fully explore the deep falsehoods of the emergency landing theory.

Most scholarship that discusses Iwo Jima justifies the battle on the basis of emergency landings of Superforts. Although early histories implied that most of the landings were of an emergency nature, subsequent authors stated it explicitly. Bill D. Ross's popular book *Iwo Jima: Legacy of Valor* (1985) provides a good example. He states, "Iwo Jima in American hands meant that 24,751 Army Air Corps crewmen would be saved from ditching disabled aircraft in the icy waters of the north Pacific with an almost certain loss of most of them. By war's end, 2,251 emergency landings had been made on the island by B-29 Superfort bombers."[76] Ross inflated the emergency landing theory to imply that every B-29 crewman who landed at Iwo Jima (all 24,751) were saved from certain death. Instead of a fresh standpoint, the author embellished upon the tales of previous generations. The theory has come under less scrutiny as time has passed.[77]

Upon close analysis, however, the theory completely collapses. To begin with, the numbers tossed around defy the laws of probability. According to the Army's official casualty report, 2,148 B-29 crewmen lost their lives as a result of combat operations. This figure includes the Superforts based in China and India.[78] The emergency landing theory claims that an additional 24,761 airmen from the Marianas alone would have died without the use of Iwo Jima. In other words, the theory claims that over *eleven times* the number of airmen actually lost in combat were saved simply by offering an alternative landing field between Saipan and Tokyo.[79]

In terms of bombers lost, an examination of the evidence generates similar results. The Twenty-First Bomber Command lost a total of 359 B-29s to all known causes. Of these, the Japanese destroyed 218 in combat-related occurrences.[80] Analyzing events statistically, the emergency landing theory suggests that the absence of one emergency landing strip would have resulted in over *ten times* (2,251) the total number of Marianas-based Superforts lost in combat (218).[81]

Historians who use the emergency landing theory have failed to recognize its absurd implication: if the emergency landing theory were valid, the strategic bombing campaign on Japan would have completely failed without

Operation Detachment. A few numbers demonstrate the improbability of this inference. At its peak, the Twenty-First Bomber Command consisted of roughly 1,000 Superforts. For 2,251 bombers to have been landed on Iwo Jima, each B-29 in the Twenty-First Bomber Command would have landed on the island an average of at least two times. Given the redundancy of the B-29's four engines, the need for so many landings is improbable enough (the bomber could actually fly on just two working engines, even if both were located on the same side). Consider the raw numbers involved. If the absence of one airfield caused two thousand planes to ditch in the Pacific, every single Superfort from the Twenty-First Bomber Command, along with a second set of replacements, would have been destroyed. But at most, only 1,000 Superforts were ever based in the Marianas. The Army Air Forces did not even have 2,251 B-29s in its total inventory at the end of the war.[82]

If all these lives were not being saved by emergency landings on Iwo Jima, why did the planes land? The vast majority of landings occurred for reasons other than emergencies. To give one example, when the 509th Bombardment Group transferred to the Pacific in late June, its crews underwent an intense series of training missions.[83] The training included five or six flights for each crew from the Marianas to Iwo Jima. These missions alone add up to over 260 landings.[84] Gen. Emmett O'Donnell also confirmed that his 73rd Bombardment Group carried out half a dozen training missions to Iwo Jima—an additional 260 landings.[85] Placing these 500 or so training missions in perspective, the 509th and 73rd were only two of twenty-one bombardment groups attached to the Marianas. If instruction for all new aircrews included flights to Iwo Jima, training made up a considerable portion of the Iwo Jima landings.

B-29s landed on Iwo Jima for several reasons other than training. Primarily, Superforts extended their range or increased payloads by refueling there. This extension of range proved particularly helpful for flights over Korea.[86] Missions to targets in northern Japan used the island as well. Additionally, instead of returning to Tinian, Guam, or Saipan, many B-29s made stopovers on the island to wait for weather conditions to clear up.[87] Once the island was captured, Gen. Curtis LeMay kept fuel at a minimum to increase bomb loads, causing many pilots to refuel on Iwo Jima.[88] Even when fueled adequately, pilots often made expenditure decisions based on the knowledge that Iwo Jima provided a safety net.[89] None of these instances should be classified as emergencies, but Army Air Forces still categorized these landings as "aborts and malfunctions."[90]

One of the reasons for landings on Iwo Jima derived from the pressure of service rivalry. Before the war ended, the Army, Navy, and Army Air Forces had begun positioning themselves for control over the postwar budget.[91] In particular, the Army Air Forces began systematic and comprehensive planning for the organization of an independent air force from at least December 1943 onward, a full year and a half before the end of hostilities.[92] In their quest to demonstrate the dominance of strategic bombing, Generals Arnold and LeMay pushed the B-29 and its crews to dangerous limits. Six months before Operation Detachment, Arnold wrote to the Commanding General of the Twenty-First Bomber Command, "Every pilot should be an expert on keeping gasoline consumption to a minimum. There is a tendency to plan missions so that the weakest pilot will have a safe reserve on return to base. This can not be tolerated."[93] This statement indicates Arnold's attitude about safety concerns even before the Marines seized Iwo Jima. Once the island had been secured, Iwo Jima provided an additional safety measure that allowed the Twenty-First Bomber Command to launch missions with precariously low fuel reserves or in the face of foul weather. Essentially, the Army Air Forces' quest to improve B-29 performance further facilitated the island's use. A better description of Iwo Jima's airfield would be "convenient" or "helpful" rather than "emergency."

Examining the usage of Iwo Jima by B-29s in May, June, and July 1945 demonstrates that the vast majority of landings served simply for refueling purposes. Unfortunately, the Army Air Forces did not make any distinction between planned stops on Iwo Jima and unplanned ones. Instead, the maintenance section on Iwo Jima regarded every touchdown as an "emergency," no matter the actual reason for landing. Of the nearly two thousand landings in these three months, more than 80 percent were for refueling. The second most common reason was for engine maintenance, but most repairs were minor, and the planes took off again within twenty-four hours. Combat damage and serious engine malfunction to aircraft was a very low percentage of the landings and tapered off as the war progressed. Remarkably, during the month of June, not a single aircraft landed on Iwo Jima due to battle damage, and June had the largest number of landings (over 800). Nevertheless, the Army Air Forces still characterized all these landings under the heading "emergency."[94]

Although it is likely impossible to discover the reasons for each landing on Iwo Jima, one can estimate the number of impromptu landings by examining the first couple of dozen touchdowns on Iwo Jima—those that occurred between 4 and 26 March. The month of March is the best time frame to examine because the condition of the unimproved landing facilities made it unlikely that a B-29 would land for reasons other than foul weather, fuel shortage, mechanical malfunction, or combat damage. It becomes more difficult to establish the motives for landings as time passed. Gen. Curtis LeMay increased the number of bomber runs on Japan to unprecedented levels in March (see table 5), and some of these Superforts landed on Iwo Jima. The proportion of those landing for unplanned reasons can then be applied to the total number of bombing missions made from the Marianas during the rest of the war.[95]

Adding up the total number of flights from table 5, during 4–24 March 1,720 B-29s dropped ordnance over Japan. Of those planes, 36 made landings on Iwo Jima (around 2 percent).[96] Many of these landings may have been avoidable. For instance, on 14 March, 9 B-29s landed, of which 8 quickly refueled and departed.[97] Only one was in need of significant repair. Crews running the air facility on Iwo Jima stated that many of the landings were of "doubtful necessity."[98] In a communiqué to the Twentieth Air Force on 13 March, airmen on Iwo Jima requested an investigation into the preceding instances and cautioned the Army Air Forces to land in future only in cases of "extreme emergencies."[99] Additionally, 16 B-29s landed on 17 March due to strong headwinds.[100] Although convenient, using the airstrip on Iwo Jima may not have been imperative since over 300 B-29s in that same mission made it back to the Marianas safely.

After the Marines secured Iwo Jima until the end of the war, an additional 19,651 Superfort missions from the Twenty-First Bomber Command were completed over Japanese targets.[101] Extending the March ratio of 2 percent to include all missions from 4 March to 14 August, it is probable that fewer

TABLE 5
Missions Launched from the Marianas, 4 to 24 March 1945

Date of Mission	Number of B-29s over Target	Target City
March 4	192	Tokyo, Japan
March 9	325	Tokyo, Japan
March 11	285	Nagoya, Japan
March 13	274	Osaka, Japan
March 16	331	Kobe, Japan
March 18	290	Nagoya, Japan
March 24	23	Nagoya, Japan

than 450 Superforts landed at Iwo Jima for unanticipated reasons.[102] This generous figure accounts for less than one-fifth of the 2,251 touchdowns popularized by the emergency landing theory.

It must further be clarified that the figure of 2,251 landings used in most Pacific war histories may not be entirely accurate. A higher number of B-29s may have used the airfields. A minority of historians argue that there were 2,400 landings, and some evidence supports that number.[103] Other evidence indicates as many as 3,000 Superforts landed. At any rate, the actual number makes little difference in regard to the emergency landing theory. The central problem with the theory is not the number of B-29s that used the island's airfields. The error is that *tallying up the total number of landings does not indicate the number of emergencies.* The theory uses erroneous logic—the vast majority of airmen that landed on Iwo Jima were not saved from an icy cold death in the Pacific Ocean.

Whatever the number of Superforts that actually landed for urgent reasons, many would have made it back to the Marianas without Iwo Jima. Common sense would say that some of the Superfort landings on Iwo Jima were dramatic emergency landings, and that the airfields on the island saved lives, but generalizing that every landing on Iwo Jima occurred for emergency purposes distorts statistics. Writers have greatly exaggerated the emergency landing theory for the purpose of justifying the heavy battle losses, and this has proven misleading in several ways. Not only was this justification for the battle erroneously constructed in hindsight, but the fixation with it has led nearly every history to overlook the actual reason for seizing the island—fighter escort. The most important aspect left to be considered is the battle's impact on Japan's defeat.

Fallout

General Arnold fixed upon the need to seize Iwo Jima as a fighter base. As those operations proved unfeasible, senior officers struggled to justify Operation Detachment. No service had more reason to doubt the necessity of the battle than the U.S. Marine Corps. In his after-action report, Gen. Holland M. Smith ignored strategic considerations entirely, maintaining instead that "since it is the final purpose of the war to impose our will on the Japanese Empire by force, and since that purpose is opposed by military forces; the destruction of those enemy forces becomes the primary mission in the conduct of war."[104] But destroying 20,000 Japanese on Iwo Jima did not necessarily best fulfill America's national objectives.

A century before Smith's time, the famous strategist Carl von Clausewitz argued that the primary objective of war was not the destruction of the enemy but of his will to resist.[105] When America launched Operation Detachment, Japan possessed meager resources to carry out offensive combat. So sure was the United States of Japan's defeat that senior commanders of the U.S. Navy had already begun positioning themselves for the postwar budget as early as December 1944.[106] In addition, the Joint Chiefs of Staff was reviewing the process of surrender formalities before the battle for Iwo Jima began.[107] The United States had much to lose with a casualty-intensive fight over a tiny island of rock, yet the Japanese had much to gain in the conflict. Operation Detachment may have hindered U.S. war aims in several ways. First, to the Japanese, Kuribayashi's "last stand" improved upon existing defense doctrine. At the very least, it confirmed the effectiveness of the static defense in depth used at Peleliu in late 1944. Second, although the loss of Iwo Jima certainly made the prospect of losing the war more real to Japanese, the magnificent defense of the island simultaneously became a useful stimulus for instilling public defiance against American aggression. Third, for the United States, the battle depleted needed manpower and weakened popular support for future ground operations.

Just as Tarawa taught the Navy and Marine Corps critical lessons for forthcoming amphibious assaults, Iwo Jima became the model for Japanese defensive tactics. In a message to Tokyo, Kuribayashi strengthened his line of reasoning, even as death closed in around him: "however firm and stout pill-boxes you may build easily at the beach they will be destroyed by bombardment of main armament of battle ships."[108] Iwo Jima proved that it was possible to nullify America's military superiority with Japanese conscripts as long as Japan organized a coordinated defense in depth. Realizing the devastating effect it had on invading forces, the Japanese military warmly embraced Kuribayashi's hotly contested shift from the traditional beach defense after the battle ended.[109] The battle served as the final transition to these new tactics. The Americans realized its importance as well. One U.S. Navy study concluded that "in defending Iwo Jima, the Japs employed one basic tactic which in a sense was a departure from the Japanese defensive operations hitherto generally encountered. This tactic was simply to occupy previously determined D-Day positions and maintain them . . . the expressed plan conceived by the Commanding General."[110]

Kuribayashi may have influenced to some extent the Japanese defenses at the subsequent battle for Okinawa in April 1945. Gen. Mitsuru Ushijima must have paid scrupulous attention to Iwo Jima communiqués from February through March. By choosing to sacrifice his beach defense, Ushijima made ample use of the island's caves and rugged terrain. The adherence to static inland fortifications suited the composition of the defense force, which included over 39,000 hastily conscripted Okinawan civilians. These conscripts would have had difficulty performing complex military operations but could still fight effectively from defensive positions. The durability of the static defense proved extremely costly to U.S. ground troops, and it also placed naval vessels in a vulnerable supporting role for an extended period. As it had done at Iwo Jima, Japan used *kamikaze* again to defend Okinawa, but in much greater numbers and to much better effect. Suicide planes wreaked havoc on American warships, causing 10,000 casualties.[111] The Japanese probably attempted to duplicate at Okinawa, as far as possible, Kuribayashi's improved defense tactics. And, they would have used Iwo Jima as the foremost example in defense preparation if the United States had invaded the mainland.

Although the loss of the Bonin Islands certainly brought the war closer to Japan, the battle for Iwo Jima may have done more to encourage its populace to continue fighting than to discourage it. The Japanese government espoused rhetoric and propaganda that the United States planned to exterminate them. Historian John Dower described Americans disembarking onto the beaches of Iwo Jima with depictions of "Rodent Exterminator" stenciled onto their helmets.[112] "Rodent Exterminators" even served as the title for an article on Iwo Jima in a major U.S. weekly, which stated that the "Pacific's nastiest exterminating job was done."[113] Since the comparison of Japanese to rats was commonplace in American periodicals, it should not come as a surprise that Japanese newspapers advertised Iwo Jima as an example of "enemy plans to wipe Japan and the Japanese people off the face of the earth."[114]

Michael Sherry in *Rise of American Airpower* (1987) argued that the United States gradually employed a policy of targeting enemy civilian populations with the B-29.[115] Undeniably, U.S. airpower became an increasingly favored tool of war. Expensive battles on land, like Iwo Jima, only served to support bombing as a preferred method. As ground fighters moved closer to the home islands, they had increased contact with Japanese civilians. When Marines encountered the civilian population on Saipan, it became difficult to kill the enemy by any means possible yet deal with the complexity of having noncombatants on the battlefield.[116] In other words, women and children in the battle space made it challenging to prosecute the aggressive tactics Americans had developed in years of island warfare.

Conducting the war from the air sanitized the entire process of killing and left little distinction between the treatment of Japanese men, women, and children. Essentially, no innocents existed. The firebombing of Tokyo in March 1945 killed as many as 120,000 Japanese, mainly noncombatants. However, aerial bombardment provided such great advantages of relative safety between the American pilots in the air and the total destruction below that such methods became preferred. Furthermore, Americans could calculate damage from aerial photographs without appreciating the true horrors on the ground, making it easier to justify the collateral damage. The intimate ferocity and moral complexity of vicious ground combat reinforced aerial bombardment as a preferable method of conducting a brutal war.

According to Thomas Searle, the Army Air Forces specifically targeted urban areas with firebombing because it "cut Japanese industrial production by (among other things) killing Japanese civilians."[117] Searle demonstrated that Japanese civilians were not collateral damage to military targets but explicitly designated as military targets. Nevertheless, the photographs that Army Air Forces Gen. Curtis LeMay exuberantly applauded, showing the gutted city districts in Tokyo, did not relate the true story of firebombing as seen from the ground. In the first Tokyo raid alone, over 270,000 residences burned—between 18 percent and 25 percent of the structures in the capital. According to a recent Air Force study, between 72,000 and 83,000 people died, and between 24,000 and 40,000 were injured. Many of the corpses, "melted together, could not be separated or even differentiated as to sex."[118] Yet due to its effectiveness and the illusions of sanitary destruction from pictures taken at 30,000 feet, bombing certainly proved a more attractive choice to the United States than horrific contests like Iwo Jima.

After the war, one of the claims about the effectiveness of air power publicized by the Army Air Forces was that "B-29s caused 330,000 fatalities and 806,000 injuries, far exceeding Japan's 780,000 combat casualties for the entire war."[119] Through technological prosecution of air war, the Army Air Forces calculated Japanese deaths in simple numerical figures, that equated the children that airpower had easily decimated to the Japanese fighting men killed at high price on islands like Iwo Jima.

If the United States sought unconditional surrender, aerial bombardment certainly did more to facilitate that goal than costly land campaigns like Iwo Jima. Setting aside the legal and moral questions concerning its prosecution, aerial bombardment was the most logical choice to bring about Japan's utter submission without paying a heavy price in American lives. While the Japanese could fight Marines and soldiers on the ground, they had few methods of combating an aerial campaign that had a terrifying effect on the population. A senior civil servant at the Japanese Air Raid Precautions Headquarters in Tokyo stated that air raids "had the worst effects and really brought home to the people the experience of bombing and demoralization of faith in the outcome of the war."[120]

As the Japanese populace reeled under the increasing anguish brought about by U.S. naval blockade and aerial Armageddon, engaging the American enemy on Iwo Jima offered the Japanese an opportunity to inflict revenge and retribution at a time when little other recourse was available. On the eve of the attack, the military released to the public stirring poems about the warriors on Iwo Jima, dedicated to defending their nation:

Samurais assigned to Iwo
Handpicked death-defying men
Enflamed in determination to beat the enemy
They wait for the action
By training themselves day and night.[121]

Iwo Jima offered a distant place, far from the homeland, for "heroic" samurai to battle "impure" barbarians. The battle facilitated romanticism and nationalism, in contrast to the harsh reality of the bombardments on Honshu. Kuribayashi's death memorialized him as a national hero, and stirred the patriotism of the Japanese people. While reading the general's final communiqué to the emperor, one radio announcer swelled with emotion and was unable to keep his composure. His inability to go on required his "fellows in the studio [to] mercifully put a record of patriotic music on the platter."[122] Before his death, Kuribayashi apologized to Japan for his failure to defend the island. But poet Ryuichi Saito exclaimed that the opposite was true—the public had failed their fallen heroes. The Japanese people needed to emulate the determination of the defenders of Iwo Jima who had taught "a sad but necessary lesson" about the spirit needed to win the war.[123] One Japanese college professor told his students, "Even in such a small island, Imperial Japanese Forces could defend and sustain Iwo Jima against large U.S. forces for more than one month. If the enemy will land on Japanese mainland, it should provide just the chance for us to overthrow them. We must make up our minds to fight and reverse the war situation."[124]

After the devastating firebombing raids in March, a government-sponsored newsreel applauded how Japanese soldiers had killed Americans on Iwo Jima. It depicted the battle as a good example of how to deal with demonic

Americans.[125] At Iwo Jima, the Japanese had caused a higher percentage of American casualties in relation to Japanese deaths than in any other major land battle. Radio in Japan broadcast that "the heroic and gallant fighting spirit of each and every one of the officers and men of the garrison defending Iwo, was a bloody epic which should be recorded and stressed in the war history of our nation, and also in the world as well, as a manifestation of the ideal perfection of the pure Japanese spirit. Our men inflicted the maximum amount of losses on the enemy . . . In a way the battle of Iwo Jima may seem to be a miraculous display of spiritual power over materialist power."[126] Iwo Jima reinforced propaganda about the superiority of the Japanese spirit.

In addition to its effect on the beleaguered Japanese home front, Operation Detachment contributed to Japan's war effort. Historian Richard B. Frank has shown that the refusal of the Japanese military to accept defeat did not simply derive from an irrational hope for victory.[127] The United States depended upon the will of its people to pursue its objective of unconditional surrender. Many in the Japanese military understood that America's advance could only be halted if the resolve of its populace to continue fighting wavered in the face of escalating casualties. By 1945 the Japanese high command harbored no illusions about winning the war. Instead, it organized its efforts to preserve Japanese sovereignty. The military believed that if it could achieve one decisive victory, Japan could force the United States to negotiate. In the words of historian Jon Hoffman, Iwo Jima "demonstrates the folly of directly taking on the enemy's strength. The Japanese specifically sought a battle of attrition in which they could maximize the cost to American manpower, and the U.S. forces obliged them in a number of ways."[128] If the Japanese built one of the greatest defenses in the history of modern warfare, all the more reason to bypass it. Essentially, just because the United States had the military might to seize objectives like Iwo Jima did not necessarily mean that doing so helped win the war.

Both American and Japanese decisions concerning strategy in 1945 also derived from ideological beliefs in personal and national honor. In Japan, nearly any sacrifice was viewed as a more acceptable choice than subjugating the nation to those viewed as foreign and impure barbarians; better for millions of Japanese to die than to allow the American "devils" into the land of Yamato (the foremost god from whom the Japanese traced their ancestry). Unconditional surrender was morally reprehensible to Japanese. The longer the war went on, the more irrational the Japanese high command became. Essentially, Japan did not offer serious proposals for a negotiated settlement until it had nothing left to negotiate with.[129] Because ultimate defeat was basi-

THE UNTOLD TRUTH

cally unconscionable and never spoken of, irrational judgment concerning the prospects of continued war against the United States pervaded Japanese society—despite the desperate circumstances. As put so profoundly by James Bradley in *Flyboys* (2003), the Hakko Ichiu (Spirit Warriors) in the military began evaluating defeats as victories, so long as the price for America was high and few Japanese surrendered.[130] For the "Spirit Warriors," Iwo Jima served as an ultimate example of *Yamato damashii* (Japanese spirit). In ideological terms, it demonstrated the power of spirit over materialism.

Conversely, American ideas about war left little compromise in terms of peace.[131] If the cause was just, then only total victory validated the principles on which the United States fought. Compromise with the enemy, who was wrong, could never result in an honorable end to the war, since the United States was right. Negotiation meant concessions, and concessions would require the United States to compromise moral principles. American commanders viewed as unacceptable any concessions to those whom they perceived as criminal and immoral. Ironically, the United States proved reluctant to prosecute its just war by conventional means, such as traditional land campaigns, because the cost in American lives exceeded the population's pain threshold. This became the moral dilemma for decision-makers. The predicament resulted in a choice of the lesser of two evils: it was better to concede on ethical issues regarding the bombardment of Japanese civilians than on the principle of unconditional surrender itself.

As a manpower-intensive battle, Iwo Jima further detracted from the American public's conviction to invade mainland Japan. Losses on Iwo Jima occurred at a difficult time for the United States. Nimitz released the shocking number of dead and wounded in mid-March. Less than thirty days later, America's most popular president died.[132] While the newly inaugurated President Harry S. Truman got acquainted with the military situation, Germany surrendered in early May. With the end in sight, the American people wanted an end to the madness and a quick resolution in the Pacific. The public would not forget the price of Iwo Jima. Instead, editorials used the cost of the battle to illustrate what an invasion of Japan would entail.[133] A *New York Times* report concluded that any future ground operations would certainly "cost us heavily in blood and tears before Tokyo is reached."[134] The frightening memory of Iwo Jima, combined with even greater losses on Okinawa, reinforced such grim predictions, which eroded public support for unconditional surrender.

Although the Japanese lost the battle, it did serve to weaken American popular support for an invasion of Japan and had a profound impact on high-level commanders in the United States. Kuribayashi's well-conceived defense began to shift America's insistence on Japan's absolute submission. Perplexed at how to end the Pacific war without more catastrophic losses of American lives, Secretary of War Henry Stimson wrote in his diary that the United States must make provisions to protect the emperor in the Japanese surrender terms "in order to save us from score of bloody Iwo Jimas and Okinawas."[135]

President Truman began to question the wisdom of an invasion of Japan, and there is little doubt that his apprehension derived from the high cost of recent operations.[136] Following the losses on Iwo Jima and Okinawa, the President's adviser Admiral Leahy proved equally reluctant. In a meeting with the President and the Joint Chiefs of Staff on 11 July, Leahy stated that "he could not agree with those who said to him that unless we obtain the unconditional surrender of the Japanese that we will have lost the war. He feared no menace from Japan in the foreseeable future, if we were unsuccessful in forcing unconditional surrender. What he did fear was that our insistence on unconditional surrender would result only in making the Japanese desperate and thereby increase our casualty lists. He did not think that this [invasion of Japan] was at all necessary."[137] This opinion mirrors his diary entry a week later, in which he wrote, "it is my opinion at the present time that a surrender of Japan can be arranged with terms that can be accepted by Japan and that will make fully satisfactory provision for America's defense against future trans-Pacific aggression."[138] In the minds of decision-makers, the combination of bloody Iwo Jima and Okinawa worked against U.S. goals for unconditional surrender.

Leahy espoused a strategy of blockade versus invasion because he believed it would force the Japanese to negotiate and would cost significantly less in American lives. He advocated the continued use of unrestricted submarine warfare, which was crippling Japan, an island nation dependent on importation of raw materials. According to Adm. Ernest J. King's final report to the Secretary of the Navy, the sinking of enemy merchant ships via submarine surpassed that of surface ships, mines, ground-based air, and carrier air combined, accounting for at least two-thirds of all enemy tonnage sunk. Submarines began the war by destroying 134 ships (580,390 tons) in 1942, increasing their effectives to 284 ships (1,341,968 tons) in 1943. Unrestricted submarine warfare reached its peak effectiveness in 1944, sinking 492 ships (2,387,780 tons). Japan's merchant shipping was so devastated by 1945 that not enough targets existed, decreasing the amount sunk to 132 ships (469,872 tons).[139]

Not only did blockade and aerial bombardment restrict the making of war materials, it also brought the Japanese populace to the brink of starvation. According to Frank's study *Downfall: The End of the Imperial Japanese Empire*, "by 1944, the Japanese daily average fell to 1,900 calories; by 1945 it sank to only 1,680. The incidences of tuberculosis, beriberi, and digestive, skin and vitamin-related diseases soared. By the end of the war, about 20 to 25 percent of the urban population suffered from serious nutritional deficiencies."[140] Several more months of blockade would have likely resulted in mass starvation.

Weighing the effectiveness of naval blockade in comparison to the high cost of seizing ground at Iwo Jima and Okinawa, Admiral Leahy believed it better to temper U.S. war aims and allow the Japanese government to participate in the surrender process than to force Japan's total capitulation. He certainly opposed the use of ground troops in costly land campaigns. As the President's adviser, Leahy had significant influence on Truman, who openly expressed doubts about the planned invasions of Kyushu and Honshu.

The reluctance of the President to invade Japan concerned both General Marshall and Admiral King. In March, Marshall had been so concerned over the casualties on Iwo Jima that he had suggested the use of poison gas on Okinawa.[141] Although the high casualties in these recent operations concerned the heads of the Army and Navy, both Marshall and King believed invasion necessary to ensure Japan's unconditional surrender. In Frank's analysis of the plan to invade southern Japan, he indicated that Marshall and King may have deliberately withheld projected casualty figures from the President.[142] In particular, General Marshall feared that Truman's apprehension over the cost of previous operations impeded his approval of an invasion of the mainland. Frank argued that "Truman was systematically denied information about the huge projections inherent in the April 25 paper of the Joint Staff Planners . . . The President was also shielded from the estimates prepared by men charged with carrying out Olympic [invasion plan for Kyushu]."[143] The Joint Staff Planners produced a summary of past battle losses for Truman's review with simple ratios. Frank suggested that Marshall chose this information to present to Truman because he "actively sought to quash" casualty estimations that would endanger the invasion of Kyushu.[144] Table 6 shows the numbers and ratios produced for the President.[145]

By far, the ratio of "U.S. to Jap[anese]" casualties on Iwo Jima posed the most troubling of the figures presented to Truman, indicating American losses nearly equal to Japanese. Yet, despite the disturbing implications of the Iwo Jima casualty ratio, the Joint Staff Planners, based on the available evidence at the time, actually underestimated American casualties while at the same time exaggerating Japanese losses. The product of the two miscalculations increased the actual casualty ratio, which was about three Americans for every two Japanese (1:.67).

For U.S. casualties, planners appear to have used the numbers announced by Nimitz over ten days before the battle ended. Since four months had passed since this first announcement, planners undoubtedly had access to substantially higher estimates. Nevertheless, they chose the smallest number. Additionally, the highest estimate by U.S. intelligence regarding Japanese defenders indicated fewer than 23,000.[146] It is uncertain how planners arrived at 25,000 Japanese casualties, but they may have exploited the hastily produced battle reports of the V Amphibious Corps. U.S. intelligence considered these preliminary reports "excessive," and believed that they did not "reveal an accurate estimate of enemy dead."[147]

One might question why planners provided numbers for the President to review that they likely knew to be less than accurate. It appears that the presentation of American losses on Iwo Jima, underappreciated or not, threatened approval for the invasion of Japan. When the President met with the Joint Chiefs, he hesitated on the direction of future operations. He reluctantly allowed the Joint Chiefs to continue planning for an amphibious invasion of the southern Japanese island of Kyushu but did not approve the invasion of the Japanese mainland.[148] The Joint Chiefs knew that public condemnation over recent losses against Iwo Jima and Okinawa concerned the President. Frank has demonstrated that Marshall and King failed to include the number of Navy deaths from the Okinawan campaign in the ratio presented to Truman.[149] In addition, Marshall and King presented

TABLE 6
Casualty Comparison Produced for the President, 11 July 1945

Campaign	US Casualties Killed, wounded, missing	Jap. Casualties Killed and Prisoners (Not including wounded)	Ratio U.S. to Jap.
Leyte	17,000	78,000	1:4.6
Luzon	31,000	156,000	1:5.0
Iwo Jima	20,000	25,000	1:1.25
Okinawa	39,000 (ground)	119,000	1:3
	7,700 (navy)	(not a complete count)	

evidence that underestimated Iwo Jima's cost. Despite attempts to calm Truman's fears, even the sanitized version of losses on Iwo Jima gave the President pause. Quite simply, the extensive manpower losses on Iwo Jima in comparison to the size of the enemy force hindered approval of future, and inherently more vital, ground offensives.

The American public's concern for casualties endangered Truman's quest for unconditional surrender and reinforced the U.S. government's adoption of increased technological solutions, including the aerial bombardment of Japan's civilian population, in order to force the enemy government's capitulation. Extensive use of firebombing by B-29s destroyed numerous Japanese cities, killing hundreds of thousands of men, women, and children. The huge intake vortexes sucked away so much oxygen that many people suffocated. The fires grew so hot that pavement erupted and rivers boiled. Despite such colossal damage, the scientific methods of dealing death from above did not come to full fruition until the Army Air Forces married the B-29 with the atomic bomb.[150] Only after the United States developed this technological tool did it achieve its desired end-state of Japan's total subjugation.

In balance, historian John Dower overstated his argument that American commanders' racial hatred for the Japanese primarily motivated a war that resembled extermination.[151] Instead, the Truman administration held strong ideas about how to achieve unconditional surrender in the most rapid and least costly way (to Americans) possible. Writer Lee Sandlin skillfully explained how tragic experiences like those on Iwo Jima facilitated decisions to use atomic bombs: "The Japanese still hadn't surrendered. It seems obvious now that they must have been about to—their situation was hopeless, and they couldn't have endured the overwhelming fury of the American firebombing raids much longer. But the Americans didn't see it that way. The logic of war had taught them to expect the exact opposite. Japanese soldiers had routinely responded to hopeless situations by fighting to the death and to the last man, and Japanese civilians throughout the Pacific had typically committed mass suicide rather than allow themselves to be captured. Their resistance had grown exponentially as the Americans approached the home islands. Why should anybody think it would break down now?"[152]

The result of American prosecution of the Pacific war and Japan's reaction to it may have resembled an extermination attempt of the kind that Dower argues, but that certainly was not the intent of most decision-makers. Instead, Japan's refusal to surrender in the face of overwhelming odds, coupled with the enormous casualties incurred while seizing strongholds on Iwo Jima and Okinawa in the final year of the war, so maddened U.S. commanders that they "didn't understand and didn't much care what the bomb did. They just wanted some big, nightmarish weapon that would break Japanese resistance once and for all—the bigger and the more nightmarish the better."[153] The primary motivation for America's fury was not racial hate but frustration.

After the first atomic bomb was dropped on Hiroshima, the *Nippon Times* surmised that the United States "was intent on killing and wounding as many innocent people as possible due to his urgent desire to end the war speedily."[154] The Army Air Forces made up a target list for President Truman consisting of four Japanese cities with the specified population size next to each name provided—the order of priority correlated (some have claimed incidentally) with the population size of the city. Of the four projected targets—Hiroshima (population 350,000), Nagasaki (population 210,000), Kokura (population 178,000), and Niigata (population 150,000)—Truman finally decided to use atomic bombs on the two with the highest concentrated populations.[155] The *Nippon Times* statement that the United States intended to kill thousands of Japanese civilians in order to force the issue of surrender quickly certainly had more than a ring of truth to it. Unfortunately, the tragic number of American losses on Iwo Jima contributed to the logical equation that made decisions about Hiroshima and Nagasaki possible.

*I remember that there seemed to be quite a bit of rivalry be-
tween the Navy and the Marines at the time of the Battle of
Iwo and preparing for the battle. Even though the Marines
are part of the Navy, there should be a great feeling of cooperation between the Navy and Marines, and at a higher level
also, that we support each other the very best we can, in
every way possible, and forget about things that divide us.*

NORBERT V. WOODS, *oral interview, April 2003*

CHAPTER 5   *Lessons*

With the start of World War II, the U.S. armed services made enormous
transitions. The size of the naval operations dwarfed anything witnessed
in American history. At the same time, the Army and Navy were forced to
work together as never before in ambitious joint operations. Since the prewar military had distinctly divided Army and Navy responsibilities based
upon geographical boundaries of land and sea, amphibious operations in
the Pacific left much ambiguity over how best to integrate service efforts.
The creation of the Joint Chiefs of Staff was a giant leap forward in unified command of the armed services. Still, the Army and Navy had great
difficulty working together, both in Washington and abroad. Intense rivalry
continued to influence problematic command arrangements and had tragic
repercussions, especially in the Pacific.

Considering Iwo Jima within the overall context of the Pacific war demonstrates that Operation Detachment was influenced by U.S. service interests. Plans to seize Iwo Jima began as a result of Army Air Forces strategy. The Army Air Forces sought to provide fighter escort from an intermediate air base between the Marianas and Japan in order to improve B-29 Superfortress performance. Although there were many small islands in the Nanpo Shoto, none had both the ideal terrain and the proper location to meet the Army Air Forces' requirements. Because General Arnold desperately sought to demonstrate the value of an independent air force through the performance of the B-29, he strongly urged the capture of the most suitable island anyway. Although Iwo Jima had an appropriate landscape for large airfields, distance from mainland Japan, adverse weather conditions, and limitations of the P-51 Mustang proved detrimental to effective U.S. fighter support. Planners from 1943 onward had expressed doubts that seizing Iwo Jima would justify its cost. They also doubted the ability of fighters to operate such long distances to mainland Japan. Admiral Spruance, the leading Navy officer to adhere to the Army Air Forces' desires, retained deep reservations about the island's value throughout the planning and preparation process. In retrospect, one could certainly question whether the price was worth the gain—an approach that strongly contrasts with the embellished justifications given in most scholarship on the subject.[1]

After investigating the existing justifications for Operation Detachment, one must conclude that most have been exaggerated. In particular, the emergency landing theory, the pillar of most historical arguments, can only be regarded as myth and a misrepresentation of the preponderance of evidence. Proposals for Operation Detachment did not mention B-29s using Iwo Jima's airfields. This justification became prominent after the seizure of Sulfur Island cost many lives. The primary justification historians have used for seizing Iwo Jima—the emergency landing theory—was erroneously generated in hindsight.

The tragic cost of Operation Detachment pressured veterans, journalists, and commanders to fix upon the most visible rationalization for the battle. The sight of the enormous, costly, and technologically sophisticated B-29 landing on the island's small airfield most clearly linked Iwo Jima to the strategic bombing campaign. As the myths about the flag-raisings on Mount Suribachi reached legendary proportions, so did the emergency landing theory, in order to justify the need to raise that flag. Of the 2,251 touchdowns popularized in most history texts, the vast majority did not result from crucial or unavoidable crises. Most landings were for the purpose of refueling, planned or otherwise.

In regard to unplanned cases, in its urgency to improve B-29 performance, the Army Air Forces pushed the envelope on several safety factors, and the seizure of Iwo Jima allowed it to do so even further. Consequently, that many B-29s landed on Iwo Jima to refuel is not surprising. Although seizure of the islands' airfields proved the only valid justification for seizing the island, the current reliance upon the emergency landing theory should change. The time has come to put this fabrication to rest.

Disregarding the hindsight argument about B-29s, the U.S. Navy seized the island for the purpose of providing fighter escort—an endeavor that failed to produce substantial results. It was only after fighter escort proved difficult and unnecessary that the island's airfields became increasingly oriented toward accommodating the B-29. The island did serve as an intermediate air base for the Superfortress, which exploited its potential and proved valuable, but this function does not justify writers labeling the battle as "inevitable" or "bound to happen."[2] In the light of critical analysis, the battle could have been avoided, and it might have proven more beneficial to do so.

The Army Air Forces pressured for Iwo Jima during a time when the Army and Navy bickered over who would command operations against Formosa. After a three-month standoff, a frustrated Nimitz finally proposed to bypass Formosa and take Okinawa instead. He suggested the seizure of Iwo Jima simultaneously, which ensured approval of Okinawa by the Joint Chiefs of Staff. Yet Admirals Nimitz, Spruance, and King made the decision to initiate the operation before they completed a thorough and updated examination of Iwo Jima's defenses. Iwo Jima had strategic relevance, but because of its distance from Japan and lack of port facilities, it was a debatable objective, which Admiral King described as a "sinkhole." When evidence surfaced about the extensive fortifications on the island, Admiral Nimitz and his Pacific commanders found it too late to reevaluate whether the cost was worth the gain. The compromise to substitute Okinawa and Iwo Jima for Formosa had solved a fierce debate between the Army and Navy over future strategy. Iwo Jima had also fulfilled the ardent requests of the Army Air Forces. Despite reservations expressed by Admiral Spruance and General Smith, once the Joint Chiefs of Staff made the decision, naval commanders could do little to change it.

Weaknesses in the decision to initiate Operation Detachment primarily derived from the organization of the Pacific Theater along service lines. Dual command in the Pacific combined with a decision-by-committee system in Washington proved a difficult leadership arrangement for proper and timely prioritization of objectives and efficient use of resources. Nearly every senior commander recognized the arrangement as flawed, but no consensus could be reached as to the solution. Although the Joint Chiefs of Staff recognized that a unified Pacific commander would have integrated efforts toward balanced and mutual objectives, the intense rivalry among the Army, Navy, and Army Air Forces proved an impermeable barrier to integrated strategy. Competition existed at all levels of the military, especially within the Joints Chiefs of Staff. By 1945 each service strongly contended for its own interest. The Joint Chiefs of Staff initiated nearly concurrent operations against Luzon (Army objective), Okinawa (Navy objective), and Iwo Jima (Army Air Forces objective) to meet each service's strategic vision.

Some have presented U.S. Pacific strategy as systematic. In reality, it was disjointed. The decision by the Joint Chiefs of Staff to split responsibility and resources contributed to problems faced at Guadalcanal (1942), Tarawa (1943), and Peleliu (1944). The institutional self-interests of the Army, Navy, and Army Air Forces influenced their schemes of maneuver, including the planning for Operation Detachment.

Once the planning for Iwo Jima began, service rivalry continued to adversely affect preparations. The United States did not properly focus its available military might against Iwo Jima. The Army refused to release the battleships and cruisers it borrowed for Luzon in time to participate. Despite the Army Air Forces' astonishingly massive air raids on Tokyo, it refused to allocate B-29s to soften up Iwo Jima. And the Navy prioritized resources for Okinawa over Operation Detachment, cutting preparatory naval bombardment from ten days to three. The scattering of forces made the battle more costly than it might have been, resulting in the bloodiest battle in Marine Corps history. The heavy losses incurred on Iwo Jima hindered important future ground operations. Scholars and military analysts can and should rationally question the decision to capture the island.

Myths created about the necessity of taking the island, emphasis on the flag-raising on Mount Suribachi, and the emergency landing theory have distorted memory of the battle. Nimitz paid apt tribute to the Marines who fought the battle when he stated that "uncommon valor was a common virtue."[3] Historians have emphasized the admiral's sentiment to the exclusion of analytic rigor. They have overlooked the strategic decisions that sent these warriors to make such horrific sacrifices. One can honor the Marines' bravery without conflating it with their commanders' wisdom. Perhaps the most appropriate tribute later generations can offer Iwo Jima's valiant dead is to ask why they had to die to secure fighter escorts that never really materialized.

PART 2

The Immortal Icon

My feeling is best expressed in the words of Major General Julian Smith who wrote to his wife after Tarawa, "I can never again see a United States marine without experiencing a feeling of reverence."

JAMES FORRESTAL, *"Arms, Character, Courage,"* March 1945

CHAPTER 6

Making Heroes into Legends

On the cold morning of 21 February, the commanding officer of Easy Company, 2d Battalion, 28th Marines, Capt. Dave E. Severance, gathered the members of his 3d Platoon around him. Since the first briefings on Operation Detachment in Hawaii months earlier, Marines had boasted about who would be the first to raise the American flag on the tallest point on the island—Mount Suribachi. Now Captain Severance initiated the order that would bring those imaginings to reality. The 2d Battalion commander, Lt. Col. Chandler W. Johnson, wanted a reconnaissance mission to scout the summit of the volcano. Third Platoon would execute it.[1]

Johnson talked to the men of 3d platoon personally: "If you're able to get up the mountain I want you to take this flag . . . If you can't make it all the way up, turn around and come back down. Don't try to go overboard."[2] Johnson handed the flag to the platoon commander, 1st Lt. Harold G. Schrier. The flag handed to Schrier had initially arrived on the sands of Iwo Jima in the map case of the battalion adjutant, 1st Lt. George G. Wells. Now it went forward to fulfill the purpose Wells had brought it for—to fly in the most prominent corner of Sulfur Island.

Schrier headed out with his entire forty-man platoon of tired, dirty, and unshaven, but thoroughly motivated Marines. The night before had been cold and wet, but the weather this morning held out and offered a fine day in the making. It was also a quiet morning, and it was apparent that organized resistance on the mountain had tailed off.[3] Instinctively recognizing a photographic opportunity, *Leatherneck* photographer Staff Sgt. Lou Lowery traveled with them. He did not want to miss the moment. Over the thick black sands that pulled at their feet, through the twisted debris of burned scrub that snagged their uniforms, and up the steep rocky slopes of the volcano that cut their hands, they traveled. The Marines followed a path that adhered to a crevice that vertically split the face of the mountain, as if a powerful stream had once flowed down there. One by one, they moved upward, Lowery stopping periodically to take pictures of the trek.

Lieutenant Schrier worried about opposition, but his men finally reached the nearly 600-foot summit without dispute. Bending over at the waist, the Marines kept a low profile along the rim of the crater since they had now silhouetted themselves on the skyline for anyone below to easily make out. Several Marines scoured the area for something to hoist up the flag and quickly returned with a long metal water pipe found nearby. Schrier and three other Marines—Ernest Thomas, Henry Hansen, and Charles Lindberg—sat down and fastened the Stars and Stripes to the makeshift flagpole, being careful to not let the flag touch the ground in the process. Incredibly, the pipe had a bullet hole in the precise place needed to tie the flag to it.[4] The four Marines made ready to raise the standard. James Michaels crouched nearby with his rifle at the ready. Lowery shouted out to wait a minute. He had run out of film. He quickly resolved the problem and got into position. Then he gave the command, "Ready."[5] At 10:20, the Marines of 3d Platoon raised the American standard on Mount Suribachi for all to see.[6] As Lindberg described it, "All hell broke loose below. Troops cheered, ships blew horns and whistles, and some men openly wept."[7] The Japanese took notice of the event, too.

A Japanese soldier came out of a nearby cave, firing a shot that nearly hit Lieutenant Schrier. Rifleman Jim Robeson pivoted from his position in the ready and unleashed several deadly rounds of fire from his Browning

Automatic Rifle (BAR). A Japanese inside the cave pulled the lifeless body of his comrade back inside. From another direction, a Japanese officer charged forth to knock down the American standard with the only tools at his disposal, spirit and flesh. He had broken his own Samurai sword in half before attacking in order to prevent the satisfaction of American souvenir-hunters. Now, he sallied forth with a broken, antiquated weapon toward a crowd of forty heavily armed Marines—his death before dishonor. Obliging his wish, the Marines cut him down. A firefight rapidly ensued, with the Japanese and Marines lobbing grenades at each other. Attempting to escape the explosions, Lou Lowery tripped and fell backward, smashing his camera beyond repair. Like a good correspondent, he made sure the film remained undamaged. Meanwhile, 3d Platoon, and eventually the rest of the company, mopped up Japanese resistance for nearly three hours with flamethrowers, destroying each cave with demolitions.[8]

For the Marines on the ground and for the sailors at sea, seeing the small flag raised on Suribachi meant a great deal. Marines fought in the midst of their most costly battle in history. The Navy recovered from a disastrous *kamikaze* raid two days earlier. Nearly everyone within eyesight of the flag stopped, looked up, and felt reenergized. All could see that the Marines had seized that damned colossal mountain, and it surely felt good! If only for a moment, sailors and Marines celebrated with each other, pointing and laughing and shouting. The event inspired some sailors on board the ships to write poems about the episode.[9] By 11:00, even Adm. Richmond Kelly Turner had joined in the festivities by congratulating the Marines in an official radio message. In a Higgins boat on its way to disembark its prestigious passengers onto the black sands of Iwo Jima, Secretary of the Navy James Forrestal put down his binoculars and declared to Gen. Holland M. Smith, "The raising of that flag on Suribachi means a Marine Corps for the next five hundred years."[10]

Of the forty men who left on that reconnaissance patrol in the early morning hours of 23 February 1945 and seized the summit of Mount Suribachi, only four would leave the island unscathed. Their impromptu acts, however, to raise the flag and the sacrifices they made thereafter would fall into obscurity. Despite the magnificent trek, the photographer who almost lost his life in a skirmish with the Japanese, and the inspirational moment that swept across the battlefield as Americans raised "Old Glory," Lowery's snapshots of a small flag hoisted by the raggedy-ass Marines of 3d Platoon simply did not make a good enough picture for front-page news. Numerous American flag-raisings accompanied island battles, and in the competitive stories of a wartime press covering both Europe and the Pacific, the pictures of the first flag-raising on Iwo Jima made little impression.

Publishing the Flag

Ecstatic over the turn of events that morning, 2d Battalion's Lieutenant Colonel Johnson decided that the diminutive flag on Mount Suribachi had to be replaced with a larger one that could be seen more clearly. Besides, some souvenir-hungry Marine might steal his battalion's trophy, and he wanted it back. Johnson gathered a few Marines and sent up a full, 96 x 56-inch standard to the now somewhat secure area. He wanted to replace his flag of significance. The battalion commander would later die on Iwo Jima, believing he had preserved the most important relic of Operation Detachment's history. Having seen the motivating capture of Suribachi from below and anxious to document the occasion, three more correspondents, Joe Rosenthal from Associated Press, Sgt. Bill Genaust from *Leatherneck*, and combat photographer private Bill Campbell decided to climb Suribachi and catch up with 2d Battalion's latest mission. As the three correspondents began the long climb up, they passed an elated Lou Lowery who headed down to the command post. Lowery jeered at them: "You guys are late!"[11]

Indeed, Rosenthal, Genaust, and Campbell had missed the inspirational moment. The three decided to make the best of it anyway. Lowery had mentioned the fabulous view from the top, so they continued—Campbell with his camera, Rosenthal with his heavy Speed Graphic, and Genaust with his motion picture camera. The second Marine patrol that climbed Suribachi arrived before the correspondents and set up a defensive perimeter "without a single enemy shot being fired."[12] In a short time, a working party of five Marines and one Navy corpsman raised the secondary, larger flag on a rusty pole, while other Marines simultaneously caught the principal flag being lowered on its original hollow water pipe.[13] Almost missing the action, Rosenthal and Genaust, who just "happened to be there at the right time," hurriedly took pictures and video of the incident from about the same angle but only focused on the new flag going up.[14] From the opposite viewpoint, Campbell took pictures of both flags being exchanged simultaneously—the original standard lowered at the same time the larger flag was raised. Then Rosenthal captured several other photos of the Marines posing around the flagpole. At that moment, no one believed the second flag-raising significant—not the servicemen on the summit, or the Marines below, or the sailors at sea, or even Rosenthal himself.

THE IMMORTAL ICON

That same afternoon, Rosenthal returned to his quarters on the command ship at sea and prepared to mail his sheet film to Guam, where it would be processed and eventually sent to New York if found commendable. Slightly misleading, the heading Rosenthal used on the envelope later led to some confusion. "Atop 565-foot Suribachi Yama, the volcano at the southern tip of Iwo Jima, Marines of the Second Battalion, 28th Regiment, 5th Marine Division, hoist the Stars and Strips, signaling the capture of this key position."[15] The title provided no context about the events that had occurred atop Mount Suribachi and made no clarification about a previous flag-raising. After viewing the pictures of the summit, one could easily misconstrue that the actions depicted "the capture of this key position."

Upon processing the twelve photos in the film pack sent by Rosenthal, John Bodkin, the Associated Press photo editor in Guam, became captivated by the tenth sheet film, exclaiming, "Here's one for all time!"[16] He immediately radiophotoed the image to Associated Press headquarters in New York, and the spark quickly became a firestorm as newspaper editors around the country looked at the photo in wonder. Against the backdrop of an overcast sky, the Stars and Strips unfurled in the wind as six Americans struggled to raise "Old Glory" on a 20-foot heavy pipe over the sacrificial hell of a tiny Pacific island. Combining the patriotic picture with the latest numbers of American dead, raising the flag on Suribachi made front-page news everywhere. The picture stirred imaginations. As a consequence, many in both the press and the public assumed that six Marines, in the chaotic fury of an epic battle, had gallantly run forward to climb the rocky summit and plant the American flag amid deadly Japanese mortar and rifle fire.

On 4 March Rosenthal traveled back to Guam, eight days after his picture had made front-page news. Like everyone else fighting on Iwo Jima, he had no idea one of his shots had captivated millions of Americans. Since Rosenthal had mailed the negatives without viewing them, he initially was unsure which picture everyone was talking about. Yet through his capture of one fantastic image, Rosenthal went from insignificance to fame—on a path to national celebrity for depicting "one of the war's greatest moments."[17] Artists re-created the picture in "paintings, statues, medallions—in oils, pastels, watercolors, stone, bronze, plaster, and wood."[18] One publication described it as "the most inspiring photograph to come out of this war—or *any* war, for that matter."[19] Once a man of obscurity, Rosenthal now found that people recognized his face and slapped him on the back. Reporters flocked to interview the war correspondent. Above all, people wanted to know the story behind the picture.

Rosenthal made for an ideal patriot. He had tried to join the service but was rejected by the Navy and Marine Corps due to poor vision. Ironically, the man with deficient eyesight took the picture that fascinated the nation. A modest "Joe," as he liked to be called, Rosenthal represented the ideal American—an average man doing everything he could do for his country, giving the kind of effort everyone needed to imitate in order to win the war.[20]

Rosenthal returned home to a hero's welcome and a flurry of banquets. His first, in San Francisco, featured an ice sculpture of his photo.[21] Associated Press gave him a pay raise, and he received a bonus year's salary in war bonds—$4,200.[22] *Camera* magazine gave him the Diamond Award (an additional $1,000), and he received a few hundred dollars more for radio

Joe Rosenthal's famous photograph of the second flag raised atop Mount Suribachi.

THE IMMORTAL ICON

From the opposite angle from Rosenthal's photo, the original flag is seen being lowered as the second one goes up.

interviews. One promoter offered him $200,000 for the rights to the picture. Unfortunately for Joe, he did not own them.[23] Next, Rosenthal traveled to New York, where he dined with Kent Cooper, the president of *Associated Press.* Rosenthal also spoke on the broadcast "We the People," selected a number of his photographs for publication in *U.S. Camera,* and lunched with New York's Dutch Treat Club. He received special plaques from the New York

Making Heroes into Legends

Photographers Association and the Catholic Institute Press.[24] Far from fading away, all of this attention only forecast even larger recognition. Rosenthal's photo would eventually be used for a U.S. Stamp, win a Pulitzer Prize, and serve as the model for the largest bronze statue in the world.

Despite attempts to clarify that there had been a previous flag-raising, Americans saw what they wanted to see in Rosenthal's photo—a symbol of the patriotism, honor, and sacrifice of the Marines' exploits on Iwo Jima. On 7 March, Democratic Representative Mike Mansfield proposed that the Treasury Department use the Suribachi photo as the symbol of the Seventh War Loan campaign.[25] During the war years, bond tours gathered crowds in stadiums and public forums around the country. Stars like Bing Crosby and Bob Hope made special radio programs to support them. They served as a national celebration of patriotism. However, six previous bond drives had already drained the pockets of Americans, and the European war had almost concluded.[26] A seventh campaign needed something exceptional to energize the public. Mansfield believed that the Iwo Jima icon would motivate Americans to contribute—challenging them to raise their patriotism at home as high as the flag waving over foreign shores abroad. James Bradley wrote, "It was an image the public had fallen in love with, seeming to find in it an affirmation of the national purpose at its very origins that no politician, no history book had ever matched. The Photograph had become The Fact. It had, in a way, become its admirers. The Mighty 7th would make this triumphal joining complete."[27]

Already concerned about the success of a seventh bond campaign, President Roosevelt thought Mansfield's idea of using the flag-raising image as its symbol was an excellent idea. On 30 March he ordered the Marine Corps to find the men in *that* picture and transfer them "immediately to us by air" in order to raise support for a war loan campaign.[28] Unfortunately, only three of the six ("Doc" Bradley, Ira Hayes, and Rene Gagnon) survived the battle.[29]

When the President's order reached the V Amphibious Corps, the three Marine divisions had already left the miserable hell of Iwo Jima and were in transit at sea. Upon hearing the news, Gagnon volunteered his name as a flag-raiser. In contrast, Hayes defied the orders of the President by saying nothing. Considering the death and despair of the battle, Hayes found the special attention given to the flag-raisers inappropriate. It drew attention away from the sacrifices made by fighting men elsewhere and focused on an insignificant (albeit symbolic) event instead. Despite his desire to remain anonymous, at least one other man knew that Hayes had been in the picture. Ira Hayes took Rene Gagnon aside and told him to keep quiet.[30]

Ira Hayes was by far the most combat-tested veteran of the three surviving Americans in Rosenthal's photo. A Native American from the Pima Tribe in Arizona, he had battled adversity before ever wearing a uniform. His family was poor and could offer little in the way of opportunities. When war broke out, he and his two brothers were anxious to volunteer (both his brothers, Leonard and Dean, joined the Army when of age and eventually won silver stars for heroism).[31] At 5 foot 9 and 155 pounds, nineteen-year-old Ira, who had played football in high school, decided on the U.S. Marines. He set out for boot camp in August 1942.[32] An idealistic youth, he signed his first letter home, "From a guy who's very proud he's a Marine and in his country's service."[33] Such commentary was typical of Ira's positive attitude and love for the Corps. His resilience to hardship, combined with the arduous training and resulting self-confidence of boot camp, transformed him into an extremely capable fighter. Discovering his newfound opportunities to excel, Hayes decided to press on to more difficult challenges—Marine paratrooper. At airborne school he earned the nickname "Chief Falling Cloud."[34] By February 1943 he had completed the training and joined Third Parachute Battalion. From October 1943 through January 1944, Hayes participated in operations in the Solomon Islands. For valid reasons, the Marine Corps decided to disband both the raider and parachutist battalions. Hayes's pay dropped from $100 a month to $50. He returned to San Diego, California, where he and his comrades were integrated into the newly formed 5th Marine Division.[35] The parachutists formed the "cream of the crop" of 5th Division, giving it the requisite experience and training needed for Operation Detachment.[36]

During his years in the Marine Corps, Hayes gained his abiding impression of the war. First, he highly valued the Marine Corps as an organization and a brotherhood in which he formed numerous personal bonds with other members. Second, any romanticism of war that Hayes may have believed before shipping out was shattered in the Solomon Islands. He lost friends there and saw the grim realities of the brutal fighting in the Pacific.[37] Still, when he returned to San Diego in 1944, Hayes remained confident and positive, believing that he served his country for a worthwhile cause. He trained with the best of Americans for Iwo Jima, ready to play his part for his country one more time.

Hayes fought the brutal contest on Iwo Jima the entire thirty-six days, landing on D-Day and persevering until the final withdrawal. Whether by luck, skill, or experience, he survived an entire month in the nightmare of Sulfur Island. He started and ended the battle in Easy Company, 2d Battalion, 28th Marines. Of the 235 original members of his company, only 35 remained unscathed at battle's end.[38] Three of the men who raised the flag with Hayes—Franklin Sousley, Harlon Block, and Mike Strank—died along the way, and both Sousley and Strank were Hayes's friends.[39] One can only imagine how traumatic the experiences of Sulfur Island must have been for Hayes.

The Pima Indian also had more intimate knowledge of the enemy he killed on Iwo Jima than most. Before entering the Marines, he had worked at a Japanese American "relocation center" in Arizona. Writer William Bradford Huie argued that for Ira, no amount of government propaganda could fit the enemy he faced into simple stereotypes. He had seen uprooted, dispossessed, and imprisoned Japanese, and held "yellow children in his arms. He had looked into innocent, frightened, yellow faces."[40] The Japanese were his enemy, and he hated them, but he could not completely dehumanize them. On the outside, Hayes did not suffer injury on Iwo Jima, but on the inside the battle had badly mauled him. He certainly did not hold the same vision of the contest that Americans saw in Rosenthal's picture. For Hayes, the combat remained much more real and tragic.

Above all, Ira Hayes wanted to exemplify a model Marine and uphold the "Semper Fidelis" ethos, but no one nominated him for a medal or recognized his efforts to conquer the Japanese. Now, the government wanted him to play a hero, not for any of the real sacrifices he had endured, not because the country appreciated the measly $50 a month for service, but because the public had fallen in love with a picture, and he just happened to be in it. The photo had already begun overshadowing the events of the battle. He had heard his buddies apply obscenities to that "flag-raising crap."[41] So when Gagnon stepped aboard a plane for Washington, D.C., Hayes stayed behind with his remaining friends and prayed for anonymity. In obscurity, perhaps he could find solace and honor those who had died. At least in the company of his platoon, he remained a good Marine, respected by those whose opinion mattered to him.

Unlike Hayes, Doc Bradley was somewhat easier to find—strapped to a hospital bed in Hawaii. Mortar fire had finally found him and a handful of other Marines halfway through the battle. After his fierce experiences in combat, Bradley was lucky only to have shrapnel in his legs. Weeks earlier, when the 28th Regiment was still trying to seize Mount Suribachi, Bradley was right in the thick of it. His son described the action best:

> He watched a Marine blunder into cross fire of machine-gun bursts and slump down to the ground. Doc did not hesitate. His telltale "Unit 3"

THE IMMORTAL ICON

bag slapping at his side, my father sprinted through thirty yards of saturating cross fire—mortars and machine guns—to the wounded boy's side. As bullets whined and pinged around him, Doc found the Marine losing blood at a life-threatening rate. Moving him was out of the question until the flow was stanched. The Japanese gunfire danced all around him, but Doc focused his mind on his training. He tied a plasma bottle to the kid's rifle and jammed it bayonet-first into the ground. He moved his own body between the boy and the sheets of gunfire. Then, his upper body still erect and fully exposed, he administered first aid.[42]

Such was only a few minutes of the typical hell and heroism on Iwo Jima. Doc Bradley would later get a Navy Cross for that exploit. Even in a hospital, he must have looked upon Hawaii as a fortunate blessing. In mid-April, the Navy transferred Bradley to Bethesda Hospital in Washington. He needed to recuperate quickly. The nation called on him to perform once again—this time as a celebrity. The Navy Department had found Gagnon and Bradley; there was just one more man to track down.

The Marine Corps finally discovered Hayes several days later. Gagnon could not stand up to the pressure of Marine brass in Washington who ordered him to identify the other flag-raiser.[43] A reluctant Hayes was eventually extracted from his regiment. He arrived in Washington on 19 April. With attitudes ranging from excited, to modest, to reluctant, the three flag-raisers had been reunited. Hayes did not kill Gagnon for ratting on him as he had promised to do, but he never forgave him either. For the next couple of months, Hayes refused to speak with Gagnon, doing so through Bradley instead.[44] The Pima Indian remained quiet most of the time, looking embarrassed by all the hoopla. But there was nowhere to hide. If anything, the furor over the photo continued to increase. Fighting on Iwo had been hell, but Americans saw heavenly virtues in the picture. On a personal level, Ira Hayes could not deal with the contradictions.

Although the three survivors had been rounded up, the Corps mistakenly identified one of the dead Marines in the photo, the one putting the pole into the ground. Much to his mother's dismay, Harlon Block had been misidentified as Hank Hanson. Mrs. Block protested loudly to anyone who would listen. She knew that was Harlon in the picture. Even the family refused to take her seriously. Having just lost her son, they attributed her claims to maternal hysteria. But upon his arrival in Washington, Ira Hayes instantly recognized the error and tried to correct it with the public relations office. Both men, Block and Hanson, were dead, and the press report had already been released. Rather than start a public commotion, a senior Marine officer told Hayes to "keep his mouth shut."[45] To let the error go uncorrected shocked Hayes. He grudgingly kept quiet, and the issue officially went unresolved for several months. In 1946 Hayes demonstrated his extraordinary integrity by hitching rides for hundreds of miles from the Pima Indian Reservation in Arizona to east Texas in order to tell the Hanson family the truth.[46] Yet for now, in 1945, the incident just added to his bewilderment. Hayes acted with the simplicity and fortitude of his heart. He held true to the unadulterated values learned from his parents, his tribe, and his Corps. The public's trendy romanticism and Washington politics baffled him.

The Treasury Department brought in artist C. C. Beall to illustrate the poster of the Seventh War Loan campaign.[47] The painting, entitled "*Now . . . All Together,*" displayed six Americans heroically raising the flag, with the Stars and Stripes waving against the beautiful horizon, complete with vibrantly colored bomb bursts in the sky. To express their approval, Commandant of the Marine Corps A. A. Vandegrift and Joe Rosenthal both attended the press conference making the poster public.[48] The Treasury Department regarded the icon as "the most dramatic poster and insignia of all the war loans."[49] It distributed over 2 million copies to War Finance Division field offices around the country, with another 1.5 million scheduled for release in the weeks ahead. Of the 3.5 million total, 1 million posters were designated for retailers, 200,000 for factories, 30,000 for railroad stations, 16,000 for theaters, and 15,000 for banks.[50] Additionally, the Treasury Department made 175,000 bus placards and 15,000 outdoor signs.[51] The already famous picture of the Marines atop Suribachi (corpsman rarely mentioned) was disseminated to schools, grocery stores, theaters, subway cars, banks, railroad stations, businesses, and military establishments. The insignia was also estimated to feature in 140,000 advertisements, 1,800 daily newspapers, 1,600 magazines, and 15,000 house organs.[52] "*Now . . . . All Together*" was expected to become as historically accepted as *The Spirit of 76* and *Washington Crossing the Delaware.* The Treasury Department pledged to display the flag-raising "more widely than any other picture has been displayed in history."[53]

American corporations quickly echoed the government's call. Bankers Trust Company, New York, took out a full-page bond ad featuring Rosenthal's photo. The caption read "Four thousand men died to plant Old Glory on Iwo Jima. Now it's *our* turn to show what that Flag means to us!"[54] Iwo Jima, the U.S. Marine Corps, and "Old Glory" all blended together—American patriotism at its best and purest.

Accompanied by Bradley, Hayes, and Gagnon, the Treasury Secretary presented the original Seventh War Loan campaign painting to Democratic President Harry Truman on 20 April.[55] Before the Seventh War Loan campaign began, Truman met with the three surviving flag-raisers in the Oval Office. He told the three men that "the spirit they had displayed had been caught by the photographer and typified the greatness of those who wore the country's uniform."[56] It was a field day for the press, making front-page news in the *Washington Post*.[57] One photo showed the three heroes with the President. "Gagnon, pointing to himself in the poster, Bradley, supported by his crutches, and Hayes looking on."[58] The body language of the three men clearly demonstrated their differing attitudes about the media hype. Hayes always appeared the reluctant warrior.

After meeting with the President, the three men visited the Senate, where they received a standing ovation. The Senate called a short recess so that each Senator could file by and shake the heroes' hands. Then, the Marines and corpsman had their first press conference on the steps of Congress and explained how they had raised the flag. Following the conference, the three were escorted to Griffith Stadium. After the Speaker of the House threw out the first ball, the loudspeaker system introduced the three surviving heroes from the picture that everyone recognized. Twenty-four thousand baseball fans stood up and cheered.[59] The three veterans had reached the status of national celebrities.

The flag-raisers got the red-carpet treatment in Washington for a couple of weeks while the bond drive finished organizing. Hayes spent most of his free time at Ninth Street bars in Washington's nightclub district.[60] He drank heavily. One bartender said, "I don't know who ever got the idea that Indians can't drink. The Chief could drink more than most these white Joes. And he was quiet—didn't have nothing to say. Never even broke a glass. He'd come in and stand there and drink; and when he was too drunk to stand, we'd prop him up in a booth and let him drink some more. We figured he deserved it."[61] Hayes was developing quite a drinking problem, exacerbated by his survivor's guilt.

The war bond tour received a big sendoff on 9 May. The Marine Band played the "Star Spangled Banner" as Bradley, Gagnon, and Hayes raised the flag from Suribachi over the Capitol. Admirals, generals, and congressmen came out to celebrate the occasion. Democratic Speaker of the House Samuel T. Rayburn gave brief remarks describing Rosenthal's iconic photograph as "a symbol of victory to Americans." Marine Commandant A. A. Vandegrift described how this flag had inspired the Marines on the ground and the sailors offshore to perform "the utmost efforts of all in the hard fighting that is yet to come." Hundreds of people showed up to watch the ritual, and many bought bonds. At sun down, the flag was retrieved to accompany the heroes on their nationwide bond campaign.[62]

The first official stop of the bond tour was New York City on 11 May. General Vandegrift and the Republican mayor of New York Fiorello H. LaGuardia oversaw the unveiling of a 50-foot-high Iwo Jima monument erected in Times Square.[63] To the tune of the "Star Spangled Banner," the Suribachi flag went up the statue's flagpole. Tens of thousands of people turned out for the event.[64] The ceremony also honored fifty wounded Marines, veterans of Iwo Jima who were brought out from a local hospital.[65] Parents of Medal of Honor winner John Basilone also attended.[66] Basilone, a national hero and star of a 1942 bond campaign, had died on Iwo Jima leading his troops forward into the teeth of the enemy defenses. In addition to New York's representation of the Suribachi scene, artist Felix de Weldon created a 9-foot-high plaster model of the flag-raising for the bond tour as well.[67] Adulation for Iwo Jima came in many forms, but the focus was always on the flag-raising.

The next day, after another crowded unveiling ceremony of the statue in Manhattan, reporters turned out to hound the three stars—Bradley, Hayes, and Gagnon. Hayes proved the toughest nut to crack. One reporter questioned his Irish name: "How'd you get a name like Ira Hayes, Chief? I never heard of an Indian with a name like that?" Hayes replied curtly, "You didn't?" Nothing followed—just silence. Another reporter asked: "How many Japs you killed Chief?" Ira just stared back, his jaw stiffening. Irritated, a reporter took the Marine press agent aside: "Listen . . . somebody's gonna bust this goddamn Indian over the head with a camera. He's a surly bastard. He's asking for it." The Marine retorted that whoever did so had "better run fast." Then, he proceeded in a protecting tone, "You fellows are not being fair with him. How the hell does he know how he got his name? And what's wrong with it? And he doesn't like to be asked about killing Japs. So lay off him."[68] Hayes later said, "You should hear the silly questions those people asked out East—like they had never seen an Indian."[69]

The celebrities continued on, touring the East Coast and Midwest at a rapid pace. They stopped at Philadelphia, Boston, New York (the Stock Exchange), Chicago, Detroit, Indianapolis, and back to Chicago again. By late May Hayes could not keep up with the first-class dining, hero worship, and incessant flag-raising reenactments. In his own words, he could not "stop thinking about all those other guys who were better men than me not coming back at all, much less to the White House."[70] Everywhere Hayes

Hayes, Gagnon, and Bradley raise the flag over the Capitol, while Washington's top brass and politicians pay tribute.

went, people shoved drinks in his hand and said he was a hero. He knew the flag-raising was a great picture, but it was not an important battle event. Yet he could not tell people that. By the time the bond drive hit Chicago, Hayes had developed such a bad drinking habit that his conduct endangered the success of the campaign. Consequently, when he requested to return to his unit, the Marine Corps approved the request and shipped him back to Hawaii. Undeterred, the bond tour continued on through July, with Bradley and Gagnon playing the leading roles.

The mighty Seventh War Loan campaign set its sights on the highest goal of any drive to date—$14 billion, $7 billion from corporate sources and $7 billion from individuals.[71] With a U.S. population of about 160 million, that meant about $100 for every man, woman, and child in America—a very large amount for a country with an average family income of $1,700.[72] As impossible as the task appeared, the Treasury Department actually collected *$26 billion,* almost double the proposed amount and more than any other war loan campaign in American history.[73] To accomplish this Herculean task, the publicity campaign for the Seventh War Loan reached unprecedented levels. At the focal point of the bond drive was the tour of the famous Marines and corpsman. But in their wake often followed the Commandant of the Marine Corps. Other services contributed to the publicity for the campaign as well. The Army Air Forces put on air shows. Army ground forces gave demonstrations. The Navy invited the public to displays of naval platforms. Admirals Leahy, King, and Nimitz even teamed up with Generals Marshall, MacArthur, and Eisenhower to endorse the bond drive in a public appeal statement designed to gain the "assurance and backing of a united people."[74] The moral was implicit: if the Army and Navy could unite, so could Americans.

Despite its rhetoric, neither Rosenthal's photo nor the bond drive had solved all the differences between the Army and Navy. What the bond drive did accomplish as a by-product, however, is quite clear: the monumental winner of the Seventh War Loan campaign was the U.S. Marine Corps. The advertising and support for the war loan simultaneously magnified the Corps' image immensely around the country. Through Rosenthal's photo, Iwo Jima received more public recognition than other Pacific campaigns. The drive celebrated a popular American icon. In so doing, it further endeared the Marine Corps in the eyes of the population. Nevertheless, in the larger story of Iwo Jima's usefulness to positive public relations for the Corps, the Seventh War Loan campaign was only the beginning.

A Star-Struck Nation

Joe Rosenthal's photo had an immediate impact on the political landscape in Washington and gave Marine Corps supporters in Congress an instrument on which to focus attention. Many of those same congressmen would later lead the way in the fight for the Corps' survival during the Armed Forces unification crisis and the budget cutbacks in the late 1940s.[75] Iwo Jima reached a pinnacle in American memory possibly unsurpassed by any previous battle in history. Rosenthal's photograph served as a vehicle for a growing national identification with Iwo Jima. Initially, the flag-raising icon symbolized the battle itself, yet it soon came to stand for the courage of all Marines. Ultimately, the image transcended the time, geography, and circumstances in which the event took place to represent the highest form of American nationalism.

The flag-raisers give their first press conference. War bonds from the Seventh War Loan campaign are already on sale in the background.

When the photo first caught media attention, the public still greatly misunderstood actual events on Iwo Jima. The realities of the first flag-raising mixed with fascination over the second, as depicted in Rosenthal's glorious picture. An editorial in the *Oregonian* stated, "The greatest war picture so far—and it won't be surpassed—is that of five marines raising Old Glory atop Suribachi, when the volcano of death had been taken. The striving figures whose hands clutch the flagstaff, the helmeted heads, and aslant above them, whipping in the sea wind, the colors. Correspondents who watched from boats off-shore of Iwo Jima, the far figures tiny to them, the flag a miniature, wrote that their hearts were lifted as their visions blurred. How the sight of it, at the summit, must have gladdened our troops. Then they knew, if ever they had doubted that the enemy could not withstand them."[76] One could almost see the whole event if one looked hard enough into the photo. The supreme affair had become immortal: "Forever America, and forever Americans. Forever the flag! The more one looks at that picture of the flag-raising on Iwo Jima the firmer becomes one's conviction of the dauntless permanency of the American spirit."[77]

It took less than a week after the photo's release for Marine Corps supporters in Congress to act. On 1 March Democratic Representative Joseph Hendricks introduced a bill to authorize the erection of an Iwo Jima monument in Washington to honor the "heroic action of the Marine Corps."[78] He stated, "Never have I seen a more striking photograph. I have provided in the bill that this picture be a model for the monument because I do not believe that any product of the mind of the artist could equal this photograph in action." Hendricks attempted to describe the symbolism of the photo:

> The base of the flag is the crowning success of the sacrifices made
> to plant it there. The base on which the feet of the four marines are
> planted is of the most rugged terrain. The action of the men is sym-
> bolic of the efforts of the Nation to crush the despicable enemy, Japan.
> Even while three of the marines grasp the flag pole the fourth is making
> every effort to help finish the job, and his upstretched hands are indica-
> tive of the fact that he had already raised the flag to his greatest height.
> The right leg of each man is bent in the same direction and each body
> leans forward, typifying concerted action and forward movement. Their
> backs are to the camera as though they were baring their breasts to
> the enemy and protecting their homeland and loved ones who are far
> behind them. Even the half-unfurled flag has a message . . ."I have not
> completely unfurled, but soon I will reach my destination and in the
> God-given air shall wave in full length over a free world."[79]

For Hendricks, the flag-raising scene represented America's virtuous crusade to conquer its evil enemies—those who would endanger the sanctity of freedom. As such, the photo deserved a statue in its likeness to commemorate that powerful sentiment for all time. Although Hendricks's proposal did not receive immediate approval, the idea of an Iwo Jima monument gained momentum over the next several years until it finally came to pass in 1954.

In their frequent memorializing of Iwo Jima, the House of Representatives and the Senate almost appeared in competition with each other—each attempting to outdo the other in recognition of the battle. On 13 March Republican Senator Raymond E. Willis supported Hendricks's idea for an Iwo Jima monument with a similar proposal in the Senate.[80] Willis prefaced his proposal with these words: "Every American has been thrilled by the hardihood, the devotion to duty, the dauntless courage, and the will to win of the United States Marine Corps." Comparing the battle to Lexington, Washington crossing the Delaware, and the signing of the Declaration of Independence, Willis argued that Rosenthal's picture contained "all the elements of the beauty of bravery and determination of the United States Marines" in all their Pacific contests from Guadalcanal to Iwo Jima. More than just another Marine conflict, he maintained that the powerful symbolism in the photo indicated the paramount battle, surpassing other Pacific contests.

From their respective legislative bodies, both Senator Willis and Democratic Representative Brooks Hays requested that the government strike a medal for Iwo Jima veterans depicting Rosenthal's photograph on the face.[81] Willis wanted the next of kin of all those who had died on the island to receive the medal. He believed the nation should pay tribute to those who planted the "the Stars and Stripes on Iwo Jima" and made sure "that it stayed there."[82] The congressional call for an Iwo Jima medal ended up as a failed Iwo Jima measure. However, it indicated the symbolic power Rosenthal's photo had on American perception of the battle. In their unprecedented request, Senator Willis and Representative Hays proposed that the government should issue a special medal for the dead of a single contest. Somehow the deaths on Iwo Jima mattered more than the hundreds of thousands of other sacrifices made by Americans in other areas of the Atlantic and Pacific. Through the power of Rosenthal's photo, those who died on Iwo Jima were seen as deserving special recognition.

Astonishingly, the photograph even suggested a change in geography. "Sulfur Island" simply did not prove appealing enough for such an important event. On 15 March Representative Hays submitted a bill that would rename Iwo Jima "Marine Island."[83] The Marines who fought and died there added new luster to the motto "Semper Fidelis." This appears to be the only instance when a member of Congress proposed that a combat space in the Pacific be named after a service. In a similar pitch, on 4 May Democratic Representative Walter K. Granger proposed the creation of a "National Marine Corps Day" to be celebrated on 10 November.[84] Although these measures did not succeed, they testify to Iwo Jima's perceived significance. The Army Air Forces, Navy, and Army participated in the seizure of Iwo Jima—though to a lesser extent than the Marine Corps—yet only the Marine Corps received recognition for its capture. Probably of more importance, Iwo Jima epitomized all Marines, including those who did not fight there. For the public, it served as a collective sacrifice. The spirit and actions of the combatants greatly aided the Marine Corps' reputation at home. The horrific battle conditions, the heavy price in blood, and the glorious scene atop Suribachi exemplified the epic victory in which Americans expected their amphibious warriors to triumph.

On 11 March Democratic Senator Joseph C. O'Mahoney asked the postmaster general to issue a special three-cent Iwo Jima stamp depicting the flag-raising on Suribachi to commemorate the Marines' valor and sacrifice in the Pacific.[85] To gain support for the stamp proposal, he wrote to both the Associated Press and the Commandant of the Marine Corps. Senator O'Mahoney then appealed to the U.S. Senate, and his initiative received broad support.

In July the Post Office released the three-cent Iwo Jima stamp in "Marine Corps green" (the first commemorative stamp of that denomination not issued in purple). Advertising the event as Marine Corps Day, Postmaster General Robert E. Hannegan presented the initial sheet of stamps to General Vandegrift with the statement, "Through this stamp the people of our country seek to identify themselves with the men who fought and bled and triumphed and died . . . the planting of this flag on the hard-won peak moved every American heart." Numerous officers, servicemen, and distinguished guests attended the ceremony, among them flag-raiser John Bradley and Senator O'Mahoney. The display of Rosenthal's picture on a stamp established a host of precedents. It was the first U.S. stamp to represent living persons. It was also the first to depict an unfurled Stars and Stripes. The Post Office serviced over 400,000 covers the first day of sale, the greatest number for any stamp ever issued.[86] Over 137 million copies were printed before the end of circulation.

Fascination with the flag-raising inspired many poems about the glory of the Suribachi scene. With a full-size image of Rosenthal's photo in the backdrop, Win Brooks published a poem in the *Boston Evening American*, "Marines on Iwo Jima," which began as follows:

> Out of the ages distant, dark and dim,
> Where decency and courage, twins, were born
> Leaped a new flame to Suribachi's rim,
> Towering high against the sullen morn,
> The sullen sea. It rose, fell, rose again,
> Burned deep, burned steep, burned bright, burned fiercely clean,
> Red from young hearts and nourished rich by pain,
> Fed from the crater of the soul unseen.[87]

In addition to the numerous pieces published in newspapers and magazines, at least two poems were read in Congress. Democratic Senator from California, Sheridan Downey, entered a poem for the record, "Report from Iwo" by Victor Heyden.[88] And Republican Representative Gordon L. McDonough presented "Iwo Jima" by Louanne Wilder.[89] The best known verse of the latter ran as follows:

> Then suddenly there came to view,
> News of a place we little knew;
> The blazing headlines told the story
> Of how our friends were making glory,
> Soon they'd be raising the Red, White, and Blue.

Fascination with the photo ranged from politicians, to poets, to impressionable children. In Roseville, California, four boys between the ages of six and eight reenacted the flag-raising scene in a cow pasture. One dwarfed in a steel helmet and another by a hunting rifle as tall as himself, the children struggled to raise a flagpole. A full-sized American flag, larger than all of them put together, waved strongly in the breeze. The picture made national news.[90]

While members of Congress used Iwo Jima to celebrate patriotism, the Marine Corps cashed in on Rosenthal's photograph with a recruiting poster. Created by Sgt. Tom Lovell, the poster used Rosenthal's photo as its centerpiece. Superimposed over the picture were displayed the unit patches of the 3d, 4th, and 5th Maine Divisions. Just right of the Stars and Stripes but at the same height and even larger than the flag, a caption declared, "IWO JIMA. Here Marine courage and skill were put to the supreme test. In 26 days of relentless assault beginning February 19, 1945, the gallant Third, Fourth and Fifth Marine Division crushed fierce enemy resistance and captured this vital base along the last miles to Japan." Below the photo, with the Eagle, Globe, and Anchor, was the message "Enlist Now: U.S. Marine Corps."[91] By juxtaposing language and symbols of the Marine Corps with Rosenthal's photo, the poster attempted to regain ownership over what had become a national icon. It did not do so very effectively, but rather cluttered up the glorious scene. Yet the poster reminded viewers that the Marine Corps had made possible the most popular picture of the day.

In the first few months following the flag-raising event, Rosenthal's picture established itself in many places in American culture: in the press, on the floor of Congress, on a U.S. stamp, and in poetry. But the public fascination with the events on Suribachi also had special significance because of the epic scale, ferocity, and sacrifice of the battle. The collision of adulation and sorrow would forever sanctify the battle.

Forever Sanctified

The tragedy of the tens of thousands of Americans who suffered on Iwo Jima profoundly affected the military community, especially those in the Navy and Marine Corps. Unlike the public, which viewed the battle from afar, the sorrow of many servicemen and their families could not be extinguished by romanticizing the second flag-raising on Mount Suribachi and glorifying patriotism. The reality of war simply was much more tragic for those who fought it—who sacrificed themselves to purchase victory. In the months following the battle, U.S. commanders mourned the losses and sacrifices on Iwo Jima by honoring both the dead and the survivors.

In a famous communiqué to the Pacific Fleet in March 1945, Adm. Chester Nimitz initiated the tone and themes of subsequent ceremonies that honored the fighting men on Iwo Jima:

> The United States Marines by their individual and collective courage
> have conquered a base which is as necessary to us in our continuing
> forward movement toward final victory as it was vital to the enemy
> in staving off ultimate defeat . . . With certain knowledge of the cost
> of an objective which had to be taken, the Fleet Marine Force sup-
> ported by the ships of the Pacific Fleet and by Army and Navy Aircraft,
> fought the battle and won. By their victory the 3d, 4th, and 5th Marine
> Divisions and other units of the V Amphibious Corps have made an ac-
> counting to their country which only history will be able to value fully.
> Among the Americans who served on Iwo Island, uncommon valor was
> a common virtue.[92]

Transcending the hell on Sulfur Island, Nimitz focused on the courage of the Marines. He reinforced the bravery of the combatants by stating that the Marines knew beforehand of the extensive cost they would pay yet heroically carried out the mission anyway. The most famous line of his address, the last sentence, powerfully immortalized the battle as an epic of valor. Although "uncommon valor was a common virtue" is an accurate assessment of the nature of the combat, Nimitz also implied that the objective had unquestion-able worth to the end of the war. As Headquarters Marine Corps became flooded with letters from families who deplored the loss of loved ones on Iwo Jima, it reacted in a corresponding manner. According to one journalist, the publicity became so negative "that Marine Corps headquarters with-held all additional news of heavy losses."[93] Instead, Headquarters Marine

Corps mimicked Nimitz by concentrating on heroic sacrifice—a powerfully attractive concept.

The tragic hell on Sulfur Island was too horrific for anyone to describe, and veterans of the battle understandably did not wish to dwell on it. Still, a few in the military attempted to put the significance of Iwo Jima into words in an appropriate way that went beyond the appeal of the flag-raising photo. In a ceremony atop Mount Suribachi in October 1945, Army Gen. Fredrick Hopkins addressed a crowd consisting mostly of soldiers and airmen: "There are no words that can adequately describe the suffering on Iwo Jima during the following twenty-five days of vicious fighting. Suffice it to say that it was the toughest in all Marine Corps history, and that service has an enviable record in the archives of our country's wars. The white crosses in our two cemeteries give mute testimony that the price of victory was not low and that the Japanese General Kuribayashi made few tactical errors in the conduct of his static defense."[94]

There are few notable aspects of Hopkins's speech, although the general's position as island commander provided him considerable insight. Foremost, he did not focus on Mount Suribachi, even though the American public had become obsessed with the flag-raising by the time he gave the address. For the audience of veterans to whom Hopkins spoke, the hallowed ground on which they currently stood required a more meaningful speech than patriotic generalities. Second, rather than paying tribute to the veterans with words like "uncommon valor," he acknowledged the tragic nature of the "vicious fighting" that characterized the battle. He concluded his remarks by challenging each in attendance to "vow on his lips to do his utmost after he leaves this island that such fighting will never again be necessary."[95] The tragic cost incurred on Iwo Jima created a yoke of responsibility for World War II veterans to carry forward. Those who survived owed a debt to those who had died—a duty to ensure that such horrors would never be revisited.

The Department of the Navy made its own attempts to honor the sacrifices of servicemen who seized Iwo Jima. The Battle of Iwo Jima accounted for 22 of the 80 Medals of Honor awarded to Marines in World War II (28 percent). The number of Medal of Honor recipients for Iwo Jima exceeds that of any other battle in Marine Corps history.[96] Additionally, the Navy Department bestowed 186 of the 1,000 Navy Crosses given to Marines in World War II (17 percent) for Iwo Jima. It awarded 892 Silver Stars to Iwo Jima veterans, 20 percent of the 4,400 total that Marines received during the war. Additionally, the dead and wounded of Operation Detachment also received thousands of Bronze Stars. In sum, Iwo Jima accounted for more decorations than any other Marine campaign.[97]

The V Amphibious Corps also earned two unit awards, a Presidential Unit Citation (PUC) and a Navy Unit Commendation (NUC). The highest military award bestowed to a unit, the Presidential Citation read as follows:

For extraordinary heroism, in action during the seizure of enemy Japanese-held Iwo Jima, Volcano Islands, February 19 to 28. Landing against resistance which rapidly increased in fury as the Japanese pounded the beaches with artillery, rocket and mortar fire, the Assault Troops of the FIFTH Amphibious Corps inched ahead through shifting black volcanic sands, over heavily mined terrain, toward a garrison of jagged cliffs barricaded by an interlocking system of caves, pillboxes and blockhouses commanding all approaches. Often drove back with terrific losses in fierce hand-to-hand combat, the Assault Troops repeatedly hurled back the enemy's counterattacks to regain and hold lost positions, and continued the unrelenting drive to high ground and Motoyama Airfield No. 1, captured by the end of the second day. By their individual acts of heroism and their unfailing teamwork, these gallant officers and men fought against their own battle-fatigue and shock to advance in the face of the enemy's fanatical resistance; they charged each strongpoint, one by one, blasting out the hidden Japanese troops or sealing them in; within four days they had occupied the southern part of Motoyama Airfield No. 2; simultaneously they stormed the steep slopes of Mount Suribachi to raise the United States Flag; and they seized the strongly defended hills to silence guns commanding the beaches and insure the conquest of Iwo Jima, a vital inner defense of the Japanese Empire.

Perhaps of greatest significance to the Marine Corps, Congress promoted Marine Commandant A.A. Vandegrift to four stars in April 1945, only one month after the seizure of Sulfur Island and in the middle of the flag-raising hoopla. Vandegrift was the first four-star active-duty general in Marine Corps history. Perceptively, Vandegrift stated in his memoir that the Battle of Iwo Jima contributed to his promotion.[98] The heroism shown and sacrifices incurred during the most brutal battle in the Pacific had finally given the Marine Corps a four-star general. Essentially, a ferocious and bloody struggle to seize a tenaciously held Pacific island simultaneously increased the Marine Corps' standing at home.

Two days before the Marine Corps birthday in November 1945, Republican Representative Otis Hal Holmes presented the House of Representatives a dedication address given at the 5th Marine Division cemetery on Iwo Jima.[99] The powerful speech, prepared by Chaplain Rolland B. Gittelsohn, focused on the sacrifices of the battle and their contribution to American society. His words placed Iwo Jima within the context of equality and freedom:

Power of speech can add nothing to what these men and the other dead of our division who are not here have already done. All that we even hope to do is follow their example. To show the same selfless courage in peace that they did in war. To swear that by the grace of God and the stubborn strength and power of human will, their sons and ours will never suffer these pains again. These men have done their job well. They have paid the ghastly price of freedom. If that freedom be once again lost, as it was after the last war, the unforgivable blame will be ours, not theirs . . . Here lie officers and men, Negroes and whites, rich men and poor—together. Here no man prefers another because of his faith or despises him because of his color. Here there are no quotas of how many from each group are admitted or allowed. Among these men there is no discrimination; no prejudices; no hatreds. Theirs is the highest and purest democracy. Any man among us, the living, who fails to understand that will thereby betray those who lie here dead. Whoever of us lifts his hand in hate against a brother or thinks himself superior to those who happen to be in the minority makes of this ceremony and the bloody sacrifice it commemorates an empty hollow mockery.

Rosenthal's photo had focused national attention on Iwo Jima in such a way that the commemoration of the battle's dead belonged in the House of Representatives. Iwo Jima had come to represent the American struggle for freedom against all who opposed it—the paramount Pacific contest symbolized the dream of democracy itself. By extension, Marines epitomized the most patriotic citizens prepared to make the necessary sacrifices to keep the nation free. In linking Iwo Jima to the ideals established in the U.S. Constitution, Chaplain Gittelsohn recognized the Marine Corps as a model American institution.

As memories of Iwo Jima began to fuse, Rosenthal's photo of Marines atop Suribachi became synonymous with the battle, but it increasingly served as an iconic representation of the Marine Corps itself. The public recognized Iwo Jima as the most prominent Marine battle, and the Marine Corps sought to capitalize on that. Immediately following the battle, it enlisted the help of the well-known film director Frank Capra to release a twenty-two-minute color film of war footage. Compiling the work of over forty combat camera-men and moving picture men, the final product depicted preliminary ship bombardment, ship-to-shore maneuver, rocket and artillery fire, and close combat with rifles and flamethrowers.[100] Capra entitled the film *To the Shores of Iwo Jima: Combined Operations in the Assault of and Capture of the "Hot Rock."* The Marine Corps released the Technicolor picture to movie theaters in June. Of course, the powerful film incorporated Sgt. Bill Genaust's footage of the second flag-raising as the capstone of the Corps' achievement in seizing the island. One press release compared the flag-raising footage to "the moment that inspired Francis Scott Key to write . . . the Star Spangled Banner." This "Star Spangled Banner" association was enhanced by depiction of night scenes of rocket fire and artillery fire.[101] The riveting piece won an Academy Award as the best documentary of 1945.

Due to the attention it received in numerous venues, Iwo Jima had reached epic proportions in public recognition by the end of 1945. The blend of real sacrifice and powerful imagery created a legendary conflict that lifted the Marine Corps to new heights in positive public perception. The image of Rosenthal's picture represented the best in American brav-ery and patriotism. In many ways, Iwo Jima served as the culmination of nearly thirty years of pioneering efforts in developing amphibious doctrine. Unlike other campaigns, the engagement was free from significant Army influence. It became the largest all-Marine operation of the war. Indeed, the V Amphibious Corps, complete with its three Marine divisions, was the largest fighting force in Marine Corps history. Additionally, the enemy proved tough as nails. Led by a well-respected opponent in General Kuribayashi, the Japanese devised some of the most thoroughly prepared fortifications ever built. At the same time, the topographical conditions both on and sur-rounding the island presented serious engineering challenges to overcome. To win the island from enemy control, the Marines suffered more casualties than in any other battle in their 179-year history. Despite great adversity, the Marines performed with remarkable proficiency and dedication—earning the accolade from Nimitz that "uncommon valor was a common virtue."

No other Pacific battle, no matter how large or significant, could measure up to Iwo Jima's prominence. Conspicuously, Iwo Jima was the only major operation in the Pacific where Marines carried out an amphibious assault without Army assistance. At Guadalcanal, Gilbert Islands, Marshall Islands, Marianas Islands, and Okinawa, Army soldiers conducted operations along-side or in conjunction with Marines. In many places, soldiers fought with distinction, but as Iwo Jima captivated the public's attention, other Central

Pacific campaigns became viewed as similar enterprises, just on a smaller scale. It appeared that the Marines had simply captured a number of Iwo Jimas from Pearl Harbor to Japan. And before long, the soldiers who fought with Marines for four grueling years in Central Pacific campaigns became vanishing footnotes in history. The conquest of Iwo Jima came to be viewed as the supreme contest in the Pacific, and the public adored the Marines who had seized it.

The characteristics of battle on Iwo Jima epitomized why the public venerated its Marines. Americans had little knowledge of amphibious war. They had scant interest in the leadership of Marine officers or the intricate amphibious operations they had developed. However, they clearly perceived the fanaticism of the Japanese enemy and feared it. To the majority of Americans, the Japanese represented a grave threat to their ideals of freedom and democracy. To the rescue of American confidence came the Marine. Marines typified an idealistic American warrior—an amphibious frontiersman who could beat the Japanese at their own game, with fiery spirit and tenacity. The Marine could not be stopped. No matter how dedicated the enemy, no matter how difficult the obstacle, no matter how many casualties incurred, the Marine charged forward into sheer death and destruction and emerged victorious. No other service exhibited those same qualities of extraordinary determination to the same degree as Marines. Nowhere else could one find that special brand of American patriotism better exemplified than at Iwo Jima.

Beyond the real aspects of the battle, Rosenthal's photo of six legendary heroes atop Mount Suribachi created a media frenzy. The photo captivated the public's imagination. The subsequent Seventh War Loan campaign reinforced the legendary status of Iwo Jima's heroes and reinvigorated the country's patriotism. Through national celebration of the photo, Iwo Jima became an American symbol. James Bradley put it this way. "The Photograph had become a receptacle for America's emotions; it stood for everything good that Americans wanted it to stand for; it had begun to act as a great crystal prism, drawing the light of all America's values into its facets, and giving off a brilliant rainbow of feelings and thoughts."[102]

The patriotic depiction in the flag-raising scene combined with the tragic cost of the operation to create a powerful national force. The proud and courageous institution of the Marine Corps, which had earned a fierce reputation in the Pacific, was carried along in the relentless momentum. As Iwo Jima reached legendary status, the heroic Marines who fought there and who had raised the Stars and Strips on Suribachi received a sacred admiration.

But these intangible factors had yet to play their greatest role. Following the war, President Truman's administration, backed by the senior leadership in the Army and Air Force, attempted to diminish the size, organization, and mission of the Marine Corps. With the institution's existence at stake, the Marines and their friends would pull no punches. Iwo Jima had yet to serve its most useful purpose—the continued survival of the U.S. Marine Corps.

The future success of the Marine Corps depends on two factors: first, an efficient performance of all duties to which its officers and men may be assigned; second, promptly bringing the efficiency to the attention of the proper officials of the Government, and the American people.

JOHN A. LEJEUNE, *13th Commandant of the Marine Corps*

In terms of cold mechanical logic, the United States does not need a Marine Corps. However, for good reasons which completely transcend cold logic, the United States wants a Marine Corps. Those reasons are strong, they are honest, they are deep rooted and they are above question or criticism. So long as they exist . . . we are going to have a Marine Corps . . . And, likewise, should the people ever lose that conviction—as a result of our failure to meet their high—almost spiritual—standards, the Marine Corps will then quickly disappear.

GEN. VICTOR "BRUTE" KRULAK, *personal letter, 5 November 1957*

CHAPTER 7

Iwo Jima
Saves the Corps

In December 1941, on a small Central Pacific island named Wake, after two weeks of fighting the Japanese and battling an amphibious assault by superior forces, Maj. James Devereux radioed a stoic communiqué back to headquarters: "issue in doubt." In the face of a rapidly advancing Japanese enemy that appeared unstoppable, Americans questioned the outcome of the entire Pacific war. Consequently, "issue in doubt" served as shorthand for America's numerous setbacks during the first six months of fighting the Japanese. Nearly two years later, one of Col. David M. Shoup's battalion commanders evoked Devereux's phrase once again on D-Day at Tarawa: "Receiving heavy fire all along beach. Unable to land. Issue in doubt."[1] Essentially, the expression continued to serve as a fitting description of an uncertain outcome in a difficult struggle.[2]

Following the Allied victory in World War II, the Cold War brought about unprecedented changes in U.S. military policy—a revolution that jeopardized the future of the Marines. Chief proponents of abolishing the Corps were the Army and Army Air Forces. In a rudimentary sense, the Army wanted more consolidated control over American ground operations, while the Army Air Forces wanted independent command of all air forces (to include Navy and Marine Corps aviation). The scheme of "unification" proposed reorganization of the Departments of Army and Navy and their respective secretaries—replacing the entire existing system with three reorganized services (Army, Navy, Air) under a Secretary of the Armed Forces. In this skirmish dubbed "the unification crisis" (1943–47), the U.S. Marine Corps came under systematic assaults that demanded its dismemberment. The offensive did not reach an end until 1952. Perhaps Devereux's perceptive phrase "issue in doubt" best describes these seven years of bureaucratic tribulations.

During this time, the Marine Corps took its case for survival to the American public. The heroism of Marines on Iwo Jima, as symbolized by Joe Rosenthal's picture, played a key role in mobilizing the support that inspired the National Security Act of 1947 and its subsequent revision in 1952—both of which saved the Marine Corps as a fighting organization.

Issue in Doubt

The intense rivalry between the Army, Army Air Forces, Navy, and Marines reached new heights during the Pacific war, and it was actually during this period that the Army Chief of Staff, Gen. George Marshall, made the first serious proposal for merging the armed services. Marshall submitted his idea to the Joint Chiefs of Staff in November 1943. His suggestion resulted in the formation of the Special Joint Chiefs of Staff Committee on Reorganization of National Defense to discuss the question. The committee convened on the subject of unification but was incapable of any real action since the Chief of Naval Operations, Adm. Ernest King, would never agree with Marshall's ideas. Since it was getting nowhere through the military bureaucracy, the Army took its proposal to Congress for legislative action in 1944.

In March 1944 Army veteran and Republican Representative James W.

THE IMMORTAL ICON

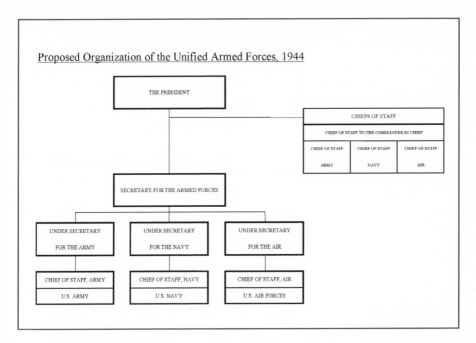

Proposed Organization of the Unified Armed Forces, 1944

THE PRESIDENT

CHIEFS OF STAFF

CHIEF OF STAFF TO THE COMMANDER IN CHIEF

CHIEF OF STAFF	CHIEF OF STAFF	CHIEF OF STAFF
ARMY	NAVY	AIR

SECRETARY FOR THE ARMED FORCES

UNDER SECRETARY	UNDER SECRETARY	UNDER SECRETARY
FOR THE ARMY	FOR THE NAVY	FOR THE AIR

CHIEF OF STAFF, ARMY	CHIEF OF STAFF, NAVY	CHIEF OF STAFF, AIR
U.S. ARMY	U.S. NAVY	U.S. AIR FORCES

Proposed organization of the unified armed forces, 1944

Wadsworth introduced a resolution in the House of Representatives that would unify the armed forces.[3] The House created the Select Committee on Post-war Military Policy to investigate the matter. The committee was more commonly referred to as the "Woodrum Committee," after its chairman, Democratic Representative Clifton A. Woodrum.[4]

Through the Woodrum Committee, Army Gen. Joseph McNarney presented the War Department's plan for unification. The plan closely resembled Marshall's previous proposal of 1943. However, it provided only a basic blueprint for a merger, nothing more definitive. Despite the lack of detail, the key areas of contention with regard to the Marine Corps rapidly became clear. The plan actually failed to mention the Marine Corps; when asked to clarify the matter, McNarney responded, "This is detail of organization which I don't believe I care to comment on at the moment."[5] With the War Department hiding its genuine intentions, the Marine Corps became gravely concerned with the Army and Army Air Forces' surreptitious designs for postwar policy. Regardless, the Woodrum Committee finally concluded that issues of unification should be revisited after war's end and surmised that the time was not "opportune to consider detailed legislation which would undertake to write the pattern of any proposed consolidation, if indeed such consolidation is ultimately decided to be a wise course of action."[6]

In the summer of 1945, as Japan's surrender appeared imminent, unification supporters started building their case again. In July the *St. Louis Post-Dispatch* ran a provocative editorial about an Army-Navy merger that clearly stated the positions of the most influential figures.[7] The two most powerful American men to hold influence over future military policy, President Harry Truman and the man who would soon become his Chief of Staff and succeeding President of the United States, Gen. Dwight D. Eisenhower, endorsed the merger proposal. The newspaper article argued that competition between the services throughout the war had caused numerous problems in wasted money, lost lives, and delays in planning. Specifically, the author pointed to Marine Gen. Holland M. Smith's firing of Army Gen. Ralph Smith on Saipan in 1944 as indicative of the severe problems with service-based rivalry in the Pacific. Now that the war was winding down, supporters for closely integrating the Army, Navy, and Air Forces appeared everywhere. At the moment, however, just how those designs would affect the Marine Corps remained less clearly defined.

As the United States faced off against the ideology and military threat of communism in 1945, it had difficult issues to solve concerning the size, organization, and mission of its military. The use of atomic bombs on Hiroshima and Nagasaki in August 1945 most strongly supported the importance of strategic air power and reduction of conventional forces, an idea that also appeared economically viable. Overwhelming air power through heavy bombers was a strategy that air enthusiasts applauded as long overdue. The fears of atomic attacks on the United States and a communist conspiracy to take over the world fueled support for the development of atomic weaponry as well as the strategic aircraft used for their delivery. Both of those developments aided the Army Air Forces' longtime goal of an independent service. The atomic era changed America's outlook on strategic delivery systems, but at the same time it endangered the Marine Corps' future.

Finding a viable mission had proven difficult throughout the Corps' history. In the early 1900s the use of steel vessels in modern navies reduced the need for marines aboard ships. In the navies of most countries, marines were relegated to garrison duty on naval bases. As opposed to its counterparts, the U.S. Marine Corps developed a new mission for itself—first in the form of colonial infantry and later in the form of amphibious assault. In the 1920s and 1930s the extraordinary prudence of Marine leadership in preparing for the Pacific war served as the greatest contribution to its later expansion in the 1940s. While retaining the impression of an all-volunteer force, the Marine Corps rapidly expanded from roughly 20,000 personnel in 1939 to almost 500,000 in 1945. To the institution's great credit, it served in some of the most difficult contests of World War II, firmly establishing an identity as amphibious assault experts. Even so, the Corps' functions and size were not clearly protected either by precedent or by law. Despite the Marines' remarkable wartime achievements, the Army and Army Air Forces questioned whether the United States would ever employ amphibious assault again.

Questions about the need for a Marine Corps did not simply derive from service rivalry but also from reasonable doubts about the future necessity of costly amphibious assault.[8] Battles against the new communist enemy in Asia, the Union of Socialist Soviet Republics, primarily required land and air forces. Even in a defensive situation, the United States had need of an army to protect its borders and an air force to counterattack with atomic warfare. But, simply stated, America no longer *needed* a Marine Corps. In the view of some, the Marine Corps had become a waste of funds. If a situation arose in which amphibious assault could be employed, the concentration of exposed naval forces required to prosecute such an endeavor made for a huge liability in an era of atomic warfare. Furthermore, many argued that the Army, which during the war had conducted larger and more numerous amphibious landings in both the Pacific and the Atlantic, could fulfill the job if necessary.

More than anyone else, senior Marine officers understood the institution's precarious position within the U.S. military. However, Marines obviously did not agree that the prestigious organization should diminish to the role of the Navy's police force—guarding ships and bases. In essence, the Corps refused relegation to the duties of other nations' marines. While it continued to argue the necessity of amphibious assault, the Marine Corps, just as it had done during its colonial infantry and amphibious assault periods, began devising a new role and mission for itself—this time as America's force-in-readiness. The basic concept argued that the Marine Corps should continue to fulfill its slogan as "first to fight" in the postwar world by remaining prepared for sea deployment at a moment's notice.

It was one thing to propose innovative ideas in times of war. It was quite another to sell an entirely new mission in a time of peace and during reductions in funding (although the Corps had done this before in regard to amphibious assault in the 1920s and 1930s). The unprecedented national debt incurred during the war logically resulted in a rapid shrinking of the military budget. President Truman and Congress cut large portions of military spending. The Navy faced reductions to its fleet, and the Marine Corps appeared one of the most superfluous institutions in the military. Due to the rivalries and jealousies between the services, Marine officers questioned whether they had many friends in the upper echelons of either the War Department or Navy Department. As the Corps attempted to define a new proposal for its future, the concept of force-in-readiness, few listened. Essentially, if the Marine Corps duplicated many aspects of the U.S. Army, then it was certainly a national luxury. To survive, the Corps had to convince the American people to retain it in something like its current form or face the prospect of reductions that would relegate it to impotence. Considering the slim resources and intense service rivalries following World War II, it is not a stretch to say that the Marine Corps' struggle to play an active part in the postwar military appeared insurmountable.

If anything, the squabble over shrinking resources in the postwar era created more open hostility between the services than there had been during the conflict itself. The opposing camps settled in for a fight. Although Democratic President Franklin D. Roosevelt, a staunch Navy enthusiast, might not have approved of unification arguments, his successor and former Army officer, President Truman, fancied the idea. Unification supporters included the President and the senior leadership in the Army and Army Air Forces. The main points of contention remained the transfer of Navy and Marine Corps air power to a newly created Air Force and the restriction of the Marine Corps to a size no larger than a regiment. The Army wanted to ensure that the Marine Corps would never resemble a regular ground army again.[9] Obviously, the Navy and Marine Corps continued to resist these ideas. At the very least, they could agree on endorsing a strong peacetime naval force instead.

Truman's support of unification actually predated his presidency. In August 1944, while still a Democratic Senator, he wrote an extensive article in *Collier's* magazine endorsing the idea.[10] Now, as President, he made unification a top priority in his administration. In mid-September 1945 he held a White House conference on the postwar Navy.[11] Present were Democratic Senator David Walsh, Chairman of the Senate Naval Affairs Committee, Democratic Representative Fred M. Vinson, Chairman of the House Committee on Naval Affairs, and James Forrestal, Secretary of the Navy. The President refused to discuss his ideas on unification for debate at this point. Nevertheless, the September meeting sparked action in the Navy Department to ensure that it coordinated its opposition to the President. The Navy did not have to wait long for Truman to make his bid for unification. In December

1945, when the Woodrum Committee disbanded, the President introduced his proposal for combining the War and Navy Departments into a single Department of National Defense.[12]

The Navy did not sit idly by as the War Department planned its postwar unification strategy. Instead, it began its own investigation for streamlining the armed services as early as May 1945.[13] Ferdinand Eberstadt completed a study that advised increased coordination between the Army and Navy rather than a merger. The Secretary of the Navy submitted the proposal to Senator Walsh, Chairman of the Naval Affairs Committee, in October, two months before Truman came public with his.[14] Remarkably, the report, which consisted of twenty-eight pages of discussion and twelve pages of conclusions, did not even mention the Marine Corps. Headquarters Marine Corps could only be found in the proposal's organizational graph underneath the Chief of Naval Operations and alongside aeronautics, ordnance, ships, yards and docks, supplies and accounts, naval personnel, Coast Guard, and medicine and surgery. Apparently, in their struggle for survival, the Marines would find few enthusiastic supporters in the Navy; instead, the Corps would have to argue on its own for its specific place and function within the revised organization of the armed forces. This lack of apparent support from the Navy impelled Marine officers to take the initiative in promoting the future direction of the Marine Corps.

Although the Navy might have failed to recognize it, Marine Corps advocates proved the strongest assets in the Navy's campaign to oppose integration of the armed services. In December 1945 the *San Francisco Chronicle* published a lengthy piece outlining the flaws of the President and the Army's plan.[15] One section, labeled "Marine Esprit," described how the enthusiasm and spirit of the Marine Corps contributed to successfully accomplishing all of its difficult missions on Pacific islands. The "fiercely proud little band of fighting men had earned with its blood the right to special consideration"; the nation could not "well afford to throw away this spirit, forged through a century and a half of training and tradition." In a unification struggle that debated the monetary cost and bureaucratic redundancy in the Army and Navy, the Marine Corps stood apart as a hallowed institution with principles like tenacity and courage, principles that paper could not convey and financial savings could not replace. The power of these intangible ideals would prove the most useful arguments against unification.

In response to what he perceived as an institutional emergency, Commandant of the Marine Corps A. A. Vandegrift formed two groups to address the unification crisis under Gens. Gerald C. Thomas and Merritt A.

Edson. Specifically, Thomas and Edson prepared position papers, monitored the actions of the executive branch and Congress, updated the press, and researched new missions for the Corps.[16] Perhaps one of the most influential groups in harnessing congressional support for the Marine Corps was the clandestine Chowder Society, made up of Marine officers working at Marine Corps Schools in Quantico, Virginia. The society was led by Cols. Merrill Twining and Victor Krulak. According to historian Allan R. Millett, the Chowder Society "developed into the Corps's political action arm, and its agents prowled the Pentagon and Congress arguing the Marine Corps case."[17]

The Marine Corps had its supporters in Congress, but the War Department held most of the bureaucratic power in the military. The struggle to gain support for or against unification quickly surfaced in the media and became a routine matter over the next several years. In December John Cowles, chairman of *Look* magazine, published an article endorsing the merger of the Navy and War Departments.[18] He leveled the accusation that the Chief of Staff of the Army, Gen. George Marshall, and the Chief of Naval Operations, Adm. Ernest King, had duplicated war efforts and had spent as much time battling each other's departments in World War II as combating the enemy. Cowles wanted one service in the future, with no distinction between servicemen. That same month, Democratic Representative Henry D. Larcade submitted a pro-integration editorial from *Collier's* magazine to Congress.[19] The editorial stated that "lack of Army-Navy cooperation" was a major factor in the disaster at Pearl Harbor and in the problems that occurred in the first few weeks after the Marines' invasion of Guadalcanal.[20]

In January 1946 the *Washington Post* published an article "No Defense Plan," which flatly put the blame on the Navy for the dual command in the Pacific war and for unreasonable debate on the postwar merging of the services.[21] Army and Army Air Forces supporters argued that service rivalry, inspired by the Navy, lay behind nearly every mistake of the war—a problem that could only now be solved by their plan for unification.

Despite the War Department's rhetoric about the dangers of service rivalry, the real issue was not "unification" itself, but rather what that term actually meant. The general plan called for the Army and newly created Air Force to absorb the Marine Corps' existing duties, manpower, and equipment. Rather than mending fences with the Navy Department, the War Department's proposal had all the appearance of a consolidation of most of the military's resources under the Army and Army Air Forces.

Marine officers began writing their members of Congress in opposition to Truman's idea, and more dissension from Congress quickly followed.[22] Republican Representative Walter C. Ploeser wrote directly to the President and got to the heart of the issue: "A plan—the War Department Plan—which talks unification in one breath and then in the other advocates a separate air force must be subject to careful examination before it is taken at face value."[23] According to Ploeser, the Army simply wanted a monopoly under the guise of unification. The creation of a separate Air Force in the War Department actually worked against the idea of unification, and Ploeser pointed out that the Navy Department, with its many organizations, was a true example of a unified system.

Based on the history of the Pacific war, Representative Ploeser made a pitch for the Marine Corps that turned the President's proposal on its head: "Had the Marine Corps been larger it might have been possible for the Navy and Marine Corps, and their Coast Guard and Seebee [sic] units, to have wrested the victory in the Pacific without the necessity of transporting millions of men all the way from Europe to the Pacific. This brings up the consideration what should be the size of the Marine Corps under the system which I propose. My estimate would be 1,000,000 men and officers trained in all phases of amphibious warfare."[24] Such an expansion of Marines had no real chance of gaining serious congressional support. However, suggesting that the Marines Corps could replace the functions of the Army indicated exactly the redundancy that the Army found objectionable. All the same, a couple of months later, a Democratic Representative from New York, Donald L. O'Toole, overtly made the argument to replace the Army with the Corps; as far as unification was concerned, the Marine Corps already worked well with the single Department of the Navy. Better to simply replace the Army by increasing the size of the Marine Corps: "Its men, noncommissioned officers, and officers have ever met the test of battle and emergency and have at all times in our history captured the imagination of the American people."[25]

As rhetoric between the Army and Marine Corps heated up, the Navy published its compromise plan in February—the one designed by Ferdinand Eberstadt for streamlining the armed services.[26] The Navy followed up with two articles opposing unification in *Seapower* magazine and another in *Naval Affairs* in March.[27] A staunch naval advocate, George Eliot, stated the Navy's fears effectively: "You [President Truman] are gambling the future of this country on the chance that your Secretary of the Armed Forces will always be impartial, uninfluenced, and evenly balanced, and that the Chief of Staff of the Armed Forces, his principal military advisor, will always, as he assumes office, forget all his ties with his own service, and at the same time acquire by some mysterious heavenly gift, a complete understanding of the needs and nature of the other two services."[28]

As the Navy openly voiced its opposition to the President's unification proposal, the Marine Corps sought to clarify its future role in the armed services. One of its most effective pitches was to advertise the importance of amphibious assault for naval warfare. On the anniversary of the Iwo Jima landings, Vandegrift contended that the battle for Iwo Jima represented the climax of years of study and training for amphibious war. It demonstrated that "no beach, however strongly defended, can be held in the face of a well-organized and resolute assault from the sea. This is the fact of vital significance to any nation whose security depends upon maintaining supremacy on, over, and under the seas which lie between it and any possible aggressor. The ability to conduct effective and successful amphibious operations is a necessary and inevitable adjunct of sea-power."[29] Nowhere could Vandegrift find a more vivid example of the Marine Corps' ability to establish footholds on enemy-held islands than Iwo Jima. In addition to its iconic importance, the battle now served as the supreme test of amphibious war.

By April 1946 President Truman had had enough with the public debate of his proposal (though only opposition to unification actually disturbed him).[30] He announced that propaganda or lobbying by active-duty officers would constitute insubordination, and he implied legal recourse for indiscretions. Truman's order dramatically put a lid on public dissent from naval officers. Nevertheless, if the Navy and Marine Corps could not speak out, their friends in the media continued to do so on their behalf. The *Utica Daily Press* in New York called the President's plan for the military "reckless" and further stated its alarm over Truman having "told its naval critics to shut up."[31] One editorial poked fun at the President's declaration by stating: "And now—discipline. If the boss wants it, you had better go along. Even if you are an expert on the science of modern naval war you better defer to the judgment of an ex-artilleryman of World War I. Or else."[32] David Lawrence in the *United States News* put it this way: "Free speech is to prevail for all but the Navy. Mr. Truman has not rebuked the many Army and air officers who have recently been making speeches in favor of his plan to merger the armed services. But he seems irritated that those who have honest convictions in opposition should express them."[33] Lawrence stated that Truman's order delivered a blow to the Navy and "gallant Marines," who had fought their way across the Pacific seizing island bases for the Army Air Forces, bases like Iwo Jima.[34]

In mid-May Republican Senator Edward Robertson presented an article to the Senate that the War Department must have found especially annoying. "Ex-Doughboy Pays Tribute to Marines" related American memory of Iwo Jima to the Corps' struggles in the unification crisis. The author, Henry McLemore (a former soldier turned Marine supporter), told Vandegrift to quit his worrying about unification. America loved its Marine Corps, and anyone in the War Department who questioned its utility should visit Iwo Jima and "imagine what it was like when the Marines went in."[35]

Despite the heated press, by the end of May the Army and Navy had compromised on many of the issues in Truman's plan. One major exception concerned the future of the Marine Corps. At least on paper, the Army's view of the functions of the Marine Corps differed only slightly from the Navy's. Both agreed that Marines should serve in the seizure and defense of advanced naval bases, as well as develop amphibious assault doctrine and equipment. However, the Army wanted to specifically direct that Marine operations should not involve "sustained land fighting."[36] The issue at stake for the Marine Corps mainly derived from differing opinions about its size and disposition. Fundamentally, the Army did not believe the Corps should resemble another land army. Meanwhile, the Marine Corps consciously realized that it needed such redundancy in order to remain a viable fighting force in America's future.

In May 1946, making one of the most powerful speeches in his career, General Vandegrift addressed the Senate Naval Affairs Committee on the subject of unification. The general's appearance seemed to embody his nickname "Sunny Jim." Legendary Marine warrior Smedley Butler once described Vandegrift as "the damndest, fightin'est hillbilly not stillin' er fuedin.' "[37] With his "cheery blue eyes and soft drawl of the spare Virginian," Vandegrift appeared before Congress, his uniform complete with seven rows of ribbons, including the Congressional Medal of Honor.[38] Vandegrift shamed the Congress into taking affirmative action on the Corps' behalf:

In placing its case in your hands the Marine Corps remembers that
it was this same Congress which, in 1798, called it into a long and
useful service to the nation. The Marine Corps feels that the question
of its continued existence is likewise a matter of determination by the
Congress and not one to be resolved by departmental legerdemain or
a quasi-legislative process enforced by the War Department General
Staff. The Marine Corps, then, believes that it has earned this right—to
have its future decided by the legislative body which created it—nothing

more. Sentiment is not a valid consideration in determining questions of national security. We have pride in ourselves and our past but we do not rest our case on any presumed ground of gratitude owing us from the nation. The bended knee is not a tradition of our Corps. If the Marine as a fighting man has not made a case for himself after 170 years of service, he must go. But I think you will agree with me that he has earned the right to depart with dignity and honor, not by subjugation to the status of uselessness and servility planned for him by the War Department.[39]

The "bended knee" speech was a resounding success in swaying congressional support. After such a dramatic address, no assurances by Secretary of the Navy James Forrestal or by Secretary of War Robert Patterson about the "safety" of the Marine Corps could measure up to the fears expressed by Sunny Jim. The War Department would have to "tell it to the Marines."[40]

Undeterred, the Army continued to push forward its plans to diminish the size and role of the Marines. In June the congressional joint committee set up to investigate the Pearl Harbor disaster released its report declaring service rivalry as a principal cause of the American defeat. In an editorial in the *Washington Post* entitled "Merger Now," unification supporters used the Pearl Harbor findings to support their case. The editorial maintained that vested service interests were holding up common-sense legislation.[41] Similarly, the *Washington Star* made the case for consolidation of all air assets into the Air Force based on the latest report from the U.S. Strategic Bombing Survey. The author claimed that the revolutionary abilities of air power could "crush a country into complete submission without invasion."[42]

Continued opposition to unification made little impact on the Army's desire to curtail the Marines, and the heated environment in Washington continued to boil over.[43] Perhaps the most provocative discourse came from Army Air Forces Gen. Frank Armstrong, who spoke at a goodwill dinner for business in Norfolk, Virginia, in December. He made the following comments to an audience consisting of the naval community:

You gentlemen had better understand that the Army Air Force is tired of being a subordinate outfit. It was a predominant force during the war, and it is going to be a predominant force during the peace . . . and we do not care whether you like it or not. The Army Air Force is going to run the show. You, the Navy, are not going to have anything but a couple carriers which are ineffective anyway, and they will probably be sunk in the first battle. Now as for the Marines, you know what the Marines are, a small bitched-up army talking Navy lingo. We are going to put those Marines in the Regular Army and make efficient soldiers out of them.[44]

General Armstrong's speech fueled the fires of controversy, and Marine Corps supporters decided to take action. In January 1947 Rep. James E. Van Zandt introduced House Concurrent Resolution 14 to "express the sense of Congress that the Navy and Marine Corps should be permitted to express views upon unification."[45] Other members of Congress made similar pleas. By June, through the Secretary of the Navy, Republican Representative Clare E. Hoffman had obtained dozens of letters from admirals and Marine generals on the subject of unification, and presented them to Congress.[46] All, to one degree or another, expressed sincere doubts on the direction and content of the unification bills, and Congress had made those opinions public knowledge despite the President's order to keep naval opposition quiet.

In another remarkable speech, given at the Navy Council Conference in February 1947, General Vandegrift made a bid for active participation within the nation's security. He concluded his remarks with these words:

> I sincerely hope that we have your confidence that the Marine Corps is aware of its responsibilities and will persist in its efforts. Your confidence is in the last analysis the thing that will determine the question of success or failure of the armed forces of a nation . . . the weapon that conquered Iwo Jima was not produced in the vast arsenal of industry, but in the hearts of the American people who were represented there by the finest they could send to do battle with our mortal enemy. It is not too much to say that the future of the Marine Corps, of the Navy, or of the Nation itself rests finally not in our hands, but in your hearts.[47]

Reference to Iwo Jima touched the heartstrings of Americans. It crowned an impassioned petition from the Marine Corps to the public for its trust and confidence. Marine veteran and Republican Representative George W. Sarbacher Jr. entered Vandegrift's comments into the *Congressional Record* with the preface, "I do hope that in future legislation we of Congress never allow the identity of this valiant organization to be lost or forgotten in the shuffle of unification."[48] With the collective memory of Iwo Jima representing the Marine Corps, it became increasingly difficult for Congress to overlook the Marines.

Following his speech at the Navy Council Conference, Vandegrift spoke before the Senate Armed Services Committee. While conceding the principle of unification, insofar as it strengthened the cooperation between services and more closely restructured the civilian chain of command with the military one, he objected to the War Department's proposal on two matters that affected the Marine Corps.

It affirms the existence of the Marine Corps without expressly stating the roles and missions which the Corps is expected to perform.

It completely excludes the Marine Corps from participation in the joint bodies and agencies which the bill would establish.[49]

Vandegrift argued that only by intervening in the language of the bill could Congress guarantee retaining a Marine Corps in its current form; not doing so would result in a fate determined by the President, the proposed Department of National Defense, or the Department of the Navy. Consequently, without specifying the roles and missions of the Marine Corps, Congress simply would not pass a unification bill. Essentially, Vandegrift's statements directly contributed to the War Department conceding on the first of his two points.[50] Concerning General Vandegrift's speech, Democratic Representative Mike Mansfield stated, "I shall personally question the value of such a merger if it contemplates subordinating the position of the corps . . . I will do my very best to see that the marines, first to fight, are not the first to be liquidated."[51]

As congressional support for the latest proposal on unification (House Bill 2319) slipped away, the press, in a feeding frenzy, increasingly pushed the case in support of the Marine Corps. In articles entitled "The Marines' Last Beachhead" and "General Vandegrift Should Be Heeded," authors used Iwo Jima as a historical example of what Marines sacrificed for an ungrateful War Department that was now attempting to dismember it. The greatest enemy to the Corps was not the "Japs or Germans" but the U.S. Army, which had "envied since time immemorial the high estate of the Marine Corps in the eyes of the public, and a few Navy admirals are not above suspicion of jealousy."[52] Public sentiment for the Marine Corps irreparably damaged congressional support for the unification proposal.

The Marine Corps had taken its case to the American people, represented by Congress, and the result left the Corps in better shape than before. House Bill 2319 was sent to Rep. Clare Hoffman's committee, "Expenditures in the Executive Department." The Chowder Society asked the father of Iwo

Jima veteran Lt. Col. James Hittle, a good friend of Hoffman, to intervene on the Corps' behalf.[53] Vandegrift subsequently assigned Lieutenant Colonel Hittle to Representative Hoffman's staff for the purpose of working on what Hoffman would later describe as the "so-called" unification bill.[54]

Since President Truman had previously forbidden military officers from speaking out publicly on the merger issue, discussions taking place in the Hoffman Committee became a platform for voicing pro-Marine sentiment. Perhaps most damaging to the War Department, the committee made one classified report public—Joint Chiefs of Staff document 1478. In that proposal General Eisenhower made the following stipulation: "Land aspect of major amphibious operations in the future will be undertaken by the Army, and consequently the Marine Corps will not be appreciably expanded in time of war . . . the Navy will not develop a land army or a so-called amphibious Army, [and] . . . Marine Corps units to be limited in size to the equivalent of a regiment."[55]

Perhaps what most concerned members of Congress, especially those who supported the Marine Corps, had to do with the manner in which the War Department debated its actual plans for the Marines in secret boards while publicly presenting more ambiguous ideas. Spelling out the mission and roles of the Marine Corps gained congressional support since the wording in the War Department's unification proposal could not be trusted. The direction of the Hoffman Committee eventually derailed H.R. 2319 so badly that supporters of unification decided to compromise in support of Hoffman's revised proposal, H.R. 4214.

In a letter sent to the Truman administration, one of the Corps' opponents best described the revisions included in H.R. 4214: "The mission of the Marine Corps is set forth in new language which has no basis of agreement among the services, limits the authority of the President over the Marine Corps, ignores the authority of the Chief of Naval Operations over the Marines, and ignores the position of the Navy in amphibious operations."[56] In other words, the Marines emerged in a stronger position in the Department of the Navy and in relation to the armed services than at any previous point in its history. And all of this had been accomplished through congressional support, despite only half-hearted assistance from the Navy and strenuous objections from the President and the War Department. David had conquered Goliath, and somewhere within the formula that had made that miracle happen was the powerful memory of Iwo Jima.

After much debate in committees and on the floors of the Senate and House, by July H.R. 4214 and its companion, Senate Bill 758, adopted the basic language the Marine Corps requested. It allowed the Marine Corps to keep the aviation and combined arms required to carry out amphibious campaigns, ensured the right to expand in times of war, and gave the broad task of performing "such duties as the President may direct."[57] H.R. 4214 eventually provided the basis for the National Security Act of 1947, which, among many other things, gave the Air Force autonomy as a separate service.[58] Signed by President Truman in July 1947, Section 206 (largely drafted by Colonel Twining and Lieutenant Colonels Krulak and Hittle) put into law the duties and functions of the Marine Corps, and at the same time restricted the President's authority to revise those definitions. Under the Department of the Navy, the Marine Corps was to provide "fleet marine forces of combined arms, together with supporting air components, for service with the fleet in the seizure or defense of advanced naval bases and for the conduct of such land operations as may be essential to the prosecution of a naval campaign."[59] As a capstone to the unification crisis, Congress nearly simultaneously passed Joint Resolution 113, which approved the erection of a Marine Corps War Memorial in Washington, D.C.—the flag-raising scene on Iwo Jima.[60] Triumph over the War Department and celebration of Iwo Jima as a national icon could not be separated.

Perhaps the most influential individual with regard to the language in the National Security Act defining the Marine Corps was Lt. Col. James Hittle, who promptly educated Marine officers on the importance of the legislation. He explained the significance of Section 206 line by line, detailing how the law established the Marine Corps' amphibious functions within a naval campaign and recognized Marines as a "fundamental feature of our nation's sea power."[61] The National Security Act was a watershed event on many levels. However, although it legally spelled out the Marine Corps' functions, it notably did not give the Commandant of the Marine Corps a position on the Joint Chiefs of Staff, and it failed to define the Corps' size and budget. As the Cold War progressed, the United States continued to redefine its military. The struggle for the future of the Marine Corps was far from over.

Spelling out the Corps' functions had not preserved it in the manner many had intended. Still, some thought it was time to celebrate. On the Marine Corps birthday, Henry McLemore wrote an editorial in the *Evening Star* to pay tribute to the organization.[62] McLemore wrote that he had saved his soldier's cap from his days in the U.S. Army, and he was glad he had done so, because he wanted to tip it: "I want to take off that cap in honor of the only fighting organization in the world that is better than the Infantry." He stated that no matter how much the soldiers, sailors, or airmen talked about who was the best, "when a marine walks in the room you gotta shut up, because his heart beats to the tune of a song that's been proved to be on the level." In answer to his brothers in the Army who might think his words treason, McLemore said, "The marine is a better soldier than the infantryman. He's meaner, and that's what makes for a good soldier." Such comments from McLemore may have sounded good to the ears of Marines, but they nettled many in the Army who objected to the notion that the United States had a second army of elite troops. The icon of the flag-raising on Mount Suribachi only served to perpetuate such popular ideas.

Army proponents in Washington could not come to grips with the fact that the War Department had lost its bid for unification. As demonstrated by the flurry of public complaints that appeared in American periodicals in May, some fruitlessly hoped that Congress would reconsider. An editor for the *Washington Post* argued that the government had not gone far enough. Simply put, "unification has not unified the armed service," and he was going to educate the "members of congress and most citizens" who assumed that it had.[63] Another writer, in the *Christian Science Monitor,* complained about the "full failure of the unification of the armed services."[64] Yet indicative of how powerful the Marine Corps' public image had become, neither of the articles mentioned the organization at all, referring instead only to the Navy. Even though the Marines had arguably done the most to derail the War Department's proposals, few directly attacked it. Indeed, just as Iwo Jima had become forever sanctified, the Marine Corps rose to near religious reverence. Criticism often proved counterproductive.

By the late 1940s only a few bold writers directly took on the Corps. One was William B. Huie. In late 1948 he restated the Army and Air Forces' arguments quite clearly.[65] America only needed one Army, not two. Maintaining a "Navy Army" was redundant and costly. Further, if the Air Force provided the Army's air support, it certainly could do the same for the Marine Corps. Huie attacked the language in the National Security Act as preposterous. He argued that "a unified force [incorporating the Marine Corps into the Army] would give America more protection, more efficiency, for less money."[66]

While the 1947 National Security Act defined the Marine Corps, it failed to protect its funding. As President Truman strove to reduce military funding to one-third of the national budget, the decrease in Marine Corps resources nearly ruined the organization as a viable fighting force. By 1948 the Corps had been reduced from its wartime high of six divisions to two skeleton ones. Commandant of the Marine Corps Clifton Cates became so concerned over the Corps' precarious position that he mandated training for all Marine officers on the language in the National Security Act of 1947.[67] Cates ordered the officer corps to review Lieutenant Colonel Hittle's essay "Seapower and a Balanced Fleet" (1948).[68] Hittle's article explained the evolution of amphibious operations, unique to the United States. He clarified that the key aspect of a balanced fleet was its ability to seize and defend advanced bases, hence the need for a Marine Corps. He then argued that "the principal means by which the war in the Pacific was fought and won" was the uniquely American naval forces. Of course, the only unique aspect of U.S. naval forces was the U.S. Marine Corps. And that was exactly the point that Hittle meant to illustrate by pointing out that Army troops used in amphibious campaigns remained under the guidance of naval commanders and that the bases used by the Army Air Forces required Marines to seize them.

The rivalry between the Army and Marine Corps continued unabated though 1948 and into 1949. In January *Infantry Journal* published an article "Who Won the War?" The editors voiced much displeasure over what they believed was the exaggerated credit given to Marine operations in the Pacific. They pointed out that soldiers had liberated much more territory than Marines and had sustained fewer casualties in the process. As a general rule, the "rush and die" procedures used by Marines were "contrary . . . to modern tactics."[69] The *Infantry Journal* piece concluded, "There has too often been the implication that the Army has fought with less valor, or against inferior odds, but for the most part, the Marines have simply applied both energy and ingenuity to making the Corps and its record known."[70] Indeed, Marine battles, Iwo Jima in particular, overshadowed the Army's larger campaigns.

The anger that the Army expressed in the *Infantry Journal* was not hollow rhetoric. It had not given up its fight to rid itself of the institution that so successfully competed for its funding and missions. In January 1949 the War Department submitted a new proposal to the President. It planned to transfer the Marine Corps to the Army and all aviation, both Navy and Marine, to the Air Force.[71] Such a proposal really had little chance of success in getting past Marine supporters in Congress. Nevertheless, the President and his new Secretary of Defense could still have an impact on the financial aspects of the military, an outlet that would soon become the primary means of influencing the disposition of the services.

Budgetary concerns exploded in one famous exchange between the Navy and the Air Force when they struggled to fund two competing projects. The

Air Force developed the B-36 very long-range bomber, and the Navy laid the keel of the USS *United States,* an immense carrier capable of launching medium bombers. Both platforms were designed to deliver atomic bombs into the interior of the Soviet Union. In 1949 Truman nominated former assistant Secretary of War Louis A. Johnson to the post of Secretary of Defense. When the Secretary of the Navy went out of town on business, Johnson single-handedly canceled construction of the *United States.* The resulting scandal, complete with congressional investigations, caused huge ripples in the Navy Department and has since been dubbed the "revolt of the admirals."[72]

As the Navy and Air Force went toe-to-toe over air power, the Army and Marine Corps squared off over ground resources. For one thing, Marines found it difficult to train for their role in amphibious operations. Secretary of Defense Johnson convinced the Chief of Naval Operations to assign nearly all amphibious shipping resources to train the Army. As if curtailing the Corps' primary mission was not insulting enough, Johnson also forbade the celebration of the Marine Corps birthday. Marine air was in jeopardy as well. Giving a speech at the Waldorf-Astoria Hotel in New York, Johnson stated that the paperwork for doing away with it was on his desk at that moment.[73] However, the most dangerous action, which nearly emasculated the Corps, was the President's cutbacks in funding. Underfunding led to severe personnel shortages. By 1947 the two active Marine divisions consisted of only eleven battalion landing teams versus the eighteen required for full strength. Although the Marine Corps insisted it needed 114,200 Marines to fulfill its peacetime obligations, manpower fell to 83,609 in 1948 and to 74,279 in 1950.[74] In the words of Gen. Victor Krulak, "we felt the dead hand of starvation everywhere."[75]

Hollywood Production

As the fights in Washington continued, Hollywood and the Marine Corps, in a pitch to secure the Corps' future, teamed up to make *Sands of Iwo Jima* (1949), a film starring John Wayne. Republic Pictures producer Edmund Grainger came up with an idea in 1948 to use Joe Rosenthal's famous Mount Suribachi picture as a backdrop for a Hollywood movie. Grainger enlisted the help of writer Harry Brown. Brown wrote the original script, which was later revised by James Edward Grant. In order to obtain official Marine Corps approval and support, Grainger promised the Corps that it would "win friends and influence legislators in Washington."[76] Fighting both the

White House and War Department for institutional survival, Commandant Cates needed little persuasion to endorse the film and reap the public relations bonanza offered by Grainger.

Kirk Douglas was first considered for the lead role, but Grainger submitted a copy of the script to John Wayne as well. At first, Wayne did not like the script, nor did he want the leading role of a gritty Sgt. John Stryker. According to Wayne's son Michael, the Commandant of the Marine Corps sent representatives to speak with his father. They pleaded with him to make the film on the basis that the Corps was fighting for its survival in Washington; if Americans saw the exploits of Marines in the Pacific, the public would want to keep the Marine Corps.[77] Supposedly, the Commandant's request helped persuade Wayne to agree to make the film. Other actors included John Agar, Forrest Tucker, and Wally Cassel. *Leatherneck* magazine's number one "pin-up girl" during the war, Adele Mara, played the leading female role. With the promise of extensive assistance from the Marine Corps, the film went into production in the summer of 1949.[78]

The Marine Corps exerted direct influence over the picture, which despite its entertainment value doubled as a recruiting and public relations piece. The beginning of the film, complete with a full-size Eagle, Globe and Anchor in the backdrop and the Marine Corps Hymn sung in the background, displayed the following text: "The United States Marine Corps whose exploits and valor left a lasting impression on the world and in the hearts of their countrymen appreciation is gratefully acknowledged for their assistance and participation which made this picture possible."[79] Technical advisers for the film included Medal of Honor winner Col. D. M. Shoup, as well as Pacific veterans Lt. Col. Henry P. Crowe and Capt. Harold G. Schrier. Even Gen. Holland M. Smith was persuaded to come out of retirement and ensure that the invasion scenes were conducted accurately. Actors underwent a type of "boot camp" training, to ensure they played the part of Marines correctly.[80]

To create a realistic combat setting and offset the cost of the picture, the Marine Corps offered its base at Camp Pendleton, California, for filming. The reenactment of battles at Tarawa and Iwo Jima required a substantial amount of assistance from the base, which provided liberal numbers of weapons, jeeps, tracked vehicles, artillery, ships, and planes.[81] Of the 16,000 Marines stationed on Camp Pendleton, 2,000 served in support of the movie, filling jobs that ranged from extras to technical advisers.[82] The Iwo Jima scene alone required 1,000 Marine extras, 30 tracked vehicles, destroyer escorts, LSTs (Landing Ship, Tanks), and two squadrons of Corsairs. According to the *New York Times*, the Marine Corps was "cooperating wholeheartedly in the venture."[83] Since this was the most expensive film Republic Pictures had ever filmed (a budget estimated at over $1 million), the studio could certainly use all the additional help it could get. Producer Edmund Grainger stated that "without Marine cooperation, the picture would have cost at least $2,500,000."[84]

Although a large portion of the movie's dialogue took place in a training area on Camp Pendleton meant to resemble New Zealand, the most epic and enthralling portions dealt with combat. The movie masterfully wove film taken at Camp Pendleton with actual battlefield footage taken at Tarawa and Iwo Jima, provided to Republic Pictures by the Marine Corps. Getting the two sets of film to match took a major effort. Parts of Camp Pendleton were transformed to resemble the Central Pacific, complete with plaster palm trees. After flamethrowers burned off the vegetation, construction crews built pillboxes and gun emplacements, and laid out rolls of barbed wire. Creating Suribachi required heavy doses of oil and lampblack mixed with water to resemble volcanic ash. Under the supervision of Howard Lydecker, nineteen special-effects men laid a mile and a half of wire, connected 2,000 sticks of dynamite, and linked up 50 black-powder bombs. On top of the explosives, they laid truckloads of sand, peat soil, and cork. Upon detonation, the blasts resembled artillery and naval gun explosions. Machine guns emitted flame spurts instead of projectiles, and air valves imitated round impacts with puffs of smoke. When Colonel Shoup saw the Tarawa set, he exclaimed "This looks so real, it scares me!"[85]

Although the screenplay told the tale of a tough sergeant who taught the boys in his squad to be Marines, the epic moment and centerpiece of the film was the reenactment of the flag-raising atop Mount Suribachi. In doing so, Hollywood worked its magic, transforming actual events on Iwo Jima to fit the imaginary tales that Americans saw in Rosenthal's famous photograph. For authenticity, the U.S. Marine Corps lent Republic Pictures the original flag raised atop Suribachi. An armed guard watched over the transfer of the Stars and Strips from the Marine Corps Museum in Quantico, Virginia, to Camp Pendleton, California.[86] Finally, the filmmakers flew in the three surviving members from the second flag-raising, Rene Gagnon, John Bradley, and Ira Hayes (Hayes proved difficult to work with, showing up on the set drunk).[87] Then, the three survivors and a couple of extras planted the flag again in a vast stone quarry on Camp Pendleton converted to resemble Suribachi. But this time, cameras rolled for American moviegoers to enjoy the entire event. Artist Felix de Weldon, who was currently working on the Iwo Jima monument for the Marine Corps, ensured that the flag-raisers restaged the flag-raising in precise parallel with Rosenthal's picture.[88] In the film, Sergeant Stryker's squad, who had just lost their leader to enemy fire, looked up from the bullet hole in his back, to find inspiration in the patriotic display on Mount Suribachi. The Marines' Hymn plays in the background as Stryker's protégé takes charge of the squad to carry on America's fight, symbolizing the transference of Marine leadership and virtues from the sacrifices of one generation to those of another.

Thanks to Rosenthal's picture, the second flag-raising meant a great deal to the American public at home. *Sands of Iwo Jima* captured the patriotic moment that Americans always wanted to believe in the photo—that it represented the first flag raised on the mountain and that it had encouraged the sailors and Marines below. Captain Schrier, the lieutenant who had led the *first* patrol up Suribachi, coached the actors and veterans of the *second* flag-raising to resemble the actions of the first. Schrier even portrayed himself in the movie, meeting with John Wayne's patrol at the bottom of Mount Suribachi.

The actual inspiring instant when 3d Platoon, 2d Battalion, 28th Marines raised the American standard above Iwo Jima had been erased from American memory. Hollywood had made the perceived events in Rosenthal's picture real. In the words of historians Karal Ann Marling and John Wetenhall, "the gap between hype and reality remained just as wide in 1949 as it had been on the 1945 bond tour. Gagnon and Bradley and Hayes were window-dressing for a reinterpretation of the war and of a symbol to which they had suddenly become so many human footnotes."[89]

In December 1949 *Sands of Iwo Jima* opened in San Francisco to the sound of the Marine Corps band, performing in full dress uniform. It finally made its way to Washington, D.C., on 24 January 1950 to premier at the Warner Theater.[90] The Marine Corps continued to assist in the film's promotion, loaning both the Suribachi flag and one of de Weldon's small-scale flag-raising models to the Warner. Both were prominently displayed in the theater lobby.[91] Even movie star John Wayne could not outshine the Corps' institutional image. Critics found the almost seamless mixture of combat footage combined with reenactment scenes at Camp Pendleton the most stirring and valuable element of the film. Audiences flocked to theaters to watch their amphibious warriors in action. The film had intentionally captured the realism of the American Marine fighting in the Pacific, "authentic to the last detail."[92] To add to this realism, John

THE IMMORTAL ICON

Wayne's character died in the film, one of only two times the actor did so in his extensive film career. In the words of critic Richard L. Coe, the fighting shots were "so good, so compelling, that the story and fictionalized scenes suffer accordingly."[93]

One of the top ten money-making films of 1950, *Sands of Iwo Jima* was nominated for four Academy Awards, including best story, best sound recording, best film editing, and best actor. It also made John Wayne the most popular star in Hollywood, graduating from his character in low-budget westerns to the role of American war hero. In the words of one film historian, from *Sands of Iwo Jima* onward, "John Wayne, rather than an actual military hero, served as the symbol of America's fighting men for a significant number of American moviegoers."[94] More important, *Sands of Iwo Jima* kept the image of Marines atop Mount Suribachi in the popular spotlight at a time when the Corps needed all the public assistance it could muster. One review commented that there was "so much savage realism in 'Sands of Iwo Jima,' so much that reflects the true glory of the Marine Corps' contribution to victory in the Pacific," that the film had "undeniable moments of greatness."[95] Arguably, despite significant attempts by the Army, Navy, and Army Air Forces to influence the writing of Pacific war history, Iwo Jima had critically influenced the perception that the Marine Corps was the leading instrument in America's victory over Japan.

In addition to the film, Iwo Jima remained in the American mainstream in a variety of ways in 1950. Five years after the battle, the captivating affair atop Suribachi continued to inspire poetry. As seen in this example, the stanzas were new but the theme remained similar:

On Suribachi's blood-stained crest,
The blood-red sun sinks slowly west,
On D-plus four, there flying high
Old Glory waves against the sky.[96]

Dozens of articles, numerous poems, and the second of two major films had now attempted to capture the heroic proportions of Rosenthal's photo. The combination of flag-raising celebrities, the sacrifice of thousands of Americans on Iwo Jima, and the national popularity of the icon had helped raise the Corps to monumental proportions in the eyes of the American public. Iwo Jima had served the Marines well in their fight for institutional survival. Now, the Marine Corps was in the process of casting the icon in bronze and transforming it into the most powerful of symbols—a living monument.

When Rep. Gordon L. McDonough wrote to Truman about his support for creating a permanent position for the Commandant of the Marine Corps on the Joint Chiefs of Staff, the President responded in August 1950: "I read with a lot of interest your letter in regard to the Marine Corps. For your information the Marine Corps is the Navy's police force and as long as I am President that is what it will remain. They have a propaganda machine that is almost equal to Stalin's. Nobody desires to belittle the efforts of the Marine Corps but when the Marine Corps goes into the army it works with and for the army and that is the way it should be."[97] President Truman believed the Marine Corps both a redundancy and an anachronism, and personally supported its transfer to the Army. However, hamstrung by the National Security Act of 1947, he continued to cut back its budget. Truman eventually planned to fund only six battalion landing teams in 1951, less than a single division. According to Marine Gen. Victor Krulak, the President "intended to diminish progressively the fighting units of the Corps and, ultimately, to transfer what remained to the Army and Air Force."[98] Just five years after its unprecedented size in the Pacific war, the U.S. Marine Corps had diminished to a tattered skeleton of its former self, but that situation drastically changed with renewed conflict in the Pacific.

One of the greatest contributors to the survival of the Marine Corps was the North Korean Communist Army, which attacked and seized most of South Korea in the summer of 1950. With a speed that can probably not be overstated, the Marine Corps quickly called in reserves and deployed the 1st Marine Brigade to defend the rapidly shrinking Allied perimeter around the port city of Pusan. Subsequently, under the direction of General MacArthur, the 1st Marine Division spearheaded the amphibious assault at Inchon in September, which instantly changed the war from a desperate defense of Pusan to total defeat of the North Korean Army. Perhaps one of the most brilliant strategic moves in military history, Inchon demonstrated the continued importance of both conventional forces and amphibious assault in the nuclear age. The Marines continued to serve with great distinction in Korea for the next three years. Their fighting withdrawal from Chosin in November–December 1950, against several Chinese divisions in temperatures of -30°F, was one of the Corps' most challenging military accomplishments. The combination of Pacific war experience with a renewed urgency to prove the Marine Corps' value to the nation resulted in martial excellence and in terms of "sheer drama, valor and hardship matched the amphibious assaults of World War II."[99] Summing up the Marines' prowess in Korea, historians Merrill Bartlett and Jack Sweetman stated, "Even the Corps's critics had to admit that the Marine Corps's performance in Korea was far superior to that of the Eighth Army and X Corps."[100] The stellar deeds of Marines in the Korean War gave added vigor to their supporters in Washington and substantiated Marine Corps claims to be a fighting elite.

A great many journalistic reports from Korea praised the Marines, while depictions of Army units were often critical. Democratic Representatives Carl Vinson and Mike Mansfield, as well as Marine veteran and Democratic Senator Paul Douglas, used the glowing accounts of Marine exploits in Korea to sponsor new legislation to expand and clarify the responsibilities of the Marine Corps, not just as an amphibious force but as the nation's force in readiness.[101] Proposals included a position for the Commandant of the Marine Corps on the Joint Chiefs of Staff and a permanent structure of no fewer than four Marine divisions and air wings. In contrast, Army generals and President Truman believed a Marine Corps conspiracy must have been slanting the truth about the performance of Marines as compared to that of soldiers in Korea. Consequently, Truman sent his former military aid, Army Gen. Frank Lowe, to the theater to assess the situation. After touring the battlefield, Lowe's reports to the President, while condemning senior Army leadership in Korea, concurrently declared that "the First Marine Division is the most efficient and courageous combat unit I have ever seen or heard of."[102] In light of such praise, new Marine Corps legislation to strengthen the organization gained support, and President Truman was unwilling to expend more political capital in blocking it.

In June 1952, President Truman signed into law an amendment to the National Security Act that gave the Commandant of the Marine Corps co-equality in the Joint Chiefs of Staff on any issue that concerned the U.S. Marine Corps. The revision included specific definitions of the size and functions of the Marine Corps that have since served as the organization's foundation. Specifically, it ensured that the minimum force structure of the Corps would "include not less than three combat divisions and three air wings."[103] As well, it set legal parameters for Marines to assume the role of the subject-matter experts on all matters of amphibious warfare, pronouncing that the Marine Corps "shall develop in coordination with the Army and Air Force, those phases of amphibious operations that pertain to tactics, technique, and equipment used by landing forces."[104]

The revisions to the National Security Act finally ensured "a Marine Corps for the next 500 years," as stated by Secretary of the Navy James Forrestal to Gen. Holland M. Smith, as he looked up at the first flag-raising on Iwo Jima. Accordingly, the Marine Corps could find no better way to celebrate its victories over the Army, Air Force, and the Presidential administration than to commemorate Rosenthal's famous photograph with the largest bronze statue in the world and place it a short distance from the halls of Congress and the White House.

The idea of creating an Iwo Jima Memorial in Washington, D.C. in the image of Rosenthal's picture had been a work in progress for years. In May 1945 Sen. Wayland C. Brooks instigated the first steps. He introduced a joint resolution that proposed that the National Park Service should initiate a study of the project's feasibility. President Truman approved that proposal in July 1945.[105] Meanwhile, artist Felix de Weldon began working on several Iwo Jima monuments. Work on some had begun just after the photo hit the press in February 1945, with the artist completing his first model flag-raising statue within forty-eight hours after seeing the picture. De Weldon presented a pilot statue to President Truman in June 1945, and another of de Weldon's statues, a soft plaster one, was put up in front of the Navy Building during the Seventh War Loan bond drive.

Marling and Wetenhall argued that "the Marine War Memorial was born from a hard-fought struggle to preserve the identity and the integrity of the United States Marines." Indeed, it had direct ties to the Corps' struggle for existence in the unification crisis. The memorial would "remind Americans that the Marines remained inseparable from Americanism—from determination, guts, drive."[106] During the unification crisis, de Weldon had continued work on the creation of larger Iwo Jima monuments. The three surviving flag-raisers posed for de Weldon to ensure an appropriate likeness, while the artist used pictures to create likenesses of the participants who had died. The artist finally completed a statue 36 feet high and weighing 20 tons. The figures stood nearly double life-size, and an American flag was hoisted from the 20-foot-high pole. Over the primary materials of plaster and clay, de Weldon covered the statue in bronze-colored paint. The 7-foot-tall base consisted of an outline of the island.

On 10 November 1945 Marine Corps Commandant Vandegrift oversaw the unveiling of de Weldon's statue at Constitution Avenue in Washington. Vandegrift dedicated the monument on the Marine Corps' one hundred seventieth birthday. The icon captured by Rosenthal's photograph had come to stand for more than the event of raising a flag on Mount Suribachi. It celebrated more than the thirty-day battle and the nearly 7,000 Americans who died. The flag-raising symbolized the Marine Corps itself—its past, its present, and its future. The Commandant remarked that Iwo Jima had become an "immortal part" of the Marine Corps' proud tradition. Yet in terms of bravery and sacrifice, the icon held significance for the entire nation, representing the highest ideals of patriotism.[107]

As he worked on smaller projects depicting the Iwo Jima icon, de Weldon continued to formulate plans for an enormous Marine War Memorial. In March 1946 Democratic Representative Brooks Hays challenged Congress to authorize fund-raising for that memorial in order to find a permanent location for the statue in Washington.[108] Although Congress authorized the project, the large national debt and budgetary cutbacks ensured that the Corps would need to raise the funds by its own efforts. A private organization, the Marine Corps League, set out to do just that. With a $20,000 start-up cost, de Weldon and his crew began work on the enormous bronze statue from a studio in Washington.[109]

The Marine Corps League's efforts to raise the necessary funds were fraught with difficulties and controversy. Historians Marling and Wetenhall chronicled the affairs that took place up through 1954, which included arguments over the size of the memorial and the proposed sites to establish it. The National Sculpture Society attacked the credibility of the artist and requested that the Marine Corps allow for an open competitive bid for the project. The Marine Corps League selected a prominent patron, Harry Dash, who had fronted the initial $20,000, to be in charge of fund-raising. Dash, however, embezzled over $100,000 before being replaced (the League eventually recovered all but $10,000). Despite that negative publicity and the fact that the cash raised could never quite keep pace with construction costs, de Weldon continued to labor.[110]

De Weldon originally plastered the six men in the nude to ensure proper bone symmetry. He used a steel framework to support the huge figures. After nine years of painstaking effort and numerous smaller versions, he finally completed his monumental statue of the Marines on Suribachi. It was then carefully disassembled into 108 pieces and trucked to an art foundry in New York, where it was cast into bronze. This bronzing process took nearly three years.[111]

In 1954 the Commandant of the Marine Corps, Gen. Lemuel C. Shepherd, inherited the cost deficiencies of the memorial, which had piled up. In need of adequate funds, he asked his officers to solicit contributions for the Iwo Jima memorial on three separate occasions.[112] He reasoned that there were 250,000 Marines and the memorial would cost $500,000; therefore, every Marine should contribute two dollars. General Shepherd's call for support netted $250,000 in 1953 and $255,000 in 1954. From other sources, the Marine Corps War Memorial Foundation (which had generally replaced the Marine Corps League by this point in regard to fund-raising for the statue) received $317,000. Total contributions in 1954 were $822,000, but an additional $47,000 rolled in by 1955.[113] Due to its positive publicity potential, the Assistant Commandant of the Marine Corps, Gen. Gerald C. Thomas, said it was "worth about a billion dollars to the Marine Corps and the Marine Corps paid for it."[114]

The final stages fell into place in the summer of 1954. After casting and further touching up by de Weldon and his crew, the 108 bronze pieces were trucked to National Capital Parks in Washington for reassembly.[115] Final assembly in Washington began in September.[116]

Once completed, the Iwo Jima statue weighed 100 tons—the largest bronze statue in the world. The six figures stand 32 feet high.[117] They erect a flag on a pole 60 feet long. The M-1 carbines carried by two of the figures are 16 feet and 12 feet long, respectively. The canteen on just one man is large enough to hold 32 gallons of water. The concrete base (66 x 46 x 10 feet) weighs 700 tons and is covered with blocks of Swedish black granite. In the upper edge of the granite were burnished in gold letters the names and dates of every major Marine Corps engagement since 1775. Also, inscribed in the base is the praise by Admiral Nimitz, "Uncommon Valor was a Common Virtue," and opposite to that, "In honor and in memory of the men of the United States Marine Corps who have given their lives to their country since November 10, 1775." Documents tracing the history of the Marine Corps and the biographies of twenty commandants were placed in a lead bomb-proof box and permanently sealed in the cornerstone. The entire sculpture, including the base, sits 78 feet tall and was placed on a 7-acre tract bordering Arlington Cemetery just at the western edge of the Memorial Bridge. The entire cost of the memorial, $850,000, was covered without the financial support of the U.S. government, through contributions of Marines, former Marines, and friends of the Corps.

The commemoration of the U.S. Marine Corps War Memorial took place on 10 November 1954, the one hundred seventy-ninth birthday of the Corps. The president of the War Memorial Foundation invited Republican President Dwight D. Eisenhower to the unveiling ceremony. Perhaps due to anxiety over Eisenhower's questionable feelings for the Corps, the audience of over 7,000 people shifted anxiously until he arrived, which he finally did minutes behind his scheduled entrance.[118] During the ceremony Gen. Holland M. Smith stated, "No American can view this symbol of heroism and suffering without a lump in his throat. Nor will they ever forget those gallant Marines."[119] For the Marine Corps, the monument stood for more than the 6,800 Marines who had died at Iwo Jima. The icon symbolized the sacrifices of every generation in its history—all Marines had paid so that America could raise that flag on Mount Suribachi. Commandant of the Marine Corps Lemuel C. Shepherd took the symbolism one step further by stating that it was "not just a monument to departed past. It is a graphic message to the future. May it stand for ages yet to come as a symbol of American courage and determination, of indestructible faith, and of unity of purpose . . . for with that spirit . . . the cause of human freedom will triumph."[120] Next, Vice President Richard Nixon put together the words that perhaps best described the significance of the statue. He stated that the monument symbolized not only "the heroism of six men and the great history of the Marine Corps," but "represented something more." It represented "the hopes and dreams of all Americans." The monument stood as a testimony to the freedom-loving values of Americans. It epitomized "America itself."[121]

The President stayed only eleven minutes—until the flag went up—and then quickly departed.[122] But the main stars stayed long enough to satisfy the cravings of the press. John Bradley, Ira Hayes, and Rene Gagnon, who sat in VIP seating in the front row, were swamped by hundreds of reporters after the ceremony concluded. Just one month earlier, Hayes had been arrested for public drunkenness in Chicago. It had become a regular pattern.[123] But no amount of trouble could change the role America perpetually wanted him to play—hero of Iwo Jima. The ceremony ended that afternoon, and the enormous icon remained.

Tragically, Ira Hayes died just three months later. He had always felt uncomfortable with the spectacle made of Rosenthal's picture. The last of six figures, a larger-than-life Hayes reached up for the flagpole—immortalized forever, not for what he had done but for the popularity of that photo. For Ira, America had gotten his story and that of the real heroes of Iwo Jima all wrong. Something about the monument, perhaps its size and grandeur, signaled his doom. After the ceremony, Hayes became extraordinarily gloomy and quiet. He had been a drunk for years, arrested for public disorder on fifty-one occasions, but this time it was different. He was in deep depression. When he returned home to Arizona to work as a cotton picker, his parents said he appeared restless. Ira promised to stop drinking, and he did so for two weeks. Then, on 23 January 1955, Hayes's two brothers and four of their friends gathered for a nightly round of cards in an abandoned adobe hut with a dirt floor. Hayes wandered into "The Place" around ten o'clock.

Despondent, he slumped down in the corner, drank muscatel from a half-filled gallon container—and cried. When the game ended, Hayes stayed behind. The next morning, authorities found him lying face down outside the hut. At the young age of thirty-two, the hero of Iwo Jima was dead.[124] He had survived the hell of Sulfur Island only to die of exposure to the elements at home.

Ira Hayes was buried at Arlington National Cemetery with full military honors, only a short distance from the new Marine Corps War Memorial. Commandant Shepherd presented Ira's mother with an American flag and the comforting words that "your son served this flag with great distinction and honor. He is immortalized in the statue which towers over his grave."[125]

Hayes was further memorialized in both film and music. In 1960 *Sunday Showcase* aired a documentary on Ira Hayes titled "The American."[126] A review of the documentary stated the main thrust of the film: "His drinking was increased because of his own awareness that he did not agree he was heroic for the reasons generally assumed. Similarly, he could not abide the dubious patriotism that prompted some of the ceremonies held in his honor."[127] Universal Studios produced a movie about Ira Hayes called *The Outsider* (1961), starring Tony Curtis as Hayes. The film explored Ira's descent into alcoholism resulting from the pressure of well-meaning Americans searching for a hero. The picture had a conscious, almost documentary-like quality, but perhaps audiences found the story too shadowy and depressing.[128] Then again, many moviegoers could simply not resist the advertisements that used the iconic image of Rosenthal's photo as the backdrop to a banner stating "Forever etched across our proudest history is the record of Ira Hayes' glory!"[129]

Peter LaFarge wrote a ballad, attempting to convey why the American hero had become so distraught. Johnny Cash recorded it in 1964. With minor changes to the lyrics, Bob Dylan recorded the same ballad again in 1971. The main chorus went:

Call him drunken Ira Hayes
He won't answer any more
Not the whiskey drinking Indian
Or the Marine that went to war

Perhaps it would be best to describe Ira Hayes as the final victim of the Battle of Iwo Jima. Time and space did not allow him to escape the horrific reality of the hellish warfare on Sulfur Island. His emotional wounds ran too deep for him to survive them. After the 6,821 dead sailors and Marines who made the heroic symbol of Iwo Jima legendary, Ira Hayes was 6,822. Rather than be memorialized in a monument, maybe he would have best liked people to remember him alongside those who had died in this epic contest. He always felt more comfortable out of the spotlight and with his buddies anyway.

Americans may rightly mourn those who paid the ultimate price in the seizure of Iwo Jima. The island did not prove as essential to winning the Pacific war as earlier histories have claimed. Nevertheless, Rosenthal's picture inspired a glorious memory of the battle that had a significant and perhaps vital impact on the Marine Corps' survival. The flag-raising photo, the euphoria of the Seventh War Loan campaign, the making of *Sands of Iwo Jima*—all popularized the tragic sacrifices of the battle and established an almost spiritual reverence for Marines. The collective memory of Iwo Jima influenced the public and its representatives in Congress to preserve the Corps as a fighting force. More than praising the Marines of generations earlier, the Marine Corps War Memorial embodied the Marine Corps' victory over the War Department and the Truman administration during the unification crisis.

In the twenty-first century, the Marine Corps continues to maintain the importance of the Marine War Memorial through ceremonies around its base. By presidential order, the U.S. flag flies eternally over the heads of the Marine legends who raised it—24 hours a day, 365 days a year. Sometimes the Marine Corps Band plays the "Marines Hymn" and other times sharply dressed young Marines silently march around the monument in perfect unison. The Suribachi statue receives thousands of visitors every year and continues to enhance the Marine Corps' public image.

As a poignant symbol of American nationalism, the Marine War Memorial has come under regular assault from a variety of sources. Artists have objected to its nationalist grandeur. Art commentator Charlotte Devree stated that it had "esthetic numbness" and was "artistically appalling."[130] With its human figures in monumental proportions, some have likened it to fascist or communist sculptures of totalitarian regimes.[131] Popular, appealing, and moving no longer seem to meet the mark in artistic circles that clamor for more "modern" styles.

In 1994, in what some have suggested as total disregard for the price Marines paid for the fighter base on Iwo Jima, the Air Force pushed a proposal through the National Park Service to build its own memorial adjacent to the Marine War Memorial. The immense project, including a 20,000-square-foot underground visitors' center, new parking lots, extensive landscaping, and road system, would transform the currently serene acreage around the Iwo Jima statue into a tribute to the Air Force. Plans include changes to the area within 500 feet of the Marine War Memorial with a series of evergreens separating the two sites. The Air Force has argued that it suffered 52,000 deaths in World War II and "deserves a similar respect" to that given to Marines. With so much Marine blood spent in purchasing airstrips for the Army Air Forces, Marine Col. Dave Severance called the Air Force proposal a historical insult.[132] More to the point, writer Larry Van Dyne described Marine sentiments about the Marine Memorial as "the most sacred spot on the earth."[133] Many Marines do not want anything to detract from their heroic sanctuary. Reinforcing that idea, former Secretary of the Navy James Webb described the plans for an Air Force memorial in the *Washington Times* in terms of pollution.[134] According to Webb, it would contaminate the clean nationalistic symbolism of Rosenthal's photo. Obviously, many Air Force veterans were offended by Webb's description of a monument dedicated to 52,000 dead airmen.

Marine supporters continue to fight the Air Force plan in Congress and the courts.[135] As of November 2001, the Air Force had embarked on a tentative deal to build at a separate location near the Pentagon.[136] Sixty years after World War II, there still exists a strong jealousy between the services. Pacific war competition has yet to end.

It was as if a part of me was left behind, as if an Iowa
farm boy was waving goodbye. We would never meet again.
Somewhere in that jagged jumble of rocks, he forever
walks with the Ghosts of Iwo.

RUSSELL WERTS, *"The Ghosts of Iwo," February 1985*

CHAPTER 8   *The Ghosts of Iwo Jima*

D efining what Iwo Jima means to Americans sixty years after the
battle is a difficult task. Joseph Rosenthal's Pulitzer Prize–winning
photo of the Stars and Stripes planted atop Mount Suribachi on
23 February 1945 immediately became a treasured icon of American patriotism. It had a significant impact on the political and cultural landscape in
the United States. As the most reproduced photograph in history, it became
the symbol of the Seventh War Loan campaign, was printed on a 3-cent
stamp, and was transformed into numerous monuments. In 2001 the icon
would even rise from the ashes of the Twin Towers of the New York World
Trade Center. Although the event Rosenthal captured on film meant little
to the combatants at the time it happened, ironically, it now overshadows
the combat itself. The battle can no longer remove the flag-raising from

its history, but, conversely, the icon can completely detach itself from the battle. The icon means something entirely on its own, completely outside the context of the event in which it took place.[1]

I think it safe to say that, in general, the public no longer remembers the Battle of Iwo Jima historically. As with most U.S. conflicts, the details of Iwo Jima have become a blur as time has passed. Of course, some people have familiarity with the subject. For instance, a few Iwo Jima veterans remain with more intimate knowledge about the operation. Unfortunately, they are rapidly disappearing. Nevertheless, World War II is an immensely popular historical subject, and history "buffs" have varying degrees of knowledge on the topic. The degree of awareness of the battle or the flag-raisings increases the depth of the icon's significance to the individual. Still, for society at large, the Iwo Jima icon remains an immortal symbol. As such, it is worth attempting to define some of its most basic connotations in the present.

Perhaps it is best to start with a simple definition of what makes the image resonate in American culture before proceeding to more complex representations. First, the abstract quality of the event depicted allows it to transcend the location where it took place. The great expanse of sky in the background is gray. The time of day, weather, and directional orientation are all mysterious. The jumbled pile of rocks and blasted landscape at the bottom of the scene hint of a battle but offer nothing definite to identify which one. The men have their backs turned. Their faces are unrecognizable. Nothing on their uniforms overtly depicts which service they belong to. Race, religion, ethnicity, and social standing are all indistinguishable as well. The ambiguity of the servicemen allows the icon to stand for any number of institutions or interest groups—they represent the common man.

Second, the incident conveys several intangible ideals. There is a startling sense of group effort and execution. The six figures work together with a unity and purpose reminiscent of the principles required for a society to triumph over adversity. The centerpiece, the American flag, adds to the picture a host of other beliefs: democracy, freedom, and patriotism. All these factors work in concert to make the Iwo Jima icon a remarkably versatile symbol for predominantly nationalistic purposes.[2]

For the Marine Corps, the significance of the Iwo Jima icon remains similar to its original symbolism in 1945, only far more intimate and intense. Perhaps because of the great value this institution places on tradition, it has continued to utilize the conventional strength of the symbol as a motivational tool. Over time, the marvel of Iwo Jima has become of pivotal importance

THE IMMORTAL ICON

for the Corps, intimately entwined both consciously and unconsciously into the fabric of its culture. Education on Iwo Jima begins early, even before boot camp. One of the latest and most popular Marine recruiting commercials debuted in thousands of movie theaters around the country on the anniversary of the Iwo Jima flag-raising, 23 February 2002. "The Climb" depicts a young rock climber making his way up the face of a monolithic cliff. As he climbs, the flag-raising scene atop Suribachi (reproduced from Sgt. Bill Genaust's film, which he captured at the same angle as Rosenthal's photo) becomes superimposed over the cliff. As the young man reaches the top, a Marine from a generation gone by—a "Ghost of Iwo"—meets the recruit at the edge and helps him up over the ledge. Only after climbing Suribachi and receiving the recognition of the historical figure does the young man receive the honor of the title Marine.

Many young Americans have become enticed by this powerful iconic message and found themselves sitting at a desk across from a sharply dressed, confident, and persuasive Marine recruiter. In the initial weeks of boot camp indoctrination, they will learn more about Iwo Jima, especially the tremendous cost incurred while seizing the island. In the final weeks of training, recruits undergo a physically grueling event dubbed "the Crucible." On the final day of the Crucible, California recruits relive the events displayed in the Rosenthal picture. Just before climbing a large mountain on Camp Pendleton called "the Reaper," recruits are told that the journey upward commemorates the seizure of Mount Suribachi in 1945. After reaching the summit, the Marines raise the Stars and Stripes on a flagpole. Afterward, drill instructors present an Eagle, Globe, and Anchor to each of the proud trainees. That exact moment, as the Marine Corps emblem is passed from the older generation to the younger, symbolizes the transformation from civilian to Marine. And for these young people, the picture taken of Marines atop Mount Suribachi represents the highest standards of cooperation, conviction, and self-sacrifice demanded of them as well.

In many ways, Marines who fought on Iwo Jima represent the model archetype desired of their heirs today. However, it is not the actual World War II standards that Marines attempt to live up to—but idealized ones. Drill instructors teach recruits that wearing the same uniform as their predecessors is a great honor and privilege, and while other services have moved on to more modern styles, the service uniforms Marines wear in the twenty-first century continue to resemble those of World War II. Recruits graduate boot camp in almost the same uniform that flag-raisers Ira Hayes and Rene Gagnon wore during the Seventh War Loan campaign. The fundamental difference is that the service uniforms of today's Marines are tailored to fit tighter and are worn in accordance with a more exacting standard.

Essentially, twenty-first-century Marines attempt to achieve the standards of legends. On average, Marines are slimmer, stronger, faster, and smarter than they were in World War II, but even better warriors cannot achieve imaginary heights. Efforts to excel above the written regulations are both expected and applauded, but for Marines in the twenty-first century, the legendary ideal is veritably unachievable. In their own minds, one's best effort could always be better—to the level of Iwo Jima's heroes. As in the recruiting commercial, Marines continue to climb Suribachi, except the steep mountain has been transformed into a nearly insurmountable cliff. Of course, Iwo Jima, in and of itself, is not responsible for the Corps' idealism. However, it has significantly contributed to the high standards and ever increasing struggle for excellence that make this institution unique. The Marine Corps has become the model of martial virtue in the United States and perhaps the world, and the memory of Iwo Jima has deeply contributed to that reputation.

The Iwo Jima icon has been used to support many forms of expression over the years, so much so that recent writers have described the image atop Suribachi as a "cliché."[3] Certainly, the proliferation of the icon in the news, commercials, political cartoons, publications, and popular media has blurred the fairly clean ideas about patriotism, sacrifice, and victory that characterized the photo in 1945. On the cover of John Kerry's book *The New Soldier* (1971), a group of Vietnam veterans, raggedly attired in mismatched military uniforms and military decorations, protest the Vietnam War by reenacting the scene atop Mount Suribachi with an upside-down flag.[4] This act figuratively and ironically turns patriotism for an unpopular war on its head. It demonstrates the iconic significance and universal recognition of the flag-raising scene as a symbol of nationalism, yet at the same time it shows an adaptability of the image to support diverse and opposing goals. During the 2003 U.S. occupation of Iraq, Sergio Langer published a political cartoon in an Argentinean publication *Clarín* in which he illustrated six American soldiers raising an oil platform in the desert.[5] The American icon has reached international application. With the exception of "Old Glory" itself, the flag-raising scene is recognized around the world more than any other symbol of American nationalism. And it can be used to chastise the use of U.S. military power as much as praise it.

Despite the many reproductions, the flag-raising icon still holds much of its original symbolism. Video games like "Elite Forces WWII: Iwo Jima" and board games like "Uncommon Valor: Battle of Iwo Jima" reinforce the battle in conjunction with the icon.[6] Scheduled to open in November 2005, the National Museum of the Marine Corps was designed to represent an enormous modern depiction of the flag-raising (a 210-foot tilted mast and glass atrium), embodying the largest reproduction of the event to date. Historical films continue to be produced on the subject, such as *Heroes of Iwo Jima* (2001) and *Inside the Great Battles: Iwo Jima* (2004).[7] Presidents persist in using Iwo Jima for nationalism. In 1980 President Jimmy Carter, in co-ordination with House Joint Resolution 469, proclaimed 19 February "Iwo Jima Commemoration Day."[8] Presidents regularly give speeches in front of the monument because it serves as the ultimate backdrop for these patriotic purposes. In 1989 President George Bush used the memorial to protest the Supreme Court's decision to permit flag-burning. The President stated that "the Nation itself was ennobled by the Battle."[9] The flag represented the nation and its most memorable sacrifices, like those at Iwo Jima. Like the flag, the prominent image of the Iwo Jima battle has become a revered symbol of our nation.

Just because the icon has proliferated in many forms does not mean that the ideas represented by the flag-raising scene are as much a "cliché" as they appear. Underestimating the "patriotic fervor" of the icon can still bring harsh criticism. Historians Karal Ann Marling and John Wetenhall recently defended their study on the Marine Memorial from accusations of inaccuracy. Because they attempted to distinguish between fact and myth, a variety of editors and critics wrote about how the authors had gotten the story all wrong. Marling and Wetenhall attributed the objections of critics to nationalist sentiment:

> It is overwhelming reverence for the heroic *feeling* of the Iwo Jima myth that still renders the *facts* of its birth—to some people, at least—irrelevant. Americans want desperately for the real-life story of the heroes of Mount Suribachi to turn out like the Duke's [John Wayne's] heart rending martyrdom in *Sands of Iwo Jima*, when his last vision was the raising of Old Glory amidst a shower of enemy fire. The famous War Bond poster—"Now all together"—made Rosenthal's image look so real that it had to be true. And the Marine Corps Memorial stands proudly as the last great vestige of monumental realism in American sculpture—big, commanding, more real than reality. In the noble cause of celebrating our nation's reverence for truth and justice, Americans prefer to let reality slip by, to ignore inconvenient facts.[10]

Essentially, Iwo Jima has two realities—the battle that took place and the perception of that battle as seen through Rosenthal's photograph. The second has proven far more resilient than the first. That reality is not simply a "cliché," but continues to manifest itself as idealism for American sacrifice and valor. The Marine Corps continues to reenact the flag-raising for public consumption—just as it did during the war bond drives of 1945.[11]

After the terrorist attack on the World Trade Center in New York on 11 September 2001, Americans anxious to reinstill public confidence resurrected Iwo Jima in their collective memory. Thomas E. Franklin's picture of three rescue workers raising the Stars and Stripes over the wreckage at Ground Zero stirred memories of America's most famous national icon. The image of this flag-raising served as a focal point for national euphoria. The photograph made front-page news around the country, aired on television networks, circulated around the Internet, and was featured in periodicals like *Time, Newsweek, Life,* and *People.* The scene was reenacted at the 2001 World Series as well as the 2002 Super Bowl. Almost immediately, requests were made to commemorate the event with a monument at the epicenter of the disaster zone. The picture won numerous awards from prestigious organizations like Associated Press and National Press Photographers Association. *People* magazine referred to it as "an echo of Iwo Jima." The weekly news broadcast *Meet the Press* referred to it as "Our New Iwo Jima." To conclude the parallels, President George W. Bush held a national press conference in the Oval Office with the firefighters and presented a 45-cent stamp in the photo's image.[12] In America's greatest hour of need, Iwo Jima returned—reinvigorating themes of patriotism, duty, unity, and self-sacrifice. The duplication of the moment did not have the same popularity as the original icon. However, in this time of great crisis, the nation certainly rallied around the flag in a fervor that matched that of the "greatest generation."[13]

Looking back sixty years later, the tragedies of the battle have dissipated, as if the "Ghosts of Iwo" have moved on. In 1947 the United States dug up the bodies of thousands of Marines and their corpsmen from the cemeteries on the island to return them stateside. In June 1968 the United States officially gave the island back to Japan.[14] The U.S. flag came down to the tune of a lone bugler playing the "Stars and Stripes." Directly afterward, the Japanese flag went up to replace it.[15] Geographical changes have accompanied the political changes. The island seized in 1945 is no longer the same. Due to volcanic activity and tidal forces, the shape of the island's southern shores has shifted, and Mount Suribachi is

President George W. Bush unveils the new flag-raising stamp in the Oval Office on 11 March 2002. From left to right are Postmaster General Jack Potter, firefighter Bill Eisengrein, firefighter George Johnson, Rep. Gary Ackerman, firefighter Dan Williams, and photographer Thomas E. Franklin. Photo by Tina Hager, provided courtesy of White House Photo Office

24 feet higher. As well, the island no longer resembles the lunar landscape that it once did. First American then Japanese engineers flattened most of the terrain to build airfields and buildings. Those fields have now overgrown with grass, flowers, trees, and thick scrub. Most times of the year, the terrain appears green, pastoral, and peaceful, with the sights and sounds of deep blue waves crashing onto the beaches. The last vestiges of U.S. presence, a weather station manned by the U.S. Coast Guard, ended in 1993. Instead of the massive fortifications they once engineered, soldiers from the Japanese Self Defense Force maintain manicured lawns and a nine-hole golf course.[16] Perhaps these changes are for the best. Few Americans remember the great destruction and tragedy of the epic contest that occurred there. Although the realities of battle have become a vague national memory, the idealism of the naval forces that seized that desolate island of hell sixty years ago live on in our society's spirit. Rosenthal's photograph pulled something out of Iwo Jima and drew it closer to our shores, much closer than that distant island

thousands of miles away. The "Ghosts of Iwo" walk among us now—just beneath our national consciousness, ready to carry the banner in triumph when called. Their actions may not be remembered, and their bodies may be broken, but the indomitable spirit they demonstrated decades ago remains stronger than ever. The specters finally came home, and through the flag-raising image, they will revisit our nation for eternity.

Postscript to Iwo

JOSEPH AUSLANDER

February returns and those five
Tremendous days return,
When a little island died—
But not the lad I mourn:
So eager, so alive,
So full of pride! . . .
The strikes, the picket lines
Are back—the old familiar signs
Of peace . . . Forget
The agony of Iwo, and the losses:
But never the opening night at the "Met,"
That drips with diamonds yet . . .
They say the shoppers last week set
New records in all the cities . . .
I read where forty-seven sub-committees
Have questioned the big bosses
For miles and miles and miles
Of conferences and files
At so much per . . .
But on a hundred windswept lone Pacific isles
The terraces of crude white crosses
Do not stir . . .
Four thousand dead men carry a flag,
Four thousand dead men hoist it on high,
Four thousand dead men crawl up a crag
To fling a banner into the sky.
Behind a handful of Leathernecks inching
Up Suribachi, clear to hell's cone,
Follow four thousand, cold-eyed, and unflinching,
To make a venomous island their own.

Our Leathernecks, wave on wave,
The bravest of the brave,
Inch in and up the landing beach,
Slog through the black soft sand to breach
A toehold on the treacherous plateau;
Enemy shells and six-inch mortars smash
Bodies and boats to a sickening mash;
A battered tank keels over, careens,
Kicking in fire, dazed with the mortal blow,
Churning the slippery sulphur ash;
And still those floating ash cans crash,
Hurling sand, water, human flesh
A hundred feet into the flaming sky:
So the Marines
On Iwo fight, dig foxholes, die;
(The gallant captains, privates, ship-to-shore men,
The quiet medical corpsmen)

Swirl past the death-spitting pillboxes, spill
Grenades and flame
Into the same,
Are killed and kill,
And wriggle forward still,
Writhing and slithering on sheer guts uphill . . .
What do the talkers who talk all night know?
Their cigars go out and glow, go out and glow;
Match after match spurts bluegreen, shrivels, chars;
Their hands make motion, disturbing the smoke of the cigars;
The ice-cubes clink as they shift in the glasses, clink
As they are shaken,
While the talkers stop talking to drink,
Then go on talking and talking and talking . . .
What do they know of the snipers stalking,
The star shell, the bullet, the stink,
The hell-defended furious ridge taken, lost, retaken,
The boys no nudge in the slack
Of pants, no ribald crack,
No bugles, no bars, no medals will awaken.
It is quite clear
The talkers know nothing of these far-away matters:

Of the cold foam-fingered face,
The intense blue stare
Of sea-washed eyes,
The slumberers rocked to the tidal lullabies,
The silvery dabble of hands and hair,
The strange inert grace
Of death's promiscuous embrace;
Abandoned battle gear,
The broken harness of combat, rags and tatters
From huge amphibious assault
Bleaching in the sun and salt;
The shambles and detritus of attack
Rolling and rotting in a vicious surf,
The landing craft, the tank, the half-track
Sprawled like a beetle on its back,
Or on its side
Still twitching in the treacherous surf and tide . . .
Night:
Hairtrigger tense,
The skin on your scalp freezing tight,
The choked-up suspense
You can almost hear, see, touch, smell;
You sweat it out—
Christ, if you could only let it out,
Let it loose in a yell . . .
Then, all of a sudden, without warning,
A phosphorus shell
Mushrooms in the air,
Hovering there
Like a star
Of morning;
It spreads, it deepens like a stain,
Fingering the lunar spectral terrain,
A huge nervous hand of light
Feeling its way
In livid Unnatural day
Over the bright
Mask of the night—
And there they are!

The little brown monkeys are there!
All around you, everywhere! . . .
And now it comes: Those squint-eyed fanatics
Raise hell with long crazy bursts from their automatics
To take your mind
Off the rats crawling in from behind,
Through the rock fissures creeping and crawling
Under the cover of the clatter and caterwauling—
You're playing a deadly hide-and-seek
In and out of this junk yard of hell,
With all the tricks and dodges of war,
Plus a few you never saw before—
(Not to mention you can wash Jap smell
In the surf and sand for a week,
And your hands still reek.)
This quicksand-surfaced hell-on-earth
Was worth
The twenty thousand Jap dead shattered
In dogged and relentless duel, scattered
Without a trace
All over the place,
Or in belched flame cremated,
Sealed up, incinerated
In their impromptu graves,

Bulldozered in their catacombs and caves,
Looking like twisted tapers
Of charred newspapers.
Yet every vicious inch of this volcanic mound
Of blood-soaked rubble and filthy slag
And slippery lava ash
Is hallowed ground,
Since men looked up with beating hearts to see
A certain sacred flag
Flutter and flash
Suddenly
From Suribachi's mountain masthead flying!
This bleak and treeless bed,
This isle of our heroic dead,
Wherever Leathernecks had fought and bled
And violently died,
And prayed, and watched the dead they prayed beside—

This ghastly citadel is henceforth and forever sanctified . . .
Listen you talkers
Who talk so loud and big, you hawkers
Of poisonous fear and hate, you squawkers
So easy with your praise
Of alien works and ways,
All you deluded starry-eyed sleepwalkers
(Haunted by nylon's pre-atomic phase)
Can you discern the blaze
Still billowing over Iwo? Have you seen
Marine after marine after marine
Dragging his guts up Suribachi's promontory
(This isn't half the story)
To plant Old Glory
Plump in the crazy middle of hell's crater? . . .
Maybe you will remember these things—later.

Notes

Preface

1. Actual headline read "Iwo Jima Casualties Total 19,938, with 4189 Dead." Battle casualties were actually much higher than those tallied in March. *Washington Post,* 17 March 1945.
2. "He Wishes There Were," *Washington Post,* 17 March 1945, 1.
3. "MacArthur Is Our Best Strategist," *San Francisco Examiner,* 27 February 1945, 1. According to the managing editor, William C. Wren, the author of the editorial was William Randolph Hearst himself. Richard F. Newcomb, *Iwo Jima* (New York: Holt, Rinehart & Winston, 1965), 238.
4. Ibid.; emphasis in original.
5. A total of 6,821 Americans died on Iwo Jima, of whom 5,931 were Marines. Since 19,733 Marines died in World War II, Iwo Jima accounts for 30 percent of those losses. For a detailed breakdown of Iwo Jima casualties, see Whitman S. Bartley, *Iwo Jima: Amphibious Epic* (U.S. Marine Corps, 1954), 218–21. For total Marine losses in World War II, see Allan R. Millett, *Semper Fidelis: The History of the United States Marine Corps* (New York: Free Press, 1980), 655.
6. "Marines Seal Off One Third of Isle; Capture Big Bomber Field," *San Francisco Examiner,* 21 February 1945, 2. The first reporter referenced is Al Dobking, a correspondent for the Associated Press. The name of the second correspondent is not given.
7. *San Francisco Examiner,* 21 February 1945, 3. Photos by Joe Rosenthal.
8. James Bradley and Ron Powers, *Flags of Our Fathers* (New York: Bantam Books, 2000), 3.
9. Robert L. Sherrod, "Another View of the Flag Raisings," *Fortitudine* (Winter 1980–81), 10.
10. Charles S. Adair, "Reminiscences of Rear Admiral Charles Adair, U.S. Navy (Retired)" (1976), 355, Special Collections, Nimitz Library, U.S. Naval Academy.

Chapter 1

1. James S. Vedder, *Surgeon on Iwo* (Novato, Calif.: Presidio, 1984), 1.
2. It is a little known fact that the original proposals for Okinawa envisioned the use of all six Marine Divisions, three of which would quickly seize Iwo Jima one month in advance. Joint Chiefs of Staff 713/18, "Future Operations in the Pacific," 2 October 1944, microfilm, *Records of the Joint Chiefs of Staff:*

1941–1945 (Frederick, Md.: University Press of America, 1982). This is explained to greater detail in the next chapter.

3. "Meat Grinder" was a term used to describe the dreadful hill no. 382 on Iwo Jima.

Chapter 2

1. Samuel Eliot Morison, *Rising Sun in the Pacific: History of United States Naval Operations in World War II*, vol. 4 (Boston: Little, Brown, 1947–64), 158. Parts of this chapter dealing with strategy have been published in *Journal of American History*. See Robert S. Burrell, "Breaking the Cycle of Iwo Jima Mythology: A Strategic Study of Operation Detachment," *Journal of Military History* 68 (October 2004): 1143–86.

2. Kenneth P. Werrell, *Blankets of Fire: U.S. Bombers over Japan during World War II* (Washington, D.C.: Smithsonian Institution Press, 1996), 116.

3. Ibid., 84–115.

4. Michael Sherry, *The Rise of American Air Power: The Creation of Armageddon* (New Haven, Conn.: Yale University Press, 1987), 183–87.

5. Ibid., 183.

6. Werrell, *Blankets of Fire*, 117.

7. R. Cargill Hall, ed., *Case Studies in Strategic Bombardment* (Washington, D.C.: Air Force History and Museums Program, 1998), 312.

8. Ibid., 316.

9. Conrad C. Crane, *Bombs, Cities, and Civilians: American Airpower Strategy in World War II* (Lawrence: University Press of Kansas, 1993), 35.

10. Raymond Spruance, interview by Philippe de Bausett, 9 July 1965, 23, Spruance Papers, Naval Historical Center, Washington Navy Yard. The specifics of the conversation between Spruance and LeMay were also discussed by Thomas Buell, *The Quiet Warrior: A Biography of Admiral Raymond A. Spruance* (1974; rpt., Annapolis, Md.: Naval Institute Press, 1987), 358.

11. E. B. Potter, *Nimitz* (Annapolis, Md.: Naval Institute Press, 1976), 358.

12. Charles S. Adair, "Reminiscences of Rear Admiral Charles Adair, U.S. Navy (Retired)" (1976), 354–55, Special Collections, U.S. Naval Academy Library. There may be other copies of this bound transcript at Naval Historical Center and at U.S. Naval Institute, Annapolis, Md.

13. World War I veteran Billy Mitchell led the fight for the creation of an independent Air Force. For more information on the struggle, see Sherry, *Rise of American Air Power*.

14. From a prewar strength of 25,000 in May 1941, the Marine Corps grew to a peak of nearly 500,000 in 1945 (the other services grew proportionally larger as well). During this period, the Navy dictated the strategy in the Central Pacific with little input from Marine leadership. Traditionally, the Marine Corps had always been subsidiary to the Navy, and it continued in that role throughout the war. For more information on the bitter relations between the Navy and Marine Corps concerning strategic decisions, see Holland M.

Smith and Percy Flinch, *Coral and Brass* (New York: Charles Scribner's Sons, 1949).

15. MacArthur's ambition to salvage his reputation by returning to the Philippines is well known. Clearly, he demonstrated a commitment to this U.S. possession long before the United States lost the islands to the Japanese. In reports entitled "The Keystone of Philippine Defense" and "The Philippines Can Be Defended" (both 1936), MacArthur demonstrated his passion for the defense of the islands. See *A Soldier Speaks: Public Papers and Speeches of General of the Army*, Douglas MacArthur, edited by Vorin E. Whan (New York: Frederick A. Praeger, 1965), 79–112.

16. E. B. Potter, "Fleet Admiral Chester W. Nimitz," in *Men of War: Great Naval Leaders of World War II*, ed. Stephen Howarth (New York: St. Martin's Press, 1993), 130.

17. Russell F. Weigley, *The American Way of War: A History of the United States Military Strategy and Policy* (Bloomington: Indiana University Press, 1973), 290–91.

18. Henry L. Stimson, "Lessons on Antisubmarine Warfare," microform, *The Official Papers of Fleet Admiral Ernest J. King* (Wilmington, Del.: Scholarly Resources, 1991), reel 6. Date of essay is likely 1945.

19. Ronald H. Spector, *Eagle against the Sun: The American War with Japan* (New York: Vintage Books, 1985), 145.

20. Louis Morton, *United States Army in World War II: The War in the Pacific, Strategy and Command: The First Two Years* (Washington, D.C.: Office of the Chief of Military History, Department of the Army, 1962), 330.

21. In August MacArthur asked Marshall to increase the focus of effort in his theater of operation. Essentially, he believed that the preponderance of military assets in the Pacific should be assigned to his theater because of the number of Japanese forces opposing him. Marshall responded that "the defense of the Pacific areas particularly in air and naval matters will depend to a large degree upon the closeness of the cooperation and coordination of the forces now available to you, Nimitz and Ghormley." (Adm. Robert L. Ghormley commanded the South Pacific Ocean Area.) The inherent difficulty was the Joint Chiefs of Staff's demand that Nimitz and MacArthur should solve the problems of dual command that the Joint Chiefs had created. The letters of both generals were submitted to the Joint Chiefs of Staff for consideration. Joint Chiefs of Staff 96, "Japanese Intentions in the Pacific Theater," 31 August 1942, in *Records of the Joint Chiefs of Staff: 1941–1945*. The index heading is reel 4, frame 0359, Japanese Intentions in the Pacific Theater, CINCSWPA (31 August 1942), 4f. (Due to a pagination error in the index, this reference appears to be reel 3 but is actually reel 4.) References to Joint Chiefs of Staff memoranda (to include Joint Staff Planners and Joint War Plans Committee) can be found in a number of places. I originally referenced many of these at San Diego State University from *Records of the Joint Chiefs of Staff*, ed. Paul Kesaris (Frederick, Md.: University Press of America, 1979–81). These papers are referred to in some circles as "ABC files," which was the subject title used by the War Department to index them. "ABC files"

is the title still used by National Archives, College Park, where they can be found in paper form in Record Group 165.9.1. For the purposes of consistency, I have made a concerted effort to reference the publication *Records of the Joint Chiefs of Staff: 1941–1945*.

22. Joint Chiefs of Staff 96, "Japanese Intentions in the Pacific Theater," 31 August 1942. In September the Joint Staff Planners finally dismissed MacArthur's estimate of the air situation in the South Pacific. Joint Chiefs of Staff 96/2, "Japanese Intentions in the Pacific Theater," 24 September 1942. Index heading is reel 4, frame 0364, Japanese Intentions in the Pacific Theater, JPS (24 September 1942), 2f. (Due to a pagination error in the index, this reference appears to be reel 3 but is actually reel 4.)

23. Joint Chiefs of Staff 287, "Strategic Plan for the Defeat of Japan," 19 May 1943. Reprinted in Morton, *United States Army in World War II*, 644–46.

24. King and Leahy continued to disagree with the emphasis on MacArthur's drive. The Navy continued to endorse Nimitz's Central Pacific push as the quickest way to defeat Japan. Joint Chiefs of Staff 508/2, "Strategy of the Pacific," 28 June 1943, microfilm, *Records of the Joint Chiefs of Staff: 1941–1945*. Index heading is reel 8, frame 0812, Strategy in the Pacific, JSC (28 June 1943), 5f.

25. Plans under review by the Joint Staff Planners at this time included follow-up operations to Operation Cartwheel (MacArthur's southern drive), as well as plans to secure the Marshalls. Joint Staff Planners 67/7, "Preparation of Plans for the Defeat of Japan," 7 July 1943, microfilm, *Records of the Joint Chiefs of Staff: 1941–1945*. Index heading is reel 4, frame 0023, Preparation of Plans for the Defeat of Japan, JPS (7 July 1943), 6f.

26. The Joint War Plans Committee "retained" its previous strategy for Nimitz to invade the Marshalls. Joint Chiefs of Staff 304, "Operations in the Pacific and Far East in 1943–1944," 12 May 1943, microfilm, *Records of the Joint Chiefs of Staff: 1941–1945*. Index heading is reel 3, frame 0875, Operations in the Pacific and Far East in 1943–44, JWPC (12 May 1943), 33f.

27. Joint Staff Planners 451/3, "Operations against the Marshall Islands," 18 June 1943, microfilm, *Records of the Joint Chiefs of Staff: 1941–1945*. Index heading is reel 11, frame 0331, Operations against the Marshall Islands, JWPC (18 June 1943), 22f.

28. Joint Chiefs of Staff 459/3, "Future Campaign Operations in the Pacific Ocean Areas," 14 June 1943, microfilm, *Records of the Joint Chiefs of Staff: 1941–1945*. Index heading is reel 8, frame 0798, Future Campaign Operations in the Pacific Ocean Areas, JPS (14 June 1943), 14f.

29. Rafael Steinberg and the editors of Time-Life Books, *Island Fighting* (Alexandria, Va.: Time-Life Books, 1978), 132.

30. Joint Staff Planners 451/3, "Operations against the Marshall Islands," 18 June 1943, Enclosure A, 9, microfilm, *Records of the Joint Chiefs of Staff: 1941–1945*. Index heading is reel 11, frame 0331, Operations against the Marshall Islands, JWPC (18 June 1943), 22f.

31. Morton, *United States Army in World War II*, 464. John W. Dower focused on

what he categorized as the Navy's vindictive desire to kill Japanese. Dower argued that the Pacific war resembled a race war and that U.S. policies increasingly focused on extermination of the Japanese rather than on rational attainment of military objectives. See John W. Dower, *War without Mercy: Race and Power in the Pacific War* (New York: Pantheon Books, 1986), 11. In discussing the Battle of Tarawa, Dower used the quote "Kill the Jap bastards! Take no prisoners!" to describe the Marines' approach toward the Japanese on the island (ibid., 68).

32. Potter, *Nimitz*, 243–45. Also see Joseph H. Alexander, *Utmost Savagery: The Three Days at Tarawa* (Annapolis, Md.: Naval Institute Press, 1995), 16. Alexander remains the foremost authority on Tarawa.

33. Holland M. Smith and Percy Finch, *Coral and Brass* (New York: Charles Scribner's Sons, 1949), 111–21.

34. Jeter A. Isely and Philip A. Crowl, *The U.S. Marines and Amphibious War: Its Theory, and Its Practice in the Pacific* (Princeton, N.J.: Princeton University Press, 1951), 207.

35. Henry I. Shaw Jr., Bernard C. Nalty, and Edwin T. Turnbladh, *Central Pacific Drive* (Washington, D.C.: Historical Division, U.S. Marine Corps, 1966), 28–29.

36. Smith and Flinch, *Coral and Brass,* 113.

37. Ibid., 111; Potter, *Nimitz,* 280.

38. Steinberg et al., *Island Fighting,* 133. For the rest of the war MacArthur repeatedly pointed out that Tarawa was a mistake. D. Clayton James, *The Years of MacArthur,* Vol. 2: 1941–1945 (Boston: Houghton Mifflin, 1975), 348.

39. Joseph H. Alexander, "Tarawa: The Ultimate Opposed Landing," *Marine Corps Gazette* (November 1993), 61.

40. Steinberg et al., *Island Fighting,* 118. Nimitz began receiving personal letters from families during this period as well. Typical accusations by mothers were "You killed my son at Tarawa." Potter, *Nimitz,* 264.

41. For a more detailed look at infantry tactics, see Robert S. Burrell, "The Prototype U.S. Marine: Evolution of the Amphibious Assault Warrior," in *Crucibles: Selected Readings in U.S. Marine Corps History,* ed. Robert S. Burrell, 2d ed. (Bell Air, Md.: Academic Publishing Services, 2004).

42. See Benis M. Frank, "Holland M. Smith," in *Men of War,* ed. Howarth, 562–86. For an overview of the Tarawa operations, see Robert S. Burrell, "Operation Galvanic: Remembering Tarawa 60 Years Later," *Shipmate* (November 2003), 20–23.

43. Capt. William A. Corn, USN, memorandum to Navy War Plans Division on seizure of Chichi Jima, 19 December 1942, Strategic Plans, boxes 40 and 153, Record Group 38.2.4, National Archives, College Park.

44. Joint Staff Planners 312, "Seizure of the Bonins," 30 October 1943, microfilm, *Records of the Joint Chiefs of Staff: 1941–1945.* Index heading reel 10, frame 0468, Seizure of the Bonins, JWPC (30 October 1943), 66f.

45. Ibid., 2.

46. Ibid., 26.

47. Ibid.

48. Joint Chiefs of Staff 742, "Optimum Use, Timing and Deployment of V.L.R. Bombers in the War against Japan," 6 March 1944, microfilm, *Records of the Joint Chiefs of Staff: 1941–1945*. Index heading is reel 1, frame 0736, Optimum Use, Timing, and Deployment of Very Long Range Bombers in the War against Japan, CG AAF (6 March 1944), 2f.

49. Ibid.

50. John W. Huston, *American Airpower Comes of Age: General Henry H. "Hap" Arnold's World War II Diaries* (Maxwell AFB: Air University Press, 2002), 310.

51. Ibid., 9. Huston questioned the spirit of Arnold's superior in this instance.

52. Ibid., 10. Huston attempted to challenge this last report with the wording from an award citation that was disapproved. The fitness report commentary was much more valid, objective, and indicative of Arnold's character than an award citation.

53. Ibid., 19.

54. Ibid., 20.

55. Ibid., 28.

56. Ibid., 33–35.

57. For a more detailed analysis of the development of U.S. air power, see Sherry, *Rise of American Air Power.*

58. Huston, *American Airpower Comes of Age*, 60–61.

59. H. H. Arnold, personal journal entry, 24 September 1942. Reprinted in ibid., 391–92.

60. Hansell maintained that the "Marianas were captured on the initiative and insistence of the Army Air Forces to serve as a base for B-29 operations in the Pacific." Haywood S. Hansell Jr., *Strategic Air War against Japan* (Washington, D.C.: U.S. Government Printing Office, 1980), 33. Hansell's book provides impressive insight and analysis on a variety of strategic air issues.

61. Huston alludes to this as well. Huston, *American Airpower Comes of Age*, 109.

62. Hansell, *Strategic Air War against Japan*, 34.

63. H. H. Arnold, personal journal entry, 19 April 1945. Reprinted in Huston, *American Airpower Comes of Age*, 246.

64. Adm. Thomas Kinkaid complained so loudly that Admiral Leahy, who was usually more concerned with events in Washington and Europe, noted the conversation in his diary. It is unlikely that Kinkaid would have done so without agreement from Admiral Nimitz. William Leahy, personal journal entry, 16 May 1945, microform, *Admiral Leahy's Diaries, 1893, 1897–1956: Naval Career Only*, from his papers in the Manuscript Division (Library of Congress, Photoduplication Service, 1977), Nimitz Library, U.S. Naval Academy.

65. Crane, *Bombs, Cities, and Civilians*, 33.

66. Hansell, *Strategic Air War against Japan*, 39. The empty weight of the B-29 was 69,610 lbs. The suggested loaded weight was 132,000 lbs. A weight of 140,000 lbs exceeded the manufacture's suggested load capacity, but was used by Superforts on bombing runs against Japan.

67. For test specifications, see ibid., 99.

68. The results of these photos and the specific dates they were taken are compiled in Joint War Plans Committee 91/3, "Plan for the Seizure of the Bonins," 12 August 1944, microfilm, *Records of the Joint Chiefs of Staff: 1941–1945*. Index heading is reel 10, frame 0544, Plans for Seizure of the Bonins, JWPC (12 August 1944), 105f.

69. Saburo Sakai, *Samurai!* ed. Martin Caidin and Fred Saito (Annapolis, Md.: Naval Institute Press, 1991), 276.

70. Chichi Jima still dominated assessments of the Bonin Islands in early 1944. See Joint Intelligence Center, Pacific Ocean Areas, "Information Bulletin No. 15-44: Southern Nanpo Shoto, Bonin and Kazan Islands," 20 March 1944, Air Force Historical Research Agency, Maxwell AFB.

71. George C. Dyer, *The Amphibians Came to Conquer: The Story of Admiral Richmond Kelly Turner*, vol. 2 (Washington, D.C.: U.S. Department of the Navy, 1972), 987.

72. Matome Ugaki, *Fading Victory: The Diary of Admiral Matome Ugaki, 1941–1945*, trans. Masataka Chihaya, ed. Donald M. Goldstein and Katherine V. Dillo (Pittsburgh: University of Pittsburgh Press, 1991), 423–24.

73. The plan did not identify "heavy bombers" as B-24s. However, the Army Air Forces considered the B-24 a "heavy bomber" and the B-29 a "very heavy bomber." The airfields on Iwo Jima were considered too short for B-29s to be stationed there. Accordingly, I assume the planning team meant B-24s. Joint War Plans Committee 244, "Immediate Occupation of Iwo Jima," 24 June 1944, microfilm, *Records of the Joint Chiefs of Staff: 1941–1945*. Index heading is reel 4, frame 0331, Immediate Occupation of Iwo Jima, JWPC (24 June 1944), 6f.

74. Joint War Plans Committee 244, "Immediate Occupation of Iwo Jima," 24 June 1944. Enclosure, 1-3, microfilm, *Records of the Joint Chiefs of Staff: 1941–1945*.

75. U.S. Pacific Fleet and Pacific Ocean Areas, "Defense Installations on Iwo Jima," CINCPAC–CINCPOA Bulletin No. 136-45, 10 June 1945, 2, Naval Historical Center.

76. Joint War Plans Committee 244, "Immediate Occupation of Iwo Jima," 24 June 1944, microfilm, *Records of the Joint Chiefs of Staff: 1941–1945*.

77. Twentieth Air Force Staff Meeting Action Assignments, 29 June 1944. Reprinted in Hansell, *Strategic Air War against Japan*, 107. A copy can also be found in Twentieth Air Force Staff Meeting documents, Air Forces Historical Research Agency, Maxwell AFB.

78. Weekly Staff Meeting of Twentieth Air Force, 29 June 1944. Reprinted in Hansell, *Strategic Air War against Japan*, 108.

79. Arleigh A. Burke, "Reminiscences of Admiral Arleigh Burke USN (Retired)" (1978), 387, Special Collections, U.S. Naval Academy Library.

80. Carrier Task Group 58.1, "Statistical Summary 30 June–9 August Inclusive," Enclosure H, 16 August 1944, microform, *U.S. Navy Action and Operational Reports from World War II: Pacific Theater*. Also see Ugaki, *Fading Victory*, 426.

81. Carrier Task Group 58.1, "Bombardment and Gunnery Report," Enclosure 1,

16 August 1944, microform, *U.S. Navy Action and Operational Reports from World War II: Pacific Theater.*

82. Joint Chiefs of Staff 924, "Operations against Japan Subsequent to Formosa," 30 June 1944, *Records of the Joint Chiefs of Staff: 1941–1945.* Index heading is reel 9, frame 0138, Operations against Japan Subsequent to Formosa, JCS (11 July 1944), 121f. This document can also be found on microfilm at San Diego State University with the cover letter date of 11 July 1944, in Records of the Joint Chiefs of Staff, ed. Kesaris. Both documents are the same, but the cover letters seem to differ.

83. Joint Chiefs of Staff 924, "Operations against Japan Subsequent to Formosa," 30 June 1944, 31, microfilm, *Records of the Joint Chiefs of Staff: 1941–1945.*

84. Joint Intelligence Committee 143/4, "Japanese Reaction to an Assault in the Nanpo Shoto," 20 July 1944, microfilm, *Records of the Joint Chiefs of Staff: 1941–1945.* Index heading is reel 10, frame 0534, Japanese Reaction to an Assault on the Nampo-Shotoana. JIC (20 July 1944), 10f.

85. Joint Staff Planners, "Future Operation in the Pacific," 9 July 1944, microfilm, *Records of the Joint Chiefs of Staff: 1941–1945.* Index heading is reel 9, frame 0259, Future Operations in the Pacific. JPS (9 July 1944), 18f.

86. CG, 20th Bomber Command, classified message to Arnold in War Department, 3 July 1944, ODP messages, Record Group 18.7.10, National Archives, College Park.

87. Thomas R. Searle, "'It Made a Lot of Sense to Kill Skilled Workers': The Firebombing of Tokyo in March 1945," *Journal of Military History* 66 (January 2002): 110.

88. Hansell, *Strategic Air War against Japan,* 31. Also see H. H. Arnold, *Global Mission* (New York: Harper & Brothers, 1949), 536–52, 561.

89. Twentieth Air Force Staff Meeting documents, Air Forces Historical Research Agency, see July–September 1944.

90. Joint War Plans Committee 91/3, "Plan for Seizure of the Bonins," 12 August 1944, microfilm, *Records of the Joint Chiefs of Staff: 1941–1945.* The specific words in the document are "heavy bombers," commonly used to describe B-24 Liberators.

91. Ugaki, *Fading Victory,* 439.

92. Joint War Plans Committee 91/3, "Plan for Seizure of the Bonins," 12 August 1944, 13, microfilm, *Records of the Joint Chiefs of Staff: 1941–1945.*

93. Bureau of Yards and Docks, Office of the Chief of Naval Operations, "Joint Preliminary Study for Advanced Base Layout: Bonin Islands, Chichi Jima and Haha Jima," August 1944, 3, Strategic Plans Division, Naval Historical Center.

94. Ugaki, *Fading Victory,* 449.

95. CINCPOA to COMINCH, Top Secret dispatches, 14 September 1944. Command Summary, Fleet Adm. C. W. Nimitz, U.S. Navy, Book Five: 1 January 1944–31 December 1944, 2356, Nimitz Papers, Naval Historical Center.

96. James H. Hallas, *The Devil's Anvil: The Assault on Peleliu* (Westport, Conn.: Praeger, 1994), ix; Spector, *Eagle against the Sun,* 421; Weigley, *American Way of War,* 300.

97. CINCPOA to COMINCH, Top Secret dispatches, 23 August 1944. Command Summary, Fleet Adm. C. W. Nimitz, U.S. Navy, Book Five: 1 January 1944–31 December 1944, 2347, Nimitz Papers, Naval Historical Center.

98. Joint Chiefs of Staff to Nimitz, MacArthur, Top Secret dispatches, 9 September 1944. Command Summary, Fleet Adm. C. W. Nimitz, U.S. Navy, Book Five: 1 January 1944–31 December 1944, 2350, Nimitz Papers, Naval Historical Center.

99. Ernest J. King, Memorandum for Joint Chiefs of Staff, "Employment of Marine Divisions in Formosa Operation," 4 September 1944, *Records of the Joint Chiefs of Staff: 1941–1945*. Index heading is reel 9, frame 0399, Employment of Marine Divisions in Formosa Operation, JCS (4 September 1944), 13f.

100. Whitman S. Bartley, *Iwo Jima: Amphibious Epic* (Washington, D.C.: Headquarters U.S. Marine Corps, Historical Branch, 1954), 21.

101. Raymond Spruance, oral interview by Philippe de Bausett, 9 July 1965, 21, Spruance Papers, Naval Historical Center. Spruance had favored the seizure of Okinawa over Formosa as early as July 1944. Raymond Spruance, "Notes for Possible Future Use," 17 April 1964, 1, Spruance Papers, Naval Historical Center.

102. CINCPOA to COMINCH, Top Secret dispatches, 14 September 1944. Command Summary, Fleet Adm. C. W. Nimitz, U.S. Navy, Book Five: 1 January 1944–31 December 1944, 2356, Nimitz Papers, Naval Historical Center.

103. Joint Chiefs of Staff 713/10, "Proposed Directive to the Commander in Chief Southwest Pacific Area, and Commander in Chief, Pacific Ocean Areas," 4 September 1944, microfilm, *Records of the Joint Chiefs of Staff: 1941–1945*. Index heading is reel 9, frame 0391, Proposed Directive to CINCSWPA and CINCPOA, JCS (4 September 1944), 8f.

104. Joint Chiefs of Staff 713/13, "Proposed Directive to the Commander in Chief Southwest Pacific Area, and Commander in Chief, Pacific Ocean Areas," 5 September 1944. This memorandum contains the minutes from the meeting on 5 September. Microfilm, Records of the Joint Chiefs of Staff: 1941–1945. Index heading is reel 9, frame 0419, Proposed Directive to CINCSWPA and CINCPOA, JSC (5 September 1944), 10f.

105. Joint Chiefs of Staff 713/15, "Future Operations in the Pacific," 22 September 1944, microfilm, *Records of the Joint Chiefs of Staff: 1941–1945*. Index heading is reel 9, frame 0478, Future Operations in the Pacific, CS USA (22 September 1944), 6f.

106. Joint Chiefs of Staff 713/16, "Future Operations in the Pacific," 25 September 1944, microfilm, *Records of the Joint Chiefs of Staff: 1941–1945*. Index heading is reel 9, frame 0505, Future Operations in the Pacific, JCS (25 September 1944), 3f.

107. Buell, *Quiet Warrior*, 309–10; Potter, *Nimitz*, 326–27.

108. Raymond Spruance, "Notes for Possible Future Use," 17 April 1964, 2, Spruance Papers, Naval Historical Center.

109. Thomas B. Buell, *Master of Seapower: A Biography of Ernest J. King* (Annapolis, Md.: Naval Institute Press, 1980), 473.

110. Ibid.; Buell, *Quiet Warrior,* 309–10; Potter, *Nimitz,* 326–27; Dyer, *Amphibians Came to Conquer,* 979.

111. Joint Chiefs of Staff 713/18, "Future Operations in the Pacific," 2 October 1944, microfilm, *Records of the Joint Chiefs of Staff: 1941–1945.* Index heading is reel 9, frame 0514, Future Operations in the Pacific, JCS (3 October 1944), 3f.

112. King later argued that "it had been anticipated that enemy resistance [on Iwo Jima] would be severe." However, when Nimitz, Spruance, and then King proposed Operation Detachment, they did not expect such large numbers of casualties. This type of statement appears after the battle. Ernest J. King and Walter Muir Whitehill, *Fleet Admiral King: A Naval Record* (New York: W. W. Norton, 1952), 598.

113. Hansell, *Strategic Air War against Japan,* 27.

114. Joint Chiefs of Staff 713/8, "Future Operations in the Pacific," 2 October 1944, microfilm, *Records of the Joint Chiefs of Staff: 1941–1945.*

115. U.S. Pacific Fleet and Pacific Ocean Areas, "Operation Detachment (Iwo Jima)," 7 October 1944, reprinted in Steven T. Ross, *U.S. War Plans* (Malabar, Fla.: Krieger Publishing, 2000), 199–201.

116. High-level Navy commanders only mentioned plans for fighter operations on Iwo Jima. However, some proposals called for one group of forty-eight B-17s or B-24s to be stationed on the island as well. See Bureau of Yards and Docks, Office of the Chief of Naval Operations, "Joint Preliminary Study for Advanced Base Layout: Iwo Jima," October 1944, Strategic Plans Division Records, Naval Historical Center.

117. Potter, *Nimitz,* 358.

118. Raymond Spruance, "Notes for Possible Future Use," 17 April 1964, Spruance Papers, Naval Historical Center; Buell, *Quiet Warrior,* 315; Potter, *Nimitz,* 358.

119. Raymond Spruance, oral interview by Philippe de Bausett, 9 July 1965, 22, Spruance Papers, Naval Historical Center.

120. Buell, *Quiet Warrior,* 315.

121. The commander of V Amphibious Corps, Harry Schmidt, realized the inadequacy of making preparations based upon maps taken months before. Schmidt did not discuss the strategic implications, but he directed criticism at tactical difficulties that resulted from the use of old photos during the battle. V Amphibious Corps 13/124, "Special Action Report, Iwo Jima Campaign," 20 May 1945, 7, microfilm, *U.S.M.C. Operations Reports, 1941–45* (Washington, D.C.: U.S. Navy Department, 1947), Nimitz Library. This is the only microfilmed copy of Marine Corps after-action reports on Pacific campaigns that I am aware of.

122. Plans to make use of the Bonin Islands go back to December 1942. As far as scrutiny of Iwo Jima in plans from 1943 onward, planners inadequately took into account the islands' difficult terrain. By early October 1944 the Joint Chiefs of Staff were still unaware of the size of the defense and the geographical complexities. Even the intelligence estimates after D-Day accounted for about half of the actual Japanese forces stationed on Iwo Jima.

Chapter 3

1. Tadamichi Kuribayashi, letter to his wife dated 9 September 1944, trans. Yoshitaka Horie, reprinted in *Marine Corps Gazette* (February 1955), 41.
2. John Toland, *The Rising Sun: The Decline and Fall of the Japanese Empire, 1936–1945* (New York: Random House, 1970), 646.
3. Jack Vincent, "Water on Iwo," *Marine Corps Gazette* (October 1945), 52.
4. Kuribayashi, letter to his wife dated 2 August 1944, 40–41.
5. Kuribayashi gave an example of his daily schedule to his wife. Ibid., 43.
6. "First Six Days on Iwo Jima," *Marine Corps Gazette* (May 1945), 2.
7. Whitman S. Bartley, *Iwo Jima: Amphibious Epic* (Washington, D.C.: Headquarters U.S. Marine Corps, Historical Branch, 1954), 15.
8. Masanori Ito, *Teikoku Rikugun No Saigo*, 4. Excerpts translated by Fred Saito; see Richard F. Newcomb, Iwo Jima Correspondence, Marine Corps Historical Library, Marine Corps Historical Center, Washington Navy Yard.
9. Kuribayashi, letter to his wife dated 2 August 1944, 40–41.
10. Howard M. Conner, *The Spearhead: The World War II History of the 5th Marine Division* (Washington, D.C.: Historical Division, Headquarters Marine Corps, 1950), 105–6.
11. Kuribayashi wrote at least two poems on Iwo Jima, "Aiba Koshin Kyoku" (a song of loving horses) and "Aikoku Koshin Kyoku" (a song of loving his nation). Yoshitaka Horie, "Explanation of the Defense Plan and Battle of Iwo Jima," 25 January 1946, Marine Corps University Library, Quantico, Va. Others have claimed that Kuribayashi was not a poet. See Fred Saito, letter to Richard Newcomb, 26 January 1964, Newcomb Papers, Marine Corps University Research Archives, Quantico, Va.
12. Fred Saito, letter to Richard Newcomb, 26 January 1964, Newcomb Papers, Marine Corps Historical Library, Marine Corps Historical Center. There is some contention whether Kuribayashi wrote this poem, or whether it was simply one of his favorites.
13. Kuribayashi, letter to Kuribayashi's wife dated 3 February 1945, trans. Yoshitaka Horie, reprinted in *Marine Corps Gazette* (February 1955), 43.
14. Yoshitaka Horie, "Explanation of the Defense Plan and Battle of Iwo Jima," 25 January 1946, Marine Corps University Library. Horie used the term paratyphus, a disease usually referred to in English as paratyphoid (sometimes called Salmonella paratyphi infection), a serious contagious disease caused by a gram-negative bacterium. Paratyphoid fever is marked by high fever, headache, loss of appetite, vomiting, and constipation or diarrhea. The patient typically develops an enlarged spleen.
15. Most of the information in this paragraph on Kuribayashi's background comes from Fred Saito, letter to Richard Newcomb, 26 January 1964, Marine Corps Historical Library, Marine Corps Historical Center.
16. Yoshitaka Horie, in *Marine Corps Gazette* (February 1955), 40.
17. Fred Saito, letter to Richard Newcomb, 26 January 1964, Marine Corps Historical Library, Marine Corps Historical Center.

18. Kuribayashi also had a sound appreciation for American industrial might. Yoshitaka Horie, "Explanation of the Defense Plan and Battle of Iwo Jima," 25 January 1946.

19. Fleet Marine Forces Pacific 274/229, "G-2 Report on Iwo Jima Operation," 1 April 1945, 10, microfilm, *U.S.M.C. Operations Reports, 1941–45* (Washington, D.C.: U.S. Navy Department, 1947), Nimitz Library.

20. Fred Saito, letter to Richard Newcomb, 26 January 1964, Marine Corps Historical Library, Marine Corps Historical Center.

21. See Toland, *Rising Sun*, 640–42. Some have labeled Yoshitaka Horie as a war criminal. See Chester Hearn, *Sorties into Hell: The Hidden War on Chichi Jima* (Westport, Conn.: Praeger, 2003), 29–39.

22. Kuribayashi, letter to his wife dated 2 August 1944, trans. Yoshitaka Horie, reprinted in *Marine Corps Gazette* (February 1955), 40–41.

23. *Japanese Monograph 51: Iwo Jima and Ryukyu Island Air Operations,* compiled by Japanese officers from Japanese sources, translated, and printed by the Office of the Chief of Military History, Department of the Army, August 1946, 3. Other Japanese sources indicate that the military believed invasion probable in February 1945; see *Japanese Monograph 48.* One of the most complete runs of Japanese Monographs is located at the Military Historical Institute, Carlisle Barracks, Pa.

24. Kuribayashi told his wife that if Iwo Jima was attacked, "we would never have any chance to escape death." Kuribayashi, letter to his wife dated 2 August 1944, trans. Yoshitaka Horie, reprinted in *Marine Corps Gazette* (February 1955), 40.

25. A Japanese POW indicated that the civilian population on Iwo Jima was evacuated in June 1944. Task Force 56, "G-2 Report No. 4," 22 February 1945, microfilm, U.S.M.C. Operations Reports, 1941–45, Nimitz Library.

26. *Japanese Monograph 48: Central Pacific Operations Record, Volume 1: Army Invasion and Defense Operations* (Office of the Chief of Military History, Department of the Army, 1955[?]), 62. This is an unedited translation by Japanese officers compiled by the U.S. Army after the war. One copy on microfilm at Military History Institute.

27. Richard Wheeler, *Iwo* (Annapolis, Md.: Naval Institute Press, 1980), 22.

28. Fred Saito, personal letter to Richard Newcomb, 27 January 1964, Newcomb Papers, Marine Corps University Research Archives and Marine Corps Historical Center Library.

29. Yoshitaka Horie, "Explanation of the Defense Plan and Battle of Iwo Jima," 25 January 1946. Japanese sources indicate around 14,000 soldiers and 6,000 sailors, for a total of 20,000 men, fewer than what American sources state. However, due to Bartley's detail in the official Marine Corps history, I adhere to his numbers. For Japanese sources, see *Japanese Monograph 48*, 63–66.

30. Most of the Imperial Army's career forces were depleted and diluted by the war in China in the late 1930s. Meirion and Susie Harries, *Soldiers of the Rising Sun: The Rise and Fall of the Imperial Japanese Army* (New York: Random House, 1991), 317–20.

31. Fred Saito, "Japanese Navy at Iwo," letter to Richard Newcomb, 1 February 1964, Newcomb Papers, Marine Corps University Research Archives.

32. For more information on the morale of Japanese soldiers, see Harries and Harries, *Soldiers of the Sun*, 319–20.

33. Bartley, *Iwo Jima*, 8, 16. One of the highest ranking Japanese survivors of Kuribayashi's command was Yoshitaka Horie, who stated that the troops disliked Kuribayashi. This likely stemmed from his well-known stern discipline, which Horie also spoke of. For more information on Japanese dislike for their stay on Iwo Jima, see V Amphibious Corps 15/131, "Special Action Report, Iwo Jima Campaign," 30 April 1945, 25, microfilm, *U.S.M.C. Operations Reports, 1941–45*, Nimitz Library.

34. Richard F. Newcomb, *Iwo-Jima* (New York: Holt, Rinehart & Winston, 1965), 11.

35. Toland, *Rising Sun*, 643.

36. Ibid., 642.

37. Bartley, *Iwo Jima*, 8.

38. Isamu Okazaki, quote translated in a personal letter from Fred Saito to Richard Newcomb, 1 February 1964, Newcomb Papers, Marine Corps University Research Archives.

39. Saburo Ienaga, *The Pacific War: World War II and the Japanese, 1931–1945* (New York: Pantheon Books, 1978), 19–23.

40. Ibid., 27–28.

41. For "corruption" of the bushido code, see *Yuki Tanaka, Hidden Horrors: Japanese War Crimes of World War II* (Boulder, Colo.: Westview Press, 1996), 206–11.

42. Ibid., 30–31.

43. Fleet Marine Forces Pacific 274/229, "G-2 Report on Iwo Jima Operation," 1 April 1945, 37, microfilm, *U.S.M.C. Operations Reports, 1941–45*, Nimitz Library.

44. Spector, *Eagle against the Sun*, 37.

45. "Famed Sword Returns to Japan," Conference Room, Holt, Rinehart & Winston, 383 Madison Avenue, New York, 24 May 1965, Newcomb Papers, Marine Corps University Research Archives.

46. Kuribayashi's resolution to initiate the primary defense after the American landing was debated at the highest levels of the Japanese military. Even from a distant post at Kyushu, Vice Admiral Ugaki was highly critical of the general's decision. Ugaki, *Fading Victory*, 540. Bartley suggests that Kuribayashi's plan to forego the defense of the beach was a point of contention within his own staff. Bartley, *Iwo Jima*, 11–12. Also see Toland, *Rising Sun*, 643–44.

47. Fred Saito, "Japanese Navy at Iwo," letter to Richard Newcomb, 1 February 1964, Newcomb Papers, Marine Corps University Research Archives.

48. *Indirect fire*, a military term, refers to the volley from weapons similar to mortars and artillery. Indirect fire weapons are designed to be fired upward, which allows the projectile to plummet downward onto the target. Unlike direct fire weapons, such as rifles, indirect fire weapons do not require the target to be within the operator's direct line of vision.

49. Robert Sherrod, "With Dignity and Courage," *Time* (12 March 1945), 33–34.

50. Fleet Marine Force Pacific 129/192, "Operations for the Capture, Occupation, and Defense of Iwo Jima," 27 March 1945, Enclosure E, 2, microfilm, *U.S.M.C. Operations Reports, 1941–45,* Nimitz Library.

51. Yoshitaka Horie, "Explanation of the Defense Plan and Battle of Iwo Jima," 25 January 1946.

52. Raymond Lamont-Brown, *Kamikaze: Japan's Suicide Samurai* (New York: Sterling Publishing, 1997), 89. A slightly different translation is found in Holland M. Smith's personal papers, D-2 Language Section, 4th Marine Division, "Courageous Battle Vow," 24 February 1945, Marine Corps University Historical Archives.

53. Dower, *War without Mercy,* 230.

54. Ibid., 231. For more information on the interplay of yamato damashii and gyokusai in Japanese propaganda, see James Bradley, *Flyboys: A True Story of Courage* (New York: Little, Brown, 2003).

55. Dower, *War without Mercy,* 231.

56. Yoshitaka Horie, "Explanation of the Defense Plan and Battle of Iwo Jima," 25 January 1946.

57. Dower, *War without Mercy,* 61, 243.

58. Fleet Marine Forces Pacific 274/229, "G-2 Report on Iwo Jima Operation," 1 April 1945, 32, microfilm, *U.S.M.C. Operations Reports, 1941–45,* Nimitz Library.

59. Walker Y. Brooks, "Engineers on Iwo," *Marine Corps Gazette* (October 1945).

60. Toland, *Rising Sun,* 644.

61. Keith Wheeler, *The Road to Tokyo* (Chicago: Time-Life Books, 1979), 42–43.

62. Bartley, *Iwo Jima,* 15. Also see Toland, *Rising Sun,* 643–44.

63. Brooks, "Engineers on Iwo," 49.

64. Bartley, *Iwo Jima,* 13.

65. Sherrod, "With Dignity and Courage," 26.

66. Isely and Crowl, *U.S. Marines and Amphibious War,* 485–86.

67. R. D. Heinl Jr., "Dark Horse on Iwo," *Marine Corps Gazette* (August 1945), 3.

68. W. J. Holmes, *Undersea Victory: The Influence of Submarine Operations on the War in the Pacific* (Garden City, N.Y.: Doubleday, 1966), 438.

69. Ibid., 438.

70. *Japanese Monograph* 51, 4.

71. Ibid.

72. *Japanese Monograph 45: History of Imperial General Headquarters,* compiled by Japanese officers from Japanese sources, translated and printed by the Office of the Chief of Military History, Department of the Army, August 1946, 257.

73. Marine Forces Pacific 274/229, "G-2 Report on Iwo Jima Operation," 1 April 1945, 16, microfilm, *U.S.M.C. Operations Reports, 1941–45,* Nimitz Library.

74. Isely and Crowl, *U.S. Marines and Amphibious War,* 487. Toland estimates 1,860. See Toland, *Rising Sun,* 644.

75. Fleet Marine Force Pacific 129/192, "Operations for the Capture, Occupa-

tion, and Defense of Iwo Jima," 27 March 1945. See Enclosure E, 1, microfilm, *U.S.M.C. Operations Reports, 1941–45*, Nimitz Library.

76. Isely and Crowl, *U.S. Marines and Amphibious War*, 486.

77. Bartley, *Iwo Jima*, 23.

78. William Frye, *Marshall: Citizen Soldier* (Indianapolis: Bobbs-Merrill, 1947), 350.

79. Originally, the Navy chain of command supported Smith's decision. Chief of Naval Operations Ernest King wrote to Nimitz in November 1944: "I concur in your view that it will be beneficial to remove any unwarranted stigma from the personnel of the 27th Division, but this matter appears to be heading toward blaming the whole affair on Holland Smith. I cannot tolerate any 'rectification' that tends to make it appear that the 27th Division was all that it should have been!" Despite such talk of supporting him, Smith eventually did take the fall for his decision on Saipan. Removed from direct command of amphibious forces and uninvited to Japan's surrender ceremonies, Smith became bitter. He eventually published a critical view of both Army and Navy conduct in the Pacific war. See Smith and Flinch, *Coral and Brass*. For King's comments see Ernest J. King, letter to Chester Nimitz, 8 November 1944, microform, *Official Papers of Fleet Admiral Ernest J. King*.

80. Holmes, *Undersea Victory*, 436.

81. Task Force 56 59/229, "State of Enemy Defenses, Iwo Jima," 13 February 1945, microfilm, *U.S.M.C. Operations Reports, 1941–45*, Nimitz Library.

82. "Fourth before Iwo," *Leatherneck* (May 1945).

83. Report No. 7, "Iwo Jima," 6, Army Air Forces Evaluation Board, Pacific Ocean Areas, 10 May 1945, Military History Institute, under the author M. F. Scanlon, General, USAAF.

84. Ibid., 17.

85. Ibid., 71. The Navy also used napalm on Iwo Jima during the battle. See "Air Support—Iwo Jima Operation," Memorandum for the Commanding General, Army Air Forces, 22 March 1945, Arnold Papers, Library of Congress, reel 107.

86. Buell, *Quiet Warrior*, 316.

87. In military terminology, a sortie is a single aircraft executing a mission. The term *mission* refers to any number of sorties flown against a desired target.

88. Fleet Marine Force Pacific 129/192, "Operations for the Capture, Occupation, and Defense of Iwo Jima," 27 March 1945, Enclosure D, 1, microfilm, *U.S.M.C. Operations Reports, 1941–45*, Nimitz Library.

89. Report No. 7. Also see Operations Analysis Section, Pacific Ocean Areas, "The Accuracy of the Bombing of Iwo Jima and Chichi Jima (3 September 1944–21 March 1945)," 1 May 1945, Air Force Historical Research Agency.

90. "Air Support—Iwo Jima Operation," Memorandum for the Commanding General, Army Air Forces, 22 March 1945, Arnold Papers, reel 107, Library of Congress.

91. In reference to the combined efforts of both the Twentieth and Twenty-first Bomber Commands before January 1945, LeMay stated that "it wasn't getting too much done." Interview with Curtis LeMay by John T. Bohn, March

Air Force Base, 9 March 1971, Curtis LeMay Museum, March Air Reserve Base, Calif.

92. H. H. Arnold, Command General, Army Air Forces, official letter to H. S. Hansell, Command General, 21st Bomber Command, 13 November 1944, microfilm, Hansell Papers, Air Force Historical Research Agency.

93. Hansell, *Strategic Air War against Japan*, 30.

94. Searle, "'It Made a Lot of Sense to Kill Skilled Workers,'" 112–13.

95. Curtis E. LeMay and Bill Yenne, *Superfortress: The Story of the B-29 and American Air Power* (New York: McGraw-Hill, 1988), 115.

96. Report No. 7, 4.

97. E. Bartlett Kerr, *Flames over Tokyo: The U.S. Army Air Forces' Incendiary Campaign against Japan, 1944–1945* (New York: Donald I. Fine, 1991), 324–25.

98. Isely and Crowl, *U.S. Marines and Amphibious War*, 437.

99. Ibid., 441. *Large-gunned vessels* refers to battleships and cruisers.

100. Paolo E. Coletta, "Richard K. Turner," in *Men of War*, ed. Howarth, 365.

101. Isely and Crowl, *U.S. Marines and Amphibious War*, 444.

102. Commander Fifth Fleet to Commander in Chief, U.S. Fleet, A16-3, "Report of Iwo Operation,"14 June 1945, microform, *U.S. Navy Action and Operational Reports from World War II: Pacific Theater.*

103. Fleet Marine Force Pacific 269/366, "Naval Gunfire Support in Operations against Iwo Jima," 1 April 1945, microfilm, *U.S.M.C. Operations Reports, 1941–45*, Nimitz Library. The Naval Gunfire Section of the report described the struggle between the Marines and Navy over preliminary fires in detail.

104. Joint Chiefs of Staff 1232, "Survey of Operations Pending Availability of U.S. Forces Now Deployed in Europe," 17 January 1945, *Records of the Joint Chiefs of Staff: 1941–1945.*

105. Turner justified the limitation of preliminary fires based upon a naval study, which indicated three days would be adequate. Turner disputed the Marine report that endorsed nine days of fires. Fleet Marine Forces Pacific 269/366, "Naval Gunfire Support in Operations against Iwo Jima, Report on, Preliminary," 1 April 1945, microfilm, *U.S.M.C. Operations Reports, 1941–45*, Nimitz Library.

106. James, *Years of MacArthur: Vol. 2, 1941–1945*, 629–31.

107. Smith and Flinch, *Coral and Brass*, 246.

108. Isely and Crowl, *U.S. Marines and Amphibious War*, 446. In his biography of Spruance, Buell disputes Isely's insinuation that Spruance "stole" the two fast battleships. Turner believed the ships were allocated to him, but the vessels were never assigned in writing to Task Force 51. The miscommunication over the use of the battleships was not uncovered until the ships were under way. Buell argued that Turner had "no right to assume that he could use them." Buell, *Quiet Warrior*, 326.

109. Dudly Brown, letter to Holland M. Smith, n.d. Excerpt reprinted in Smith and Flinch, *Coral and Brass*, 248.

110. A.A. Vandegrift, *Once a Marine: The Memoirs of General A. A Vandegrift*, ed. Robert B. Asprey (New York: W. W. Norton, 1964), 281–82.

111. Clifton B. Cates, oral history transcript (1973), 187, Marine Historical Center.
112. Task Force 58 reported 500 Japanese planes destroyed in the raid with the loss of nearly 50 U.S. planes in the process. In contrast, the Japanese government testified that Spruance's carrier attack had destroyed a total of 162 planes on the ground and in the air. "Magic"—Diplomatic Summary 1069, 24 February 1945, War Department, Office of the Assistant Chief of Staff, G-2, Magic Files microfilm, *Intercepted Japanese Messages* (Operation MAGIC) (Wilmington, Del.: Michael Glazier, 1979). For a detailed report on the carrier attacks, see "United States Naval Activity in the Pacific during Operations 'Iceberg' and 'Detachment,'" Army Air Forces Evaluation Board, Pacific Ocean Areas, 7 June 1945, Military History Institute.
113. According to intercepted Japanese messages, 50–60 Japanese planes failed to return from suicide attacks launched at Spruance. These planes could have been sent to Iwo Jima. "Magic"—Diplomatic Summary 1066, 24 February 1945, War Department, Office of the Assistant Chief of Staff, G-2, Magic Files, microfilm, *Intercepted Japanese Messages* (Operation MAGIC).
114. "Biggest Carrier Fleet Hits Heart of Japan," *San Francisco Examiner,* 16 February 1945, 1.
115. Buell, *Quiet Warrior,* 318–19.
116. Craig L. Symonds, *Historical Atlas of the U.S. Navy* (Annapolis, Md.: Naval Institute Press, 1995), 184.
117. "Biggest Carrier Fleet Hits Heart of Japan," *San Francisco Examiner,* 16 February 1945, 2.
118. U.S. intelligence continued to push the probability of a Japanese all-out counterattack weeks into the invasion. Despite mounting evidence to the contrary, intelligence stubbornly predicted *banzai* attacks on many days in the battle. Only a few, mostly small, counter-offensives actually occurred. For a specific reference to counterattacks see Task Force 56, "G-2 Report No. 1," 19 February 1945, microfilm, *U.S.M.C. Operations Reports, 1941-45,* Nimitz Library.
119. U.S. Pacific Fleet and Pacific Ocean Areas, "Iwo Jima," 4, CINCPAC-CINPOA Bulletin No. 9-45, 10 January 1945, Library of Congress.
120. Norbert V. Woods, interview by Christopher F. Woods, 10 March 2003, Special Collections, Nimitz Library.
121. Peter Isely and Philip Crowl conducted the most detailed examination of the tactical combat on Iwo Jima in *U.S. Marines and Amphibious War.* Instead of writing an official government history, which tends to timidly discuss or simply ignore controversial issues, Isely and Crowl relentlessly pursued provocative facets of the battle in a seemingly impartial manner. See Isely and Crowl, *U.S. Marines and Amphibious War,* 432–530.
122. Based on the examination of Iwo Jima after the battle, Isely stated that "there remained after three days of fire a great number of dual purpose guns, covered artillery pieces, blockhouses, and pillboxes" (ibid., 449).
123. Saito, "Japanese Navy at Iwo," letter to Richard Newcomb, 1 February 1964, Newcomb Papers, Marine Corps University Research Archives.

124. Toland, *Rising Sun,* 649.

125. Isely and Crowl, *U.S. Marines and Amphibious War,* 478.

126. Commander Transport Group 53.2, Action Report, 13 April 1945, Enclosure C, Beach Master Report, 2, microfilm, *USMC Operations Reports, 1941–45,* Nimitz Library.

127. Bryce Walton, "D-Day on Iwo Jima," *Leatherneck* (May 1945).

128. Gerald C. Thomas, oral history transcript (1973), 615, Marine Historical Center. Thomas said the attitude after the naval gun fire was "We've killed them all." But after the Marines got ashore, "they found out that wasn't quite correct."

129. "First Six Days on Iwo Jima," *Marine Corps Gazette* (May 1945), 3.

130. Thomas Lyons, oral interview printed in *Into the Rising Sun,* ed. Patrick K. O'Donnell (New York: Free Press, 2002), 230.

131. Isely and Crowl, *U.S. Marines and Amphibious War,* 479.

132. Sherrod, "With Dignity and Courage," 26.

133. Ibid., 27.

134. *Heroes of Iwo Jima,* Arnold Shapiro Productions (New York: A&E Home Video, 2001).

135. Wesley Frank Craven and James Lea Cate, *The Army Air Forces in World War II, Vol. 5: The Pacific: Matterhorn to Nagasaki, June 1944 to August 1945* (Chicago: University of Chicago Press, 1953), 589. Also see war plans devised by the V Amphibious Corps from October 1944 through February 1945, Marine Corps University Research Archives.

136. Potter, *Nimitz,* 362.

137. V Amphibious Corps 15/131, "Special Action Report, Iwo Jima Campaign," 30 April 1945, 9, microfilm, *U.S.M.C. Operations Reports, 1941–45,* Nimitz Library.

138. Task Force 56, "G-2 Report No. 10," 28 February 1945, Annex A, microfilm, *U.S.M.C. Operations Reports, 1941–45,* Nimitz Library.

139. A Marine Corps assessment of the island's defenses after the battle concluded that 88 percent of the defense installations were intact when the assault force landed. Isely and Crowl, *U.S. Marines and Amphibious War,* 473.

140. "Iwo: The Red Hot Rock," *Collier's* (14 April 1945), 14.

141. Ibid., 15.

142. T. Grady Gallant, "The Friendly Dead," in *United States Marine Corps in World War II,* ed. S. E. Smith (New York: Random House, 1969), 748.

143. F. A. Stott, "Ten Days on Iwo Jima," *Leatherneck* (May 1945).

144. Sherrod, "With Dignity and Courage," 27.

145. Isely and Crowl, *U.S. Marines and Amphibious War,* 488.

146. Richard Wheeler, *The Bloody Battle for Suribachi* (1965; rpt., Annapolis, Md.: Naval Institute Press, 1994), 106.

147. Ibid., 109.

148. Isely and Crowl, *U.S. Marines and Amphibious War,* 513.

149. Ibid., 498. Also see Clifton B. Cates, oral history transcript (1973), 195, Marine Historical Center.

150. Most American military histories estimate 50 Japanese attack planes, but a recent study indicates 32. See Rikihei Inoguchi and Tadashi Nakajima, *The Divine Wind: Japan's Kamikaze Force in World War II*, ed. Roger Pineau (1958; rpt., Annapolis, Md.: Naval Institute Press, 1994), 129–31.

151. Isely and Crowl, *U.S. Marines and Amphibious War*, 490.

152. Bartley, *Iwo Jima*, 5.

153. Edgar L. Jones, "To the Finish: A Letter from Iwo Jima," *Atlantic Monthly* (April 1945), 50–51.

154. G. B. Erskine, Commanding General 3d Marine Division, "Action Report, Iwo Jima Operation," 30 April 1945, microfilm, *U.S.M.C. Operations Reports, 1941–45*, Nimitz Library.

155. Graves B. Erskine, oral history transcript (1975), 357, Headquarters U.S. Marine Corps, History and Museums Division.

156. Walker Y. Brooks, "Engineers on Iwo," *Marine Corps Gazette* (October 1945).

157. "First Six Days on Iwo Jima," *Marine Corps Gazette* (May 1945), 6.

158. Isely and Crowl, *U.S. Marines and Amphibious War, 497;* "Present for the General," *Newsweek*, 19 March 1945, 37; Heinl, "Dark Horse on Iwo," 59.

159. Russell Werts, "The Ghosts of Iwo," *Marine Corps Gazette* (February 1985), 43.

160. Ibid., 43.

161. Bartley, *Iwo Jima*, 154–55.

162. Fred Saito, "Japanese Navy at Iwo," letter to Richard Newcomb, 1 February 1964, Newcomb Papers, Marine Corps University Research Archives.

163. Accounts differ on the circumstances under which Inouye gave his orders.

164. Tedd Thomey, *Immortal Images: A Personal History of Two Photographers and the Flag Raising on Iwo Jima* (Annapolis, Md.: Naval Institute Press, 1996), 134–38.

165. Carl William Proehl, *The Fourth Marine Division in World War II* (Washington, D.C.: Infantry Journal Press, 1947), 159.

166. George W. Nations, "Iwo Jima: One Man Remembers," May 1985, Iwo Jima folders, Historical Reference Section, Marine Corps Historical Center.

167. Bartley, *Iwo Jima*, 221.

168. Heinl, "Dark Horse on Iwo," 3.

169. Jones, "To the Finish," 53.

170. Erskine, oral history transcript (1975), 359, Headquarters U.S. Marine Corps, History and Museums Division.

171. Ibid., 360.

172. Unless stated otherwise, information concerning the last days of Kuribayashi comes from Yoshitaka Horie, "The Last Days of Kuribayashi," *Marine Corps Gazette* (February 1955), 39–43.

173. Hiroaki Sato, *Legends of the Samurai* (Woodstock, N.Y.: Overlook Press, 1995), xxxi.

174. Isely and Crowl, *U.S. Marines and Amphibious War*, 501.

175. After the war, Japanese officers explained Kuribayashi's importance to the defense of Iwo Jima: "Finding himself in this painful position [fighting a superior force in terms of numbers and equipment and with no support from home] he often had thoughts of evading his responsibilities and

affection toward his troops by making a suicidal all-out counter attack against superior forces, but evidently, he came to the conclusion that a premature 'banzai' charge would have no favorable bearing on Japan's general operation, especially on the preparations for the defense of the homeland, and so by continuing his delaying actions, he decided to take the maximum toll on the enemy. Besides he did not disclose anything in his reports to the Imp. Hq. pertaining to his difficulties and needs in carrying out the defensive operation. On the contrary, his reports were always filled with words expressing his anxieties about the preparations for the homeland defense. No suitable or sufficient words could be found to express our respect and admiration for him" (*Japanese Monograph 48*, 74).

176. James J. Ahern, "The Iwo Jima Campaign: 147th Infantry Regiment," Addendum, Military History Institute. Lieutenant Colonel Ahern (USA ret.) was a second lieutenant on Iwo Jima.

177. Toland, *Rising Sun*, 737.

178. Charles W. Tatum, *Iwo Jima: Red Blood, Black Sand, Pacific Apocalypse* (Charles W. Tatum Publishing, 1995).

179. For medical statistics see the surgeon's report in Fleet Marine Force Pacific 10/247, "Medical Report, Iwo Jima," 28 March 1945. Also see the medical plans leading up to the operation, Marine Corps University Research Archives.

180. The 5,000 available beds were used as a planning factor and remained the same though February. See Commander Amphibious Forces, U.S. Pacific Fleet, CTF 51, Operation Plan No. A25-44, "Medical Plan," 27 December 1944.

181. Jim Bishop, *FDR's Last Year: April 1944–April 1945* (New York: William Morrow, 1974), 479. For a more specific date, see Thomey, *Immortal Images*, 60.

182. Newcomb, *Iwo Jima*, 30–32.

183. "Flag on Iwo Jima," Appendix to the Congressional Record, 1945, A1039. Forrestal's entire 25 February address is transcribed.

184. "Organized Jap Resistance Ends with Capture of Kitano Point," *Washington Post*, 17 March 1945, 1.

185. C. W. Nimitz, "Communiqué No. 300," U.S. Pacific Fleet and Pacific Ocean Areas, Advance Headquarters Guam, 17 March 1945.

186. Isely and Crowl, *U.S. Marines and Amphibious War*, 499–500.

187. Nimitz, "Communiqué No. 300."

188. H. H. Arnold, *Global Mission* (New York: Harper & Brothers, 1949), 567.

189. H. H. Arnold, personal journal entry, 15 June 1945. Reprinted in Huston, *American Airpower Comes of Age*, 331. Also see Arnold, *Global Mission*, 567.

190. Bartley, *Iwo Jima*, 218–21.

191. Marine Forces Pacific 274/229, "G-2 Report on Iwo Jima Operation," 1 April 1945, 41, microfilm, U.S.M.C. *Operations Reports, 1941–45*, Nimitz Library.

192. Richard B. Frank, *Downfall: The End of the Imperial Japanese Empire* (New York: Random House, 1999), 140. Planners likely produced the figure of 25,000 from action reports of the 3d, 4th, and 5th Marine Divisions. However, U.S.

intelligence admitted that these estimates were excessive. For a more accurate tally, historians fashioned casualty estimations based upon the number of actual defenders. Since no intelligence estimates that I am aware of placed the number of Japanese defenders as high as 25,000, it seems illogical for that figure to be proposed.

193. Wheeler's popular history, *Road to Tokyo* (41), uses the 21,000 figure. Ross states that 22,000 defenders fought to the last man (Bill D. Ross, *Iwo Jima: Legacy of Valor* [New York: Vintage Books, 1985], xiii).

194. Bartley decided that the estimate of between 20,530 and 21,060 defenders was the most accurate. However, U.S. intelligence offered conflicting reports. The highest figure appears in a report released in April 1945—a total of 22,817 defenders. This document admitted that the numbers presented were not definitive, and Bartley appears to have ignored it. Due to the historian's expertise and proximity to events, I have chosen to rely on Bartley's judgment. For the April approximation, see Marine Forces Pacific 274/229, "G-2 Report on Iwo Jima Operation," 1 April 1945, 30, microfilm, *U.S.M.C. Operations Reports, 1941–45*, Nimitz Library.

195. Bartley, *Iwo Jima*, 193.

196. Headquarters 147th Infantry Regiment, "Report of Operations against the Enemy," Iwo Jima, 11 June 1945, 147th Independent Infantry Regiment Papers, Record Group 338.5, National Archives, College Park. The records of the 147th are detailed and reliable. They also contain numerous maps of cave installations.

197. I have chosen to use a single source for the battles for the purpose of comparison: Michael Clodfelter, *Warfare and Armed Conflicts: A Statistical Reference to Casualty and Other Figures, 1618–1991*, vol. 2, 1900–1991 (Jefferson, N.C.: McFarland, 1991). Most of these data derive from official casualty reports after the war and align with other studies. Due to the lack of Japanese records, historians consistently estimate Japanese fatalities. The number of Japanese dead on Iwo Jima that I provide is the average of the figure used in table 1. I did not include Iwo Jima's combat fatigue casualties because those on many other islands are not included. As campaigns became longer, increased cases of mental breakdowns occurred. Data not available in Clodfelter are identified with *N/A*.

198. John W. Dower, *Embracing Defeat: Japan in the Wake of World War II* (New York: W. W. Norton, 1999), 60. In addition to a dozen other awards, *Embracing Defeat* won a Pulitzer Prize in Letters (2000). For more information on the return of Japanese servicemen, see pp. 58–61.

199. Karal Ann Marling and John Wetenhall, *Iwo Jima: Monuments, Memories, and the American Hero* (Cambridge, Mass.: Harvard University Press, 1991), 223.

200. See Toland, *Rising Sun*, 737n. The information preceding the quote is only a slight modification of Toland's extensive footnote.

201. E. B. Sledge, *With the Old Breed at Peleliu and Okinawa* (Oxford: Oxford University Press, 1981), 147.

202. Ibid., 147.

203. From a rifleman's perspective, see Howard Baxter, oral interview transcribed in O'Donnell, *Into the Rising Sun*, 247–249.

204. Sledge, *With the Old Breed*, 74.

205. Fleet Marine Force Pacific 10/247, "Medical Report, Iwo Jima," 28 March 1945, microfilm, *U.S.M.C. Operations Reports, 1941–45*, Nimitz Library. Also see Bartley, *Iwo Jima*, 194.

206. Cates, oral history transcript (1973), 201, Marine Historical Center.

207. For an analysis of the Marine Corps view of combat fatigue on Okinawa, see Craig Cameron, *American Samurai: Myth Imagination, and the Conduct of Battle in the First Marine Division, 1941–1951* (Cambridge: Cambridge University Press, 1994), 157–65.

208. Bartley, *Iwo Jima*, 220.

209. Ernest J. King. "First Report to the Secretary of the Navy," 23 April 1944, reprinted in *U.S. Navy at War, 1941–1945: Official Reports to the Secretary of the Navy* (Washington, DC: U.S. Navy Department, 1946), 20.

210. King, *U.S. Navy at War, 1941–1945*, 221.

211. Fleet Marine Force Pacific 129/192, "Operations for the Capture, Occupation, and Defense of Iwo Jima," 27 March 1945, Enclosure E, microfilm, *U.S.M.C. Operations Reports, 1941–45*, Nimitz Library.

212. James Ware, "Combat Casualties: Strategic, Operational, and Tactical Implications," Individual Research Paper, Marine Corps University Library, 1990.

213. Cameron, *American Samurai*, 138.

214. See Table 2 in Cameron, *American Samurai*, 58.

Chapter 4

1. U.S. Fleet, messages from "South and Central Pacific," 5 March 1945, microform, *Map Room Files of President Roosevelt, 1939–1945;* XXI Bomber Command, Combat Staging Center, History: March–June, 1945, 14 August 1945, 1–10, Air Force Historical Research Agency. Parts of this chapter have been published previously; see Robert S. Burrell, "Breaking the Cycle of Iwo Jima Mythology: A Strategic Study of Operation Detachment," *Journal of Military History 68* (October 2004): 1143–86. A smaller article on the emergency landing theory has been accepted for publication in *U.S. Naval Institute Proceedings.*

2. "Seabees Rebuild Airstrip on Iwo under Fire of Japanese Snipers," *New York Times*, 28 February 1945.

3. XXI Bomber Command, Combat Staging Center, History: March–June, 1945, 14 August 1945, 1–10.

4. F. H. Barr, "Why It's Possible," 4 March 1945, Communiqué No. 428 to U.S. Marine Corps, William P. McCahill Papers, Marine Corps University Research Archives.

5. One copy of this photo is reproduced in Whitman S. Bartley, *Iwo Jima: Amphibious Epic* (Washington, D.C.: Headquarters U.S. Marine Corps, Historical Branch, 1954), 113.

6. Jones, "To the Finish," 52.

7. Bartley, *Iwo Jima*, 113.

8. Joint War Plans Committee 91/3, "Plans for Seizure of the Bonins," 12 August 1944, *Records of the Joint Chiefs of Staff: 1941–1945*. The first four objectives are stated verbatim on Enclosure A, 1. The last statement is paraphrased from page 37, stating that "an important object of the BONINS operation is to precipitate this decisive naval engagement." The plans to seize the Bonin Islands, eventually approved by the Joint Chiefs of Staff, were formulated before the battle of Leyte Gulf in October 1944 and continued to emphasize the need for a Mahanian-style final battle. For more information on Mahan and his ideas on seapower, see Alfred Thayer Mahan, *The Influence of Sea Power upon History, 1660–1783* (1890; rpt., Boston: Little, Brown, 1918); Alfred Thayer Mahan, *The Influence of Sea Power upon the French Revolution and Empire, 1793–1812*, vol. 1 (Boston: Little, Brown, 1892). See also Jon Tetsuro Sumida's study of Mahan, *Inventing Grand Strategy and Teaching Command: The Classic Works of Alfred Thayer Mahan Reconsidered* (Washington, D.C.: Woodrow Wilson Center Press; and Baltimore: Johns Hopkins University Press, 1997).

9. George C. Marshall, "Biennial Report of the Chief of Staff of the United States Army; 1 July 1943 to June 30, 1945; to the Secretary of War," 1 September 1945. Reprinted in *The War Reports* (New York: J. B. Lippincott, 1947), 239.

10. King, U.S. *Navy at War, 1941–1945*, 174.

11. Assistant Chief of Air Staff, "Iwo, B-29 Haven and Fighter Springboard," *Impact* (September–October 1945), 64.

12. Buell, *Quiet Warrior*, 307.

13. Hansell, *Strategic Air War against Japan*, 60.

14. Craven and Cate, *Army Air Forces in World War II*, Vol. 5, 586.

15. For a good example, see ibid., 586 and 598–99.

16. Justifications 1–5 can be found in Joint War Plans Committee 91/3, "Plans for Seizure of the Bonins," 12 August 1944, *Records of the Joint Chiefs of Staff: 1941–1945*. I am not sure when the sixth justification first became prominent, but Spruance gave this reason to his autobiographer, Thomas B. Buell, in 1974. I believe reasons 7 and 8 first appeared in the Army Air Forces September publication of *Impact*. Justifications based on emergency landings probably began soon after the capture of Iwo Jima or perhaps even during the battle itself. Several publications, including *Impact*, refer to emergency landings on Iwo Jima in September 1945, which is the date given in table 6.

17. Joint Chiefs of Staff 713/18, "Future Operations in the Pacific," 2 October 1944, *Records of the Joint Chiefs of Staff: 1941–1945*.

18. R. K. Turner, "Shipboard Briefing of Correspondents by ComPhibPac on Iwo Jima Operation," 16 February 1945, Turner Papers, Naval Historical Center.

19. John A. Russ, "VLR (Very Long Range)! VII Fighter Command Operations on Iwo Jima, April–August 1945," *Air Power History* 48 (Fall 2001): 21.

20. Harry C. Crim, "Dante Could Have Used Iwo as Model of Hell," *The Global*

Twentieth: An Anthology of the 20th Air Force in World War II, ed. Chester Marshall and others, vol. 3 (Memphis: Global Press, 1988), 366.

21. Russ, "VLR (Very Long Range)!" 20–22.

22. In one mission on 1 June, the VII Fighter Command lost 27 out of 54 planes due to a thunderstorm, or roughly one-fourth of the one hundred-odd fighters on Iwo Jima. Twenty-four of the pilots were never recovered. See Craven and Cate, *Army Air Forces in World War II, Vol. 5*, 641. Werrell gives a more comprehensive explanation of the VII Fighter Command's problems; see Werrell, *Blankets of Fire*, 183–86. The Japanese also had much difficulty reaching Iwo Jima when they encountered the tough weather conditions in the Nanpo Shoto. See Saiki, *Samurai!* ed. Caidin and Saito, 277–78.

23. Russ, "VLR (Very Long Range)!" 22. One Army Air Force magazine stated that ten missions were flown, but this source likely included the March training missions to Saipan. See Assistant Chief of Air Staff, "Iwo, B-29 Haven and Fighter Springboard," 69–71.

24. David C. Evans and Mark R. Peattie, *Kaigun: Strategy, Tactics, and Technology of the Imperial Japanese Navy, 1887–1941* (Annapolis, Md.: Naval Institute Press, 1997), 366.

25. Hansell, *Strategic Air War against Japan*, 36–37.

26. Ibid., 48.

27. LeMay and Yenne, *Superfortress*, 124.

28. Russ, "VLR (Very Long Range)!" 23–24.

29. Craven and Cate, *Army Air Forces in World War II, Vol. 5*, 635. Some in the VII Fighter Command have claimed much higher rates of success than most Army Air Force studies. It is true that fighter operations significantly improved when the weather cleared up in the summer of 1945. According to one recent study, the VII Fighter Command flew 51 missions, of which 41 were considered effective. The 4,172 sorties destroyed 1,062 aircraft, 254 surface vessels, 134 locomotives, 355 railroad cars, 246 buildings and hangars, 16 radio stations, 10 oil tanks, and 13 trucks. The VII Fighter Command lost 157 aircraft and 91 pilots. See Russ, "VLR (Very Long Range)!" 23–25. Following Craven and Cate in their sifting through Army Air Force reports (which often tend to exaggerate and are difficult to evaluate, especially as time passes), I have decided to rely on the numbers that the official Army Air Force history utilized for the sorties of April–June as most indicative of the VII Fighter Command's efforts.

30. Craven and Cate, *Army Air Forces in World War II, Vol. 5*, 635.

31. Werrell, *Blankets of Fire*, 187.

32. Ernest J. King, Conference at Casablanca, 14 January 1943. Reprinted in Hans-Adolf Jacobsen and Arthur L. Smith Jr., *World War II: Policy and Strategy, Selected Documents with Commentary* (Santa Barbara, Calif.: Clio Books, 1979), 247.

33. Combined Chiefs of Staff 676, "U.S. Progress Report on Pacific Operations," 12 September 1944. Reprinted in Jacobsen and Smith, *World War II: Policy and Strategy*, 294.

34. Joint Staff Planners 312, "Seizure of the Bonins," 30 October 1943, *Records of the Joint Chiefs of Staff: 1941–1945.*

35. Craven and Cate, *Army Air Forces in World War II*, Vol. 5, 581–82.

36. LeMay and Yenne, *Superfortress*, 108.

37. Report No. 7; *Japanese Monograph 51*, 4.

38. H. S. Hansell Jr., letter to Commanding General U.S. Army Air Forces from Commanding General Twentieth Air Force, 22 November 1944. Reprinted in Hansell, *Strategic Air War against Japan*, 132–33. For Japanese plans to attack the Marianas under full moon, see *Japanese Monograph 51*, 3.

39. Craven and Cate, *Army Air Forces in World War II*, Vol. 5, 586.

40. *Japanese Monograph 48*, 68–69.

41. Conner, *Spearhead*, 35–36.

42. Bartley, *Iwo Jima*, 16.

43. Landings on Iwo Jima accounted for only 8.5 percent of all Marianas-based missions. For total missions, see Hansell, *Strategic Air War against Japan*, 86.

44. LeMay stated that after the first big firebombing raids in March, the XXI Bomber Command lacked incendiaries to continue the "maximum effort." The Okinawa campaign further drained the command's resources for a continual bombardment of Japan. It was not until June that the XXI was able "to undertake a *sustained* strategic offensive against Japan" (LeMay and Yenne, *Superfortress*, 131; original emphasis).

45. Craven and Cate, *Army Air Forces in World War II, Vol. 5,* 597.

46. King, *U.S. Navy at War, 1941–1945,* 120–23.

47. Joint War Planning Committee 306/1, "Plan for the Seizure of Rota Island," 25 January 1945, *Records of the Joint Chiefs of Staff: 1941–1945.*

48. Raymond A. Spruance, Commander Fifth Fleet A16-3(2e), "Report of Iwo Jima Operation," 14 June 1945, microform, *U.S. Navy Action and Operational Reports from World War II: Pacific Theater.*

49. Buell, *Quiet Warrior*, 307.

50. Sakai, *Samurai!* ed. Caidin and Saito, 282.

51. Radar on Iwo Jima gave the Japanese about two hours' warning of incoming raids. Isely and Crowl, *U.S. Marines and Amphibious War*, 434.

52. Wheeler and others, *Bombers over Japan*, 137.

53. LeMay and Yenne, *Superfortress*, 95. Arnold stated that "they [the Navy] wanted control of all Superforts."

54. Data taken from Craven and Cate, *Army Air Forces in World War II, Vol. 5,* 606.

55. Wesley Frank Craven and James Lea Cate, *The Army Air Forces in World War II, Vol. 7: Services around the World* (Chicago: University of Chicago Press, 1958), 500.

56. VII Fighter Command on Iwo Jima, A Statistical Summary, Statistical Control Section, 1 September 1945, 70, Air Force Historical Research Agency.

57. King, *U.S. Navy at War, 1941–1945,* 129.

58. Bartley, *Iwo Jima*, 20.

59. The senior officer from Kuribayashi's command element left on Chichi Jima was Yoshitaka Horie, who later wrote several works on the Japanese defense

of the Bonin Islands. For more information, see Yoshitaka Horie, *Tokin Io Jima* (Tokyo: Kobunsha, 1965).

60. Yoshitaka Horie, "Japanese Defense Plans for Chichi Jima," *Marine Corps Gazette* (July 1953), 36–40. Again, some have portrayed Horie as a perpetual liar. Author Chester Hearn did so, and I have also read this in letters from Fred Saito to Richard Newcomb. See Hearn, *Sorties into Hell*, 29–40. Horie did become a "turncoat" for the United States after the war in a criminal trail regarding atrocities on Chichi Jima. His being a man with conflicting loyalties renders the motive behind his statements all the more questionable. However, Horie had intimate knowledge of Chichi Jima, as he was stationed there in a prominent position. He was a prolific writer in both the United States and Japan. Of all the written evidence I have seen, Horie's testimony on Chichi Jima's defenses, a topic on which he gave lectures on to U.S. officers following the war, seems the most credible.

61. Dyer, *Amphibians Came to Conquer*, 987.

62. Joint War Plans Committee 91/3, "Plan for the Seizure of the Bonins," 12 August 1944, 34, *Records of the Joint Chiefs of Staff: 1941–1945*.

63. Bureau of Yards and Docks, Office of the Chief of Naval Operations, "Joint Preliminary Study for Advanced Base Layout: Bonin Islands, Chichi Jima and Haha Jima," August 1944, Naval Historical Center.

64. For example, Pacific war historian Ronald Spector stated: "Japanese aircraft operating from that island [Iwo Jima] . . . could harass B-29s en route to Japan. To avoid the neighborhood of Iwo, the big bombers were obliged to fly a long dog-leg course which complicated navigation, consumed precious fuel, and reduced the bomb load they could carry" (Spector, *Eagle against the Sun*, 494).

65. Japanese naval air officer Mitsuo Fuchida explained how Iwo Jima fit its strategic purpose in Pacific operations in *God's Samurai: Lead Pilot at Pearl Harbor*, ed. Gordon W. Prange, Donald M. Goldstein, and Katherine V. Dillon (Washington, D.C.: Brassey's, 1990), 109–11.

66. Craven and Cate, *Army Air Forces in World War II, Vol. 5*, 559.

67. Report No. 7.

68. Craven and Cate, *Army Air Forces in World War II, Vol. 5*, 586.

69. William V. Pratt, "What Makes Iwo Jima Worth the Price," *Newsweek*, 2 April 1945, 36.

70. Commander Fifth Fleet to Commander in Chief, Pacific Ocean Areas, A16-3, "Iwo Jima and Okinawa—Air Craft Complements For," 7 March 1945, 1, Spruance Papers, Naval Historical Center.

71. "Motoyama Airfield No. 1," *Leatherneck* (June 1945); "Iwo Pays Off," *All Hands* (September 1945), 10; "P-51 Escort from Iwo," *Impact* (June 1945), 38.

72. Navy Department, Immediate Release, Press and Radio, "Barren Iwo Jima Played Part in Japanese Agriculture Economy," 28 May 1945, Naval Historical Center. The paper card index at Naval Historical Center has this document catalogued under the heading "Iwo Jima" with a description stating

that the island played a "vital role" in the Japanese economy. The document itself does not use the word vital, but the idea was explicit enough for the Naval Historical Center to pick up on it. Japan actually did use the island for some crops, but not to an extent that would warrant the inference that it played a valuable part in Japan's economy. Further, after the air raids in 1944, Iwo Jima certainly was not used for this purpose.

73. Assistant Chief of Air Staff, "Iwo, B-29 Haven and Fighter Springboard," 64. The Army Air Forces had been using this type of "emergency landing" reasoning for some time before September, from at least June 1945 onward, but September represented the latest and largest tally of landings, which is the number historians later adopted. The earliest Marine Corps monograph on Iwo Jima cites one Army Air Forces report from June that discusses 800 landings and uses the same logic of lives saved. Obviously, the Army Air Forces had been using this type of statistics and reasoning from the first B-29 touchdown in March 1945 onward. See Clifford Phelps Morehouse, *The Iwo Jima Operation* (Washington, D.C.: Headquarters, U.S. Marine Corps, 1946[?]).

74. Isely and Crowl, *U.S. Marines and Amphibious War,* 529.

75. Spector, *Eagle against the Sun,* 502.

76. Ross, *Iwo Jima,* xiv.

77. For one recent example, see Michael C. Howard, "Operation Detachment: The Supreme Test at Iwo Jima," *Marine Corps Gazette* (February 1995), 59.

78. Office of the Adjutant General, Statistical and Accounting Branch, *Army Battle Casualties and Nonbattle Deaths in World War II: Final Report, 7 December 1941–31 December 1946,* 93.

79. The number 24,761 divided by 2,148 equals 11.5.

80. H. H. Arnold, "Third Report of the Commanding General of the Army Air Forces: November 12, 1945 to the Secretary of War." Reprinted in *War Reports,* 444. Also see 33rd Statistical Control Unit, Twentieth Air Force, "Analysis of B-29 Losses to Enemy Action: March–15 July," 7 August 1945, Air Force Historical Research Agency.

81. The suggested number of B-29s (2,251) divided by the actual number lost (218) equals 10.33.

82. Although the emergency landing theory claims that Iwo Jima saved 2,251 Superforts, there were 2,242 B-29s of all varieties at the end of the war. Le-May and Yenne, *Superfortress,* 163.

83. Ibid., 149–50. Also see Craven and Cate, *Army Air Forces in World War II, Vol. 5,* 708.

84. Multiplying the 48 Superforts in the 509th by 5.5 equals 264 landings.

85. Toland, *Rising Sun,* 627.

86. Arnold, "Third Report of the Commanding General of the Army Air Forces," 443. Also see Craven and Cate, *Army Air Forces in World War II, Vol. 5,* 673.

87. Craven and Cate, *Army Air Forces in World War II, Vol. 5,* 598.

88. Ibid., 599.

89. Ibid., 598.

90. Twentieth Air Force, "Operational Engineering and Maintenance Sections—20th Air Force: Narrative History, Document 117," September 1945[?], Air Force Historical Research Agency.

91. William F. Halsey, "Future National Policy for the Composition, Command, Training, and Maintenance of the U.S. Armed Forces," U.S. Pacific Fleet, Third Fleet, 10 December 1944, microform, *Official Papers of Fleet Admiral Ernest J. King.* Also see official correspondence from Ernest J. King to James Forrestal. Chief of Naval Operations FF1/A16-3, "The United States Navy (Postwar)—Basis for Preparation of Plans," 3 March 1945, 1–4.

92. Barney M. Giles, "Post War Air Force," Headquarters of the Army Air Forces, Washington, D.C., 12 December 1943, Central Decimal Files, Record Group 338.4.2, National Archives.

93. H. H. Arnold, Commanding General, Twentieth Air Force, official correspondence to H. S. Hansell, Commanding General, 21st Bomber Command, 22 September 1944. Found on microfilm in Hansell's papers at Air Force Historical Research Agency.

94. Twentieth Air Force, "Operational Engineering and Maintenance Sections—20th Air Force: Narrative History, Document 117," September 1945[?], Air Force Historical Research Agency.

95. Data taken from LeMay and Yenne, *Superfortress,* 191.

96. Actual number is .0209. For the number of B-29s that landed on Iwo Jima, see Bartley, *Iwo Jima,* 113. Bartley's number contradicts a historical monograph at Air Force Historical Research Agency that indicated 65 landings in the same period; see XXI Bomber Command, Combat Staging Center, History: March—June, 1945, 14 August 1945, 3. Bartley's precise history offers the most authoritative account.

97. CG U.S. Army Forces Pacific Ocean Areas, Incoming Classified Message to War Department, 15 March 1945; microform, *Map Room Files of President Roosevelt, 1939–1945.* Disparity between landing on 14 March and the table indicating a flight on 13 March had to do with the length of the mission, which crossed into the next day.

98. CTF 93 to CTF 93.2, secret communiqué, 13 March 1945, incoming telecons to the Twentieth Air Force, Air Force Historical Research Agency.

99. Ibid.

100. U.S. Fleet, messages from "South and Central Pacific," 18 March 1945; microform, *Map Room Files of President Roosevelt, 1939-1945.* Also see the description on the back of a picture taken of the B-29s (Marine Corps University Research Archives, box 5, folder 12/5, picture 236). The description reads "Forced Down—Strong headwinds forced these B-29 Superfortresses to put down on Motoyama Airfield Number Two for refueling after a raid on Kobe, Japan. Eighteen of the ships landed for additional gas before continuing on to their base in the Marianas." The number on the fleet message indicated 16, not 18, bombers. Of the two, the message holds greater credibility on the issue of numbers, but both describe the same event.

101. Data taken from LeMay and Yenne, *Superfortress*, 191–202.

102. The number 21,371 multiplied by .0209 equals 446.65. The rounded number of 447 is too large considering that Japan's ability to defend itself against air attack was decreasing during the period. More important, the performance of B-29s with regard to engine malfunction greatly improved during the course of the war. For example, 167 airmen were forced into the Pacific in March out of 2,196 missions. In July, the number dropped to 120 even though the number of missions had more than doubled (5,755). For downed airmen, see Craven and Cate, *Army Air Forces in World War II, Vol. 5*, 598–607. For total sorties, see LeMay and Yenne, *Superfortress*, 191–201. In the Iwo Jima folders of the Marine Corps Historical Reference Section, Marine Corps Historical Center, there is a document submitted by Robert C. Hagopian, who claims to have worked as an Army Air Forces officer in the Statistical Control Center of the 20th Air Force. He submitted a copy of a document, with no date, that includes a statistical summary of combat operations at Iwo Jima from 4 March to 15 August 1945. The document states that 3,055 B-29s landed on Iwo Jima and 3,027 took off; 2,506 (81 percent) landed for refueling; 576 (18 percent) landed for maintenance; and 10 (1 percent) landed for other reasons. None of the pages has an official letterhead, address, or date. The cover page has a cartoon drawing of a B-29 with "Headquarters, Twentieth Air Force Combat Staging Center" in either pen or pencil. Cartoons are actually common on official Army Air Forces documents. I have no way to verify this copy's authenticity, yet some of the statistical breakdowns prove intriguing. The document does not mention landings due to training missions. I would assume that the 2,506 mentioned as having landed for refueling includes all planned landings as well as unplanned refueling touchdowns. That would leave 576 landings for maintenance reasons, of which the majority were minor repairs.

103. Twentieth Air Force, "A Brief Summary of B-29 Strategic Air Operation: 5 June 1944–14 August 1945" (n.d.), 52, Air Force Historical Research Agency.

104. Fleet Marine Force Pacific, "Action Report: Seizure, Occupation, and Defense of Iwo Jima (19 February 1945–16 March 1945)," 1 April 1945, 2.

105. Carl von Clausewitz, *The Book on War* (New York: Modern Library, 2000), 264.

106. Halsey, "Future National Policy for the Composition, Command, Training, and Maintenance of the U.S. Armed Forces."

107. Joint Chiefs of Staff 1275, "Unconditional Surrender of Japan," 15 February 1945, Appendix B, 1, *Records of the Joint Chiefs of Staff: 1941–1945*.

108. Yoshitaka Horie, "Explanation of the Defense Plan and Battle of Iwo Jima," 25 January 1946, i.

109. The Japanese first used this type of inland static defense at Peleliu in 1944, but many in the Japanese Army and Navy remained unconvinced that beach defenses should be abandoned. The effective defense of Iwo Jima certainly solidified acceptance of the new doctrine.

110. U.S. Pacific Fleet and Pacific Ocean Areas, "Defense Installations on Iwo Jima," CINCPAC–CINCPOA Bulletin No. 136-45, 10 June 1945, 4.

111. For more information on the battle for Okinawa, see Gerald Astor, *Operation Iceberg: The Invasion and Conquest of Okinawa in World War II—An Oral History* (New York: Donald I. Fine, 1995); or Robert Leckie, *Okinawa: The Last Battle of World War II* (New York: Penguin Books, 1995.)

112. Dower, *War without Mercy,* 92.

113. "Rodent Exterminator," *Time,* 19 March 1945, 32.

114. Dower, *War without Mercy,* 57.

115. Sherry, *Rise of American Air Power.*

116. Lewis Meyers, "Japanese Civilians in Combat Zones," *Marine Corps Gazette* (February 1945), 11–17.

117. Searle, "'It Made a Lot of Sense to Kill Skilled Workers,'" 121.

118. Hall, ed., *Case Studies in Strategic Bombardment,* 321.

119. G. Scott Gorman, "Endgame in the Pacific," in *Fairchild Paper* (Maxwell AFB: Air University Press, 1963), 57.

120. Akabane Yutaka, as quoted in Dan Van der Vat, *The Pacific Campaign: World War II, the U.S.–Japanese Naval War, 1941–1945* (New York: Simon & Schuster, 1991), 373.

121. Ito, *Teikoku Rikugun No Saigo,* 4.

122. Fourteenth Naval District, District Intelligence Office, "Digest of Japanese Broadcasts for 22 March 1945," 29 March 1945, 2, Naval Historical Center.

123. Propaganda Analysis Division, News and Intelligence Bureau, "Japanese Propaganda," 22 March 1945, 2, Naval Historical Center.

124. Fuutaro Yamada, *Senchu Ha Fusen Nikki: A Diary of Wartime Younger Generation Who Did Not Fight* (Tokyo: Kodansha, 1985), 96. This excerpt was translated by Ken-ichi Arakawa at the Japanese National Defense Academy, 11 August 2003.

125. Dower, *War without Mercy,* 248–49.

126. Fourteenth Naval District, District Intelligence Office, "Digest of Japanese Broadcasts for 21 March 1945," 23 March 1945, 1–2, Naval Historical Center.

127. Frank, *Downfall,* 84.

128. Jon T. Hoffman, "The Legacy and Lessons of Iwo Jima," *Marine Corps Gazette* (February 1995), 77.

129. Lee Sandlin, "Are We Finally Losing the War?" *Chicago Reader* (7 and 14 March 1997). This citation comes from a combined manuscript, page 30 of 42 in a printed digital copy.

130. Bradley, *Flyboys,* 77–78, 141–43.

131. Russell F. Weigley, "How Americans Wage War: The Evolution of National Strategy," in *Major Problems in American Military History: Documents and Essays,* ed. John Whitclay Chambers and G. Kurt Piehler (Boston: Houghton Mifflin, 1999), 1–6.

132. Commenting on the death of the president, Leahy stated: "This world tragedy deprives the Nation of its leader at a time when the war to preserve civilization is approaching its end with accelerated speed, and when a vital need for competent leadership in the making and preservation of the world peace

is at least seriously prejudiced by the passing of Franklin Roosevelt who was a world figure of heroic proportions" (William Leahy, personal journal entry, 12 April 1945, microform, *Admiral Leahy's Diaries, 1893, 1897–1956: Naval Career Only,* from his papers in the Manuscript Division (Library of Congress, Photoduplication Service, 1977), Nimitz Library, U.S. Naval Academy).

133. Hanson W. Baldwin, "This Is the Army to Defeat," *New York Times,* 29 July 1945, 37. Baldwin argued that "the defense of Iwo Jima and Okinawa . . . showed far more tactical skill and appreciation of defensive needs than any previous Japanese operations in the Pacific."

134. Ibid., 38.

135. Henry L. Stimson, diary entry of 24 July 1945, in *The Henry Lewis Stimson Diaries in the Yale University Library* (New Haven: Yale University Photographic Service, 1973).

136. For the minutes of the meeting between the president and the Joint Chiefs of Staff that took place on 18 June 1945, see Joint Chiefs of Staff 1388/1, "Details of the Campaign against Japan," 20 June 1945, *Records of the Joint Chiefs of Staff: 1941–1945.* Index heading is reel 2, frame 0274, Proposed Changes to Details of the Campaign against Japan, CINCUSF/CNO (20 June 1945), 10f.

137. Joint Chiefs of Staff 1388/4, "Details of the Campaign against Japan," 11 July 1945, *Records of the Joint Chiefs of Staff: 1941–1945.* Index heading is reel 2, frame 0288, Details of the Campaign against Japan, JPS (11 July 1945), 32f.

138. William Leahy, personal journal entry, 18 June 1945, microform, *Admiral Leahy's Diaries, 1893, 1897–1956: Naval Career Only, Leahy Papers, Manuscript Division* (Library of Congress, Photoduplication Service, 1977), Nimitz Library.

139. King's summary of U.S. submarine operations can be found in his *Official Reports to the Secretary of the Navy.*

140. Frank, *Downfall,* 350–56.

141. David McCullough, *Truman* (New York: Simon & Schuster, 1992), 441. Gas was also considered on Iwo Jima; see Gerald C. Thomas, oral history transcript (Washington, D.C.: Headquarters U.S. Marine Corps, Historical Division, 1973), 637.

142. Frank, *Downfall,* 144–47. For a detailed analysis of the casualty estimates for the invasion of Japan, see D. M. Giangreco, "'A Score of Bloody Okinawas and Iwo Jimas': President Truman and Casualty Estimates for the Invasion of Japan," *Pacific Historical Review* 72 (February 2003): 93–132.

143. Frank, *Downfall,* 145.

144. Ibid., 146.

145. Table 6 gives the original figures and language in Joint Chiefs of Staff 1388/4, "Details of the Campaign against Japan," 11 July 1945, *Records of the Joint Chiefs of Staff: 1941–1945.* The joint staff planners recommended that these figures be shown to the president.

146. Fleet Marine Forces Pacific, "Report of the ACofS, G-2, Expeditionary Troops, Task Force 56, on Iwo Jima Operation," 1 April 1945, 17–30,

microfilm, *U.S.M.C. Operations Reports, 1941–45* (Washington, D.C.: U.S. Navy Department. 1947), Nimitz Library.

147. Task Force 56, "G-2 Report, No. 16," 6 March 1945, 3, microfilm, *U.S.M.C. Operations Reports, 1941–45.*

148. Joint Chiefs of Staff 1388/1, "Details of the Campaign against Japan," 20 June 1945, *Records of the Joint Chiefs of Staff: 1941–1945.*

149. Frank, *Downfall,* 144–47.

150. Gorman, "Endgame in the Pacific,"14.

151. Dower, *War without Mercy,* 11.

152. Sandlin, "Are We Finally Losing the War?"

153. Ibid.

154. Toland, *Rising Sun,* 799.

155. John N. Stone, Memorandum to General Henry Arnold, "Groves Project," dated 24 July 1945. Found in *Documentary History of the Truman Presidency,* ed. Dennis Merril, vol. 1 (Lanham, Md.: University Press of America, 1995), 152. Truman argued that he hit the targets in the priority of their military value rather than the population levels. See Harry S. Truman, *Memoirs by Harry S. Truman: Vol. 1, Year of Decisions* (Garden City, N.Y.: Doubleday, 1955), 419–20.

Chapter 5

1. To argue the battle necessary or not requires a degree of perspective. In the early twenty-first century, the government placed unprecedented value on limiting casualties. In today's military, casualties are the number-one planning factor. This was not the case in 1945, when casualties were one of many concerns. One could possibly argue that improving Superfortress performance was worth the 28,000 American dead and wounded. But, even by 1945 standards, that line of reasoning would likely not have proven persuasive. Otherwise, it might have surfaced previously and precluded the need for misleading statistics.

2. Frank O. Hough, *The Island War: The United States Marine Corps in the Pacific* (New York: J. B. Lippincott, 1947), ix. Hough's investigation of the necessity of the battle of Iwo Jima typifies conventional studies. He referred to Iwo Jima as "the inevitable island" and argued that the battle "was bound to happen."

3. C. W. Nimitz, "Communiqué No. 300," U.S. Pacific Fleet and Pacific Ocean Areas, Advance Headquarters Guam, 17 March 1945.

Chapter 6

1. Accounts of the first flag-raising can be found in, but are not limited to, the following works: "Iwo: The Red Hot Rock," *Collier's,* 14 April 1945; Richard Wheeler, "The First Flag Raising on Iwo Jima," *American Heritage, June 1962,* 104–5; *History of the Iwo Jima Flag Raising, Biographies of the Flag Raisers,* Marine

Corps Historical Reference Series No. 14: (Washington, D.C.: Headquarters U.S. Marine Corps, Historical Branch, 1959); Robert L. Sherrod, "Another View of the Flag Raisings," *Fortitudine* 10 (1980–81): 7–10; Joseph H. Alexander, *Closing In: Marines in the Seizure of Iwo Jima* (Washington, D.C.: Headquarters U.S. Marine Corps, Historical Division, 1994); Bernard C. Nalty and Danny J. Crawford, *The United States Marines on Iwo Jima: The Battle and the Flag Raisings* (Washington, D.C.: Headquarters U.S. Marine Corps, History and Museums Division, 1995). See also Tom Bartlett, "Charles W. Lindberg: Atop Suribachi Again," *Leatherneck* (July 1995), 16–19; Norm Hatch, "Two Flags," *Leatherneck* (February 1995), 24–29; interview with Charles Lindberg in "Iwo Jima's Final Flag Raiser," in *Uncommon Valor: 50th Anniversary of the Battle of Iwo Jima* (Tampa, Fla.: Faircount International, 1995), 19–32; Robert Hugh Williams, "Up the Rock on Iwo the Hard Way," *Marine Corps Gazette* (August 1945), 26–28; "The Famous Iwo Flag-Raising," *Life*, 26 March 1945, 17–18; J. Campbell Bruce, "The Picture That Thrilled the Nation," *Readers Digest* (February 1955), 87; James Bradley, *Flags of Our Fathers* (New York: Bantam Books, 2000); "Shot of a Lifetime," *San Francisco Chronicle*, 19 February 1995. Karal Ann Marling and John Wetenhall, *Iwo Jima: Monuments, Memories, and the American Hero*, present the story most accurately. I have generally relied on their analysis to describe the first flag-raising.

2. Marling and Wetenhall, *Iwo Jima: Monuments, Memories, and the American Hero*, 43.
3. Williams, "Up the Rock on Iwo the Hard Way," 28.
4. Interview with Charles Lindberg in "Iwo Jima's Final Flag Raiser," 25.
5. Nalty and Crawford, *United States Marines on Iwo Jima*, 5.
6. Williams, "Up the Rock on Iwo the Hard Way," 28.
7. Marling and Wetenhall, *Iwo Jima: Monuments, Memories, and the American Hero*, 48.
8. "The Famous Iwo Flag-Raising," 17–18; Marling and Wetenhall, *Iwo Jima: Monuments, Memories, and the American Hero*, 52.
9. Richard E. Franklin, "On Suribachi's Peak," 10 March 1945, Iwo Jima Papers, Marine Corps Historical Center.
10. Marling and Wetenhall, *Iwo Jima: Monuments, Memories, and the American Hero*, 52.
11. "Shot of a Lifetime"; Marling and Wetenhall, *Iwo Jima: Monuments, Memories, and the American Hero*, 65.
12. John Bradley, "Flag Raised on Mt. Suribachi" (interview by Captain Wright, 15 May 1945), 2, Naval Historical Center.
13. For a personal description of the event, see "Hayes Left Own Account of Historic Flag Raising," *Knoxville News–Sentinel*, 28 January 1955.
14. Bradley, "Flag Raised on Mt. Suribachi" (interview by Captain Wright, 15 May 1945), 3.
15. Joe Rosenthal, and W. C. Heinz, "The Picture That Will Live Forever," *Collier's*, 18 February 1955, 62–66.
16. Parker Bishop Albee Jr. and Keller Cushing Freeman, *Shadow of Suribachi: Raising the Flags on Iwo Jima* (Westport, Conn.: Praeger, 1995), 72.

17. Words taken from the introduction of his Pulitzer prize awarded at Columbia University in May. See Bradley, *Flags of Our Fathers*, 285. Staff Sgt. Lou Lowery's pictures of the journey up Suribachi and the first flag-raising, which had inspired American fighters at Iwo Jima, received scant attention in comparison to Rosenthal's. Initially, the press confused Rosenthal's picture with the first flag-raising. But as the picture gained popularity, some have suggested that the commandant of the Marine Corps, Gen. Alexander A. Vandegrift, made a policy decision to perpetuate that myth for two and a half years. Although the public had access to the first flag-raising pictures, and *Life* magazine printed them in March 1945, the Marine Corps did not publish the photos that Lowery had taken of Operation Detachment's most inspirational moment until 1947. Thomey, *Immortal Images*, 147.

18. Bruce, "Picture That Thrilled the Nation," 87.

19. "Masterpiece," *New Yorker*, 7 April 1945, 17.

20. Shirley Povich, "How Photographer Made Flag Picture: Epic Photo of Marines Raising Ensign Likely to Adorn Calendars for Years," *Washington Post*, 13 March 1945; "Shot of a Lifetime."

21. Bruce, "Picture That Thrilled the Nation," 87.

22. Ibid.

23. Associated Press gave all proceeds from the photo to the Navy Relief Society.

24. " . . . Sincerest Flattery," *Newsweek*, 16 April 1945, 82; "Masterpiece," 17–18.

25. "The Flag on Mount Suribachi," appendix to the Congressional Record, 1945, A1061–62.

26. Bradley, *Flags of Our Fathers*, 266.

27. Ibid., 268.

28. Albee and Freeman, *Shadow of Suribachi*, 96.

29. The six flag-raisers were John Bradley, Franklin Sousley, Harlon Block, Ira Hayes, Rene Gagnon, and Mike Strank. Initially, Block had been misidentified as another dead Marine named Hansen. Although both Hayes and Gagnon told officials that Block was the Marine in the picture, they were told to keep quiet about it.

30. Bradley, *Flags of Our Fathers*, 218.

31. William Bradford Huie, *The Hero of Iwo Jima* (New York: Signet Books, 1962), 10. One of the Hayes brothers, Dean, won his silver star in Korea.

32. Huie, *Hero of Iwo Jima*, 14.

33. Ira Hayes, letter to mother, Nancy Hayes, 29 August 1942, in Huie, *Hero of Iwo Jima*, 14–15.

34. Huie, *Hero of Iwo Jima*, 16.

35. Albert Hemmingway, *Ira Hayes: Pima Marine* (Lanham, Md.: University Press of America, 1988), 1–41.

36. Gerald C. Thomas, oral history transcript (Washington, D.C.: Headquarters Marine Corps, Historical Division, 1973), 540–43.

37. According to one author, "Hayes watched his buddies hacksaw gold teeth from Japanese heads. He saw them hang heads out to 'dry' and be cleaned by tropical insects, then display skulls from tent poles." Huie, *Hero of Iwo Jima*, 26.

38. Hemmingway, *Ira Hayes*, 111.

39. Huie, *Hero of Iwo Jima*, 35.

40. Ibid., 28.

41. Ibid., 35.

42. Bradley, *Flags of Our Fathers*, 185.

43. Ibid., 269.

44. Ibid., 275.

45. Ibid., 275, 297–301, 311; Marling and Wetenhall, *Iwo Jima: Monuments, Memories, and the American Hero*, 111.

46. James Bradley does an outstanding job telling this story. Bradley, *Flags of Our Fathers*, 309–11.

47. "This Week's Work," *Collier's*, 12 May 1945, 74.

48. Marling and Wetenhall, *Iwo Jima: Monuments, Memories, and the American Hero*, 104.

49. Ibid., 104.

50. "Famous War Picture Inspires War Bond Insignia," *New York Times*, 25 March 1945.

51. Bob Ashley, "A Tale of Two Flags," in *Uncommon Valor*, 91.

52. "Famous War Picture Inspires War Bond Insignia."

53. Ibid.

54. "Now It's Our Turn," *Newsweek*, April 1945.

55. "Senate Honors Three Who Helped Raise Iwo Flag," *Washington Post*, 21 April 1945. Also see *Congressional Record*, 20 April 1945, 3611.

56. Harry S. Truman, *Memoirs by Harry S. Truman, Vol. 1: Year of Decisions* (Garden City, N.Y.: Doubleday, 1955), 67.

57. "President Receives War Loan Painting," *Washington Post*, 21 April 1945.

58. Albee and Freeman, *Shadow of Suribachi*, 108.

59. Marling and Wetenhall, *Iwo Jima: Monuments, Memories, and the American Hero*, 102.

60. Huie, *Hero of Iwo Jima*, 35.

61. Ibid., 36.

62. "Iwo Heroes Raise Famed Iwo Flag from Suribachi over Capitol," *Washington Post*, 10 May 1945; Marling and Wetenhall, *Iwo Jima: Monuments, Memories, and the American Hero*, 111.

63. "Statue to Stand in Times Square for War Loan Drive," *New York Times*, 27 April 1945; Marling and Wetenhall, *Iwo Jima: Monuments, Memories, and the American Hero*, 114–15.

64. Bradley, *Flags of Our Fathers*, 285.

65. Huie, *Hero of Iwo Jima*, 38.

66. Marling and Wetenhall, *Iwo Jima: Monuments, Memories, and the American Hero*, 114.

67. "Marine Corps War Memorial Sculptor Dies," *Marine Corps Gazette* (July 2003), 6.

68. The preceding dialogue is taken almost verbatim from Huie, *Hero of Iwo Jima*, 41.

69. "Suribachi to Skid Row," *Newsweek*, 26 October 1953, 44.
70. Ibid.
71. Laurence M. Olney, *The War Bond Story*, (Washington, D.C.: Government Printing Office, 4 August 1975), 93, Library of Congress.
72. Bradley, *Flags of Our Fathers*, 281.
73. Olney, "War Bond Story," 96.
74. "For a United People," *Time*, 28 May 1945, 14.
75. For greater detail on the unification struggle, see chapter 7.
76. "The Flag above Iwo Jima," *Oregonian*, 3 March 1945.
77. Ibid.
78. "Reports of Committees on Public Bills and Resolutions," *Congressional Record*, 1 March 1945, 2079; "Monument Based on Flag Photo Asked Congress," *Washington Post*, 2 March 1945.
79. "Planting the Flag on Iwo Jima," appendix to *Congressional Record*, 1945, A929.
80. "Proposed Memorial to Marine Corps and Capture of Iwo Jima," *Congressional Record*, 13 March 1945, 2077.
81. Marling and Wetenhall, *Iwo Jima: Monuments, Memories, and the American Hero*, 88.
82. "Proposed Memorial to Marine Corps and Capture of Iwo Jima," *Congressional Record*, 13 March 1945, 2077.
83. "The Marines' Island: Iwo Jima," *Congressional Record*, 15 March 1945, 2273.
84. "National Marine Corps Day," appendix to *Congressional Record*, 1945, A2067.
85. "Special Stamp Commemorating Valor of United States Marines on Iwo Jima," appendix to *Congressional Record*, 1945, A1133; "Flag Raising Stamp," *Washington Star*, 12 March 1945; James Waldo Fawcett, "Stamps," *Washington Sunday Star*, 11 March 1945.
86. Press releases from Information Service, Post Office Department, 11 and 18 July 1945, Vandegrift Papers, Marine Corps University Research Archives.
87. Win Brooks, "Marines on Iwo Jima," *Boston Evening American* (clipping, March 1945?), Holland M. Smith Papers, Marine Corps University Research Archives.
88. "Report from Iwo," appendix to *Congressional Record*, 1945, A4040 (entered on 25 September 1945).
89. "Iwo Jima," appendix to *Congressional Record*, 1945, A2627.
90. " . . . Sincerest Flattery," 82.
91. Photo in Marling and Wetenhall, *Iwo Jima: Monuments, Memories, and the American Hero*, 110.
92. Jane Blakeney, *Heroes: The U.S. Marine Corps, 1861–1955: Armed Forces Awards, Flags, Reference Book* (Washington, D.C.: Guthrie Lithograph, 1957), 563.
93. Thomey, *Immortal Images*, 46.
94. Blakeney, *Heroes*, 563–64.
95. Ibid., 564.
96. Ibid., 563. Five Medals of Honor were awarded to Navy personnel.
97. Ibid., 94–245.

98. A. A. Vandegrift, "My Presence Could Have Yielded Little," in *United States Marine Corps in World War II*, ed. S. E. Smith (New York: Random House, 1969), 834.

99. "Address at Dedication of Fifth Marine Division Cemetery on Iwo Jima," appendix to *Congressional Record*, 1945, A4782.

100. *The Marines at Tarawa and To the Shores of Iwo Jima*, video recording, U.S. Navy, Office of War Information, distributed by United American Video Corp., 1991.

101. *To the Shores of Iwo Jima*, Publicity Bureau, Depot of Supplies, USMC, Philadelphia, 15 May 1945. Although Rosenthal received great credit and even a Pulitzer Prize for his photograph, the man who filmed the second flag-raising from almost the exact same angle, Sgt. Bill Genaust, died in obscurity on Iwo Jima. Of the varying accounts of his death, it appears most probable that Genaust and a fellow Marine tried to escape the rain by entering a cave, but it had not been sufficiently cleared of the enemy. Thomey, *Immortal Images*, 48, 117–23.

102. Bradley, *Flags of Our Fathers*, 282.

Chapter 7

1. Michael Kernan, " . . . Heavy Fire . . . Unable to Land . . . Issue in Doubt," Smithsonian (November 1993), 118; Steinberg et al., *Island Fighting*, 112.

2. Parts of this chapter have been previously published in "'Issue in Doubt': The Unification Crisis," in *Crucibles: Selected Readings in U.S. Marine Corps History*, 2d ed., ed. Robert S. Burrell (Bell Air, Md.: Academic Publishing Services, 2004).

3. H.R. 465, "Public Bills and Resolutions," *Congressional Record*, 9 March 1944, 2398.

4. "Committee on Post-War Military Policy," *Congressional Record*, 24 March 1944, 3250.

5. Demetrios Caraley, *The Politics of Military Unification: A Study of Conflict and the Policy Process* (New York: Columbia University Press, 1966), 28.

6. H.R. Report No. 1356, "Postwar Military Policy," 10 December 1945. Also see "Reports of Committees on the Public Bills and Resolutions," *Congressional Record*, 15 June 1944 and 27 November 1944.

7. "For Army-Navy Merger," *St. Louis Post-Dispatch*, 22 July 1945.

8. Some Marine Corps proponents have argued that questions about the need for the Marines derive from professional jealousies. For one such essay, see Robert D. Heinl Jr., "The Cat with More Than Nine Lives," in *Crucibles*, ed. Burrell, 21–42.

9. Caraley, *Politics of Military Unification*, 66–69.

10. Harry S. Truman, "Our Armed Forces Must Be United," *Collier's*, 26 August 1944, 16, 63–64.

11. Harold D. Smith, diary entry, "White House Conference on the Postwar Navy," 14 September 1945. Found in Truman Papers. See *Documentary History*

of the Truman Presidency, ed. Dennis Merrill, vol. 10 (Lanham, Md.: University Press of America, 1996).

12. Harry S. Truman, "Special Message to the Congress Recommending the Establishment of a Department of National Defense," *Congressional Record,* 19 December 1945.

13. James Forrestal, Secretary of the Navy, official correspondence to David Walsh, Chairman of the Committee on Naval Affairs, 27 May 1945, in *Documentary History of the Truman Presidency,* vol. 10.

14. James Forrestal, Secretary of the Navy, official correspondence to David Walsh, Chairman of the Committee on Naval Affairs, 18 October 1945, in *Documentary History of the Truman Presidency,* vol 10.

15. "Unification Neurosis," *San Francisco Chronicle,* 1 December 1945.

16. Millett, *Semper Fidelis,* 458.

17. Ibid.

18. John Cowles, "We Must Unify Our Armed Forces," appendix to *Congressional Record,* 1945, A5464–65.

19. "Merger of the Army, Air Corps, and Navy," appendix to *Congressional Record,* 1945, A5594. Transcribed from article with the same title in *Collier's,* 22 December 1945.

20. Ibid.

21. Joseph and Stewart Alsop, "No Defense Plan," *Washington Post,* 30 January 1946.

22. "Unification of the Armed Forces," appendix to *Congressional Record,* 1946, A232.

23. Walter C. Ploeser, Representative, to Harry S. Truman, President of the United States, official correspondence, 11 January 1946, copy found in appendix to *Congressional Record,* 1946, A113.

24. Ibid.

25. Donald L. O'Toole, remarks in the House of Representatives, 17 April 1946, "Unification of the Armed Services," appendix to *Congressional Record,* 1946, A2226.

26. "The Merger Issue," Naval Affairs (February 1946), also transcribed in appendix to *Congressional Record,* 1946, A718.

27. George Fielding Eliot, "Major Eliot Doubts Benefits of Unification," *Seapower* (February 1946), 4, 30; Ralph A. Bard, "A Plan to Protect the Peace," *Seapower* (February 1946), 3; "One Department or Three Departments," *Naval Affairs* (March 1946), also transcribed in appendix to *Congressional Record,* 1946, A1142.

28. Eliot, "Major Eliot Doubts Benefits of Unification," 3.

29. A.A. Vandegrift, address on the anniversary of Iwo Jima, 19 February 1946, Vandegrift Papers, Marine Corps University Research Archives.

30. "New Factor in Unification," *Sun* (12 April 1946?), transcribed in appendix to *Congressional Record,* 1946, A2217.

31. "Truman's Dangerous Policy," *Utica Daily Press* (18 April 1946?), transcribed in appendix to Congressional Record, 1946, A2283.

32. "The Navy's Divergence," *Omaha World Herald*, 3 May 1946, transcribed in appendix to *Congressional Record*, 1946, A2441.

33. David Lawrence, "Why Punish the Navy?" *United States News*, 19 April 1946.

34. Ibid.

35. Henry McLemore, "Ex-Doughboy Pays Tribute to Marines," appendix to *Congressional Record*, 1946, A2678.

36. Robert P. Patterson, Secretary of War, and James Forrestal, Secretary of the Navy, to Harry S. Truman, President of the United States, official correspondence, 31 May 1946, *Congressional Record*, 25 June 1946, 7426.

37. "Merger: Tell It to the Marines," *Newsweek*, 5 May 1947, 26.

38. Ibid.

39. A. A. Vandegrift, *Once a Marine: The Memoirs of General A. A. Vandegrift*, ed. Robert B. Asprey (New York: W. W. Norton, 1964), 317–18.

40. "Merger: Tell It to the Marines," 26.

41. "Merger Now," *Washington Post*, 26 July 1946.

42. "The Air and the Future," *Washington Star*, 26 July 1946.

43. James Forrestal, memorandum to Clark M. Clifford, 7 September 1945. See *Documentary History of the Truman Presidency*, vol. 10.

44. Caraley, *Politics of Military Unification*, 151n.

45. "Public Bills and Resolutions," *Congressional Record*, 14 January 1947, 330.

46. "The National Defense Establishment," *Congressional Record*, 30 June 1947, 7944.

47. "The United States Marine Corps and Its Part in National Security," appendix to *Congressional Record*, 1947, A1222.

48. Ibid., A1220.

49. A. A. Vandegrift, statement to Senate Armed Services Committee, 22 April 1947. See *Documentary History of the Truman Presidency*, vol. 10.

50. T. A. Simms, letter to W. Stuart Symington, 23 April 1947. See *Documentary History of the Truman Presidency*, vol. 10.

51. "The Marines' Last Beachhead?" appendix to *Congressional Record*, 1947, A2229 (specific source and date unclear).

52. Ibid.; "General Vandegrift Should Be Headed," News of Elmira N.Y., n.d. (quotations). See appendix to *Congressional Record*, 1947, A2229.

53. Millett, *Semper Fidelis*, 462–63.

54. Clare E. Hoffman, Representative, to A. A. Vandegrift, Commandant of the Marine Corps, official correspondence, 24 July 1947, Vandegrift Papers, Marine Corps University Research Archives.

55. Richard Tregaskis, "The Marine Corps Fights for Its Life," *Saturday Evening Post*, 5 February 1949.

56. Clark M. Clifford, presidential adviser, memorandum to President Harry Truman, 22 July 1947. See *Documentary History of the Truman Presidency*, vol. 10.

57. "Unification of the Armed Services—Conference Report," *Congressional Record*, 24 July 1947, 9912.

58. Millett, *Semper Fidelis*, 463–64.

59. Gordon W. Keiser, *The U.S. Marine Corps and Defense Unification, 1944–47* (Baltimore: Nautical & Aviation Publishing, 1996), 113.

60. U.S. Congress, J.R. 113, 1 July 1947.

61. James D. Hittle, "The Marine Corps and the National Security Act," *Marine Corps Gazette* (October 1947), 57–59.

62. Henry McLemore, "McLemore Is Glad He Saved Cap to Tip to Marines," Evening Star (10 November 1947), transcribed in appendix to *Congressional Record,* 1947, A4198.

63. Marshall Andrews, "Cry of Unification Still Far Cry from It," *Washington Post* (3 May 1948?), appendix to *Congressional Record,* 1948, A2685.

64. Roscoe Drummond, "State of the Nation—Behind Armed Services Disunification," Christian Science Monitor (13 May 1948?), appendix to *Congressional Record,* 1948, A3028.

65. William Bradford Huie, "Shall We Abolish the Marine Corps?" *American Mercury* (September 1948), 273–80.

66. Ibid., 280.

67. C. B. Cates to all commanding officers in the Marine Corps, "Support of the National Security Act," 3 March 1948, Cates Papers, Marine Corps University Research Archives.

68. James D. Hittle, "Seapower and a Balanced Fleet," *Marine Corps Gazette* (February 1948).

69. "Who Won the War?" *Infantry Journal* (January 1949), 2–3.

70. Ibid.

71. W. Stuart Symington, memorandum with attached proposal to Clark M. Clifford, 14 January 1949. See *Documentary History of the Truman Presidency,* vol. 10.

72. Jeffrey G. Barlow, *Revolt of the Admirals: The Fight for Naval Aviation* (Washington, D.C.: Department of the Navy, Naval Historical Center, 1994), xvii–xviii.

73. Victor H. Krulak, *First to Fight: An Inside View of U.S. Marine Corps* (Annapolis, Md.: U.S. Naval Institute, 1984), 120–23.

74. Millett, *Semper Fidelis,* 465.

75. Krulak, *First to Fight,* 123.

76. Randy Roberts and James S. Olson, *John Wayne: American* (New York: Free Press, 1995), 319.

77. Michael Wayne. See "making of the film" section of DVD edition of *Sands of Iwo Jima,* directed by Allan Dwan, starring John Wayne, Republic Entertainment, 2000. Other accounts state that John Wayne requested the part and needed no coaxing from the Marine Corps.

78. William Milhon, "Sands of Iwo," *Leatherneck* (November 1949), 8–11.

79. *Sands of Iwo Jima* (DVD).

80. Lawrence H. Suid, *Guts and Glory: The Making of the American Military Image* (Lexington: University of Kentucky Press, 2002), 120.

81. Ezra Goodman, "From the Halls of Montezuma to Hollywood," *New York Times,* 7 August 1949.

82. Ibid.; William Milhon, "Sands of Iwo," *Leatherneck* (November 1949), 8.

83. Goodman, "From the Halls of Montezuma to Hollywood."

84. Ibid.

85. Ibid.

86. Marling and Wetenhall, *Iwo Jima: Monuments, Memories, and the American Hero*, 129.

87. Ibid., 143.

88. Milhon, "Sands of Iwo."

89. Marling and Wetenhall, *Iwo Jima: Monuments, Memories, and the American Hero*, 131.

90. Ibid., 141–42.

91. Richard L. Coe, " 'Iwo' Magnificent in Fighter Shots," *Washington Post*, 25 January 1950.

92. Goodman, "From the Halls of Montezuma to Hollywood."

93. Coe, " 'Iwo' Magnificent in Fighter Shots."

94. Suid, *Guts and Glory*, 135.

95. T. M. P., " 'Sands of Iwo Jima,' Starring John Wayne, At the Mayfair," New York Times, 31 December 1949.

96. Ernest R. Tinkham, "Iwo Jima," *Leatherneck* (December 1950), 17.

97. "From the Halls of Montezuma to the Shores of Korea—The Marines Can Win If We Give Them a Chance," *Congressional Record*, 1 September 1950, A6323. Truman apologized to the commandant of the Marine Corps, Clifton Cates, on the language he used in responding to McDonough. See Harry Truman, President, personal apology to Clifton Cates, Commandant of the Marine Corps, 6 September 1950, Clifton Cates Papers, Marine Corps University Research Archives.

98. Krulak, *First to Fight*, 121.

99. Millett, *Semper Fidelis*, 481.

100. Merrill L. Bartlett and Jack Sweetman, *The U.S. Marine Corps: An Illustrated History* (Annapolis, Md.: Naval Institute Press, 2001), 244.

101. Millett, *Semper Fidelis*, 497.

102. Ibid., 498.

103. Committee on Armed Services, U.S. House of Representatives, *National Security Act of 1947* (Washington: U.S. Government Printing Office, 1973), 16–17.

104. Ibid.

105. U.S. Congress, Senate, J.R. 112 and 113. See "Bills and Joint Resolutions Introduced," *Congressional Record*, 9 May 1947, 4847.

106. Marling and Wetenhall, *Iwo Jima: Monuments, Memories, and the American Hero*, 149.

107. Due to new construction, the 20-ton statue was moved to Quantico, Virginia, in 1947. It sat outside the main entrance to the military base until 1951, when the Marine Corps commissioned de Weldon to replace it with a sturdy limestone version. It appears that this original statue eventually found its way back to de Weldon's studio, where it sat in serious disrepair for forty years. It was eventually restored in 1995, with $300,000 of repair work, and now sits in front of the Intrepid Sea, Air and Space Museum in New Jersey. "The Iwo Jima Statue," appendix to *Congressional Record*, 1946, A1083–84; Marling and Wetenhall, *Iwo Jima: Monuments, Memories, and the American Hero*, 146–50, 160–61.

108. "Public Bills and Resolutions," *Congressional Record*, 15 March 1945; "Iwo Jima Statue," appendix to Congressional Record, 1945, A1083–1084.

109. Marling and Wetenhall, *Iwo Jima: Monuments, Memories, and the American Hero*, 150.

110. Ibid., 150–63.

111. "Huge Statue of Mt. Suribachi Heroes Arrives Unscathed at Arlington after Difficult Journey," *Evening Star*, 3 September 1954.

112. Lemuel C. Shepherd, oral history transcript (Washington, D.C.: Headquarters U.S. Marine Corps, Historical Division, 1967), 29.

113. Lemuel C. Shepherd, Marine Corps Memorandum 84-54, "Marine Corps Memorial Fund Drive," 27 September 1954, Iwo Jima Folders, Marine Historical Reference Section, Marine Historical Center; Marine Corps War Memorial Foundation, Inc., "Statement of Cash Receipts and Disbursements for the Period October 1, 1950 through April 30, 1955," 12 May 1955, Iwo Jima Folders, Marine Historical Reference Section, Marine Historical Center.

114. Gerald C. Thomas, oral history transcript (Washington, D.C.: Headquarters U.S. Marine Corps, Historical Division, 1973), 951.

115. "The United States Marine Corps War Memorial," U.S. Department of the Interior, National Park Service, Washington, D.C., 8 September 1973.

116. "Huge Statue of Mt. Suribachi Heroes Arrives Unscathed at Arlington after Difficult Journey," *Evening Star*, 3 September 1954.

117. Despite the prevailing myth, there is no "thirteenth hand" in the statue, just twelve hands and feet for the six flag-raisers. Thomas W. Miller, "The Iwo Jima Memorial and The Myth of the 13th Hand," Arlington, Virginia, 1999, Library of Congress.

118. J. W. Moreau, letter to Dwight D Eisenhower, 2 July 1954, Moreau Papers, Marine Corps University Research Archives.

119. "Rites of Statue Mark Iwo Jima Anniversary," unidentified clipping, Holland M. Smith Papers, Marine Corps University Research Archives.

120. "Marine Memorial Dedicated by U.S.," *New York Times*, 11 November 1954.

121. For Nixon's comments see ibid.; also Richard L. Lyons, "Marines Dedicate Iwo Jima Memorial," clipping (11 November 1954?), William P. McCahill Papers, Marine Corps University Research Archives.

122. Marling and Wetenhall, *Iwo Jima: Monuments, Memories, and the American Hero*, 11–16.

123. "Suribachi to Skid Row," *Newsweek*, 26 October 1953, 44.

124. "Heroes: Then There Were Two," *National Week*, 8 March 1946; "Flag Hero Found Dead," New York Times, 25 January 1955; Huie, *Hero of Iwo Jima*, 64.

125. Huie, *Hero of Iwo Jima*, 67.

126. "Television: Two Flags on Iwo," *New York Times*, 28 March 1960.

127. Ibid.

128. "'The Outsider' Opens with Tony Curtis in the Starring Role," *New York Times*, 8 February 1962.

129. "Tony Curtis: The Outsider," advertisement in *New York Times*, 7 February 1962.

130. Sanka Knox, "Public Sculpture in U.S. Is Deplored," *New York Times*, 31 March 1955.

131. Marling and Wetenhall, *Iwo Jima: Monuments, Memories, and the American Hero*, 196.

132. Kate O'Beirne, "Memorial Daze," *National Review*, 28 June 1999, 34–36; "Update on War Memorial Struggle," *Marine Corps Gazette* (July 1998), 4.

133. Larry Van Dyne, "Over My Dead Body," *Washingtonian* (November 1999), 159.

134. Ibid., 160.

135. Fredrick Kunkle, "Tentative Deal Would Move Planned Air Force Memorial," *Washington Post*, 29 November 2001.

136. Ibid.

Chapter 8

1. An earlier version of this chapter has been accepted for publication in *U.S. Naval Institute Proceedings*.

2. Janis L. Edwards and Carol K. Winkler, "Representative Form and the Visual Ideograph: The Iwo Jima Image in Editorial Cartoons," *Quarterly Journal of Speech 83* (August 1997): 299; Robert Hariman and John Louis Lucaites, "Performing Civic Identity: The Iconic Photograph of the Flag Raising on Iwo Jima," *Quarterly Journal of Speech* 88 (November 2002): 268–370.

3. Edwards and Winkler, "Representative Form and the Visual Ideograph," 289; Hariman and Lucaites, "Performing Civic Identity," 368.

4. John Kerry and Vietnam Veterans Against the War, in *The New Soldier*, ed. David Thorne and George Butler (New York: Macmillan, 1971).

5. This image can be found online at http://cagle.slate.msn.com/news/Iraq-WorldAfter/1.asp (accessed 24 June 2004).

6. Video game, "Elite Forces WWII: Iwo Jima," *Valuesoft*, 1 October 2001; board game, "Uncommon Valor: Battle of Iwo Jima," Critical Hit, unknown release date.

7. *Heroes of Iwo Jima*, Arnold Shapiro Productions (New York: A&E Home Video, 2001); *Inside the Great Battles: Iwo Jima* premiered on the History Channel in May 2004.

8. Proclamation 4724 of 19 February 1980, *Federal Register* 45, no. 36 (21 February 1980).

9. George Bush, "Remarks Announcing the Proposed Constitutional Amendment of Desecration of the Flag," 30 June 1989, George Bush Presidential Library and Museum, College Station, Texas.

10. Karal Ann Marling and John Wetenhall, "Point of View," *Chronicle of Higher Education*, 29 September 1993, A52.

11. Skye Jones, MCAS Miramar Combat Correspondent, "Marines Raise Nation's Flag, Spirits during Historical Re-enactment," document found online at: www.usmc.mil (accessed 11 March 2004).

12. Information from this paragraph comes from Hariman and Lucaites, "Performing Civic Identity," 383–84.

13. This term refers to the generation of Americans who fought and won World War II, both on the home front and abroad. See Tom Brokaw, *The Greatest Generation* (New York : Random House, 1998).

14. Ceremony of the Return of Iwo Jima, official document between United States and Japan, 26 June 1968, Air Force Historical Research Agency.

15. History of the 6100th Support Wing, April–June 1968, Fifth Air Force, Pacific Air Forces, 26 September 1968, Special Addendum, i–ii, Air Force Historical Research Agency.

16. Thomey, *Immortal Images*, 158; Marling and Wetenhall, *Iwo Jima: Monuments, Memories, and the American Hero*, 223.

Joseph Auslander, "Postscript to Iwo," *Marine Corps Gazette* (May 1946), 32–34. This poem is reprinted in its entirety with permission of *Marine Corps Gazette*. The accompanying pictures are by retired Colonel and Iwo Jima veteran Charles H. Waterhouse and can be found in *Marines and Others: The Paintings of Colonel Charles Waterhouse* (Edison, N.J.: Sea Bag Productions, 1994), 183, 184, 194, 196. They are reprinted by permission of the artist.

Bibliography

A Note about Military Documents

For the Navy and Marine Corps, communiqués, after-action reports, operational orders, and planning documents are located in several different places. Most prominent among these are the Navy and Marine Corps historical centers, which are currently located at the Washington Navy Yard. The Navy Historical Center still has the most information related to Iwo Jima strategy, as well as sets of personal papers. The Marine Corps Historical Center has more detailed data about the battle itself. It also contains recordings of thousands of interviews. However, due to personnel shortages, most of the recorded interviews have not yet been transcribed and prove time-consuming to work with. Both the Navy and Marine Corps recently moved a large portion of their World War II records to the National Archives, College Park, Maryland. Having only recently received such large treasures, the archivists at College Park are not yet familiar with the material and will likely never attain the same degree of familiarity as the personnel at the Navy Yard. For the time being, the best approach for researchers is to talk with the knowledgeable personnel at the Navy Yard before heading over to College Park. The Nimitz Library at the U.S. Naval Academy and the Marine Corps University in Quantico, Virginia, offer additional information. Marine Corps University has numerous personal papers of important Marine figures. Nimitz Library has Marine Corps World War II operations reports on thirty-five reels of microfilm, a valuable source and the only such source that I am aware of. Further, Nimitz Library has hundreds of reels of Navy documents on microfilm.

For the Army, most records are available at the National Archives. The archivists have used them for years, and provide capable and helpful advice to researchers. More records are available at the Military History Institute at Carlyle Barracks, Pennsylvania. The institute also has copies of the "Japanese Monographs" on microfilm. The Army completed the monographs after the war, with Japanese officers. Although the details in the monographs derive mostly from memory and are generally unreliable, these translated studies impart a Japanese perspective on the Pacific war—and this is their value.

Army Air Forces documents can also be found at the Military History Institute, but most Army Air Forces documentation resides at Air Force Historical Research Agency, located at Maxwell Air Force Base, Alabama. The electronic search engine at Air Force Historical Research Agency is the best and most precise I have ever encountered in Pacific war archives. Each individual item is cataloged, usually with an accompanying description of the document or text, and the location where it can be found. Unfortunately, the database can only be accessed from that location and not via the World Wide Web. The Air Force is the only service not to have turned over most of its World War II archives to the National Archives. Histories and reports from the Twentieth Air Force, Twenty-First Bomber Command, and 7th Fighter Command are located there. The personal papers of Henry Arnold and Curtis LeMay can be found at the Library of Congress, although the Air Force Historical Research Agency retains some limited copies of these.

Albee, Parker Bishop, Jr., and Keller Cushing Freeman. *Shadow of Suribachi: Raising the Flags on Iwo Jima.* Westport, Conn.: Praeger, 1995.

Alexander, Joseph H. *Closing In: Marines in the Seizure of Iwo Jima.* Washington, D.C.: Historical Division, U.S. Marine Corps, 1994.

————. *Utmost Savagery: The Three Days at Tarawa.* Annapolis, Md.: Naval Institute Press, 1995.

Arnold, H. H. *Global Mission.* New York: Harper & Brothers, 1949.

Astor, Gerald. *Operation Iceberg: The Invasion and Conquest of Okinawa in World War II: An Oral History.* New York: Donald I. Fine, 1995.

Barlow, Jeffrey G. *Revolt of the Admirals: The Fight for Naval Aviation.* Washington, D.C.: Naval Historical Center, Department of the Navy, 1994.

Bartlett, Merrill L., and Jack Sweetman. *The U.S. Marine Corps: An Illustrated History.* Annapolis, Md.: Naval Institute Press, 2001.

Bartley, Whitman S. *Iwo Jima: Amphibious Epic.* Washington, D.C.: Historical Branch, G-3 Division, U.S. Marine Corps, 1954.

Bishop, Jim. *FDR's Last Year: April 1944–April 1945.* New York: William Morrow, 1974.

Bradley, James. *Flyboys: A True Story of Courage.* New York: Little, Brown, 2003.

Bradley, James, and Ron Powers. *Flags of Our Fathers.* New York: Bantam Books, 2000.

Brokaw, Tom. *The Greatest Generation.* New York: Random House, 1998.

Buell, Thomas B. *Master of Seapower: A Biography of Ernest J. King.* Annapolis, Md.: Naval Institute Press, 1980.

————. *The Quiet Warrior: A Biography of Admiral Raymond A. Spruance.* Boston: Little, Brown, 1974.

Cameron, Craig. *American Samurai: Myth Imagination, and the Conduct of Battle in the First Marine Division, 1941–1951.* Cambridge: Cambridge University Press, 1994.

Caraley, Demetrios. *The Politics of Military Unification: A Study of Conflict and the Policy Process.* New York: Columbia University Press, 1966.

Clodfelter, Michael. *Warfare and Armed Conflicts: A Statistical Reference to Casualty and Other Figures, 1618–1991.* Vol 2. Jefferson, N.C.: McFarland, 1991.

Conner, Howard M. *The Spearhead: The World War II History of the 5th Marine Division.* Washington, D.C.: Historical Division, U.S. Marine Corps, 1950.

Crane, Conrad C. *Bombs, Cities, and Civilians: American Airpower Strategy in World War II.* Lawrence: University Press of Kansas, 1993.

Craven, Wesley Frank, and James Lea Cate. *The Army Air Forces in World War II. Vol. 5: The Pacific: Matterhorn to Nagasaki, June 1944 to August 1945.* Chicago: University of Chicago Press, 1953.

————. *The Army Air Forces in World War II. Vol. 7: Services around the World.* Chicago: University of Chicago Press, 1958.

Dower, John W. *Embracing Defeat: Japan in the Wake of World War II.* New York: W. W. Norton, 1999.

————. *War without Mercy: Race and Power in the Pacific War.* New York: Pantheon, 1986.

Dyer, George C. *The Amphibians Came to Conquer: The Story of Admiral Richmond Kelly Turner.* Vol. 2. Washington, D.C.: Department of the Navy, 1972.

Estes, Kenneth W. *The Marine Officer's Guide.* Annapolis, Md.: Naval Institute Press, 1996.

Evans, David C., and Mark R. Peattie. *Kaigun: Strategy, Tactics, and Technology of the Imperial Japanese Navy, 1887–1941.* Annapolis, Md.: Naval Institute Press, 1997.

Frank, Richard B. *Downfall: The End of the Imperial Japanese Empire.* New York: Random House, 1999.

Frye, William. *Marshall: Citizen Soldier.* Indianapolis: Bobbs-Merrill, 1947.

Gilderhus, Mark T. *History and Historians: A Historiographical Introduction.* Englewood Cliffs, N.J.: Prentice Hall, 1996.

Hall, R. Cargill, ed. *Case Studies in Strategic Bombardment.* Washington, D.C.: Air Force History and Museums Program, 1998.

Hallas, James H. *The Devil's Anvil: The Assault on Peleliu.* Westport, Conn.: Praeger, 1994.

Hansell, Haywood S., Jr. *Strategic Air War against Japan.* Washington, D.C.: U.S. Government Printing Office, 1980.

Harries, Meirion, and Susie Harries. *Soldiers of the Rising Sun: The Rise and Fall of the Imperial Japanese Army.* New York: Random House, 1991.

Hashimoto, Mochitsura. *Sunk: The Story of the Japanese Submarine Fleet, 1941–1945.* New York: Henry Holt, 1954.

Hayashi, Saburo, and Alvin D. Coox. *Kogun: The Japanese Army of the Pacific War.* Quantico, Va.: Marine Corps Association, 1959.

Hearn, Chester. *Sorties into Hell: The Hidden War on Chichi Jima.* Westport, Conn.: Praeger, 2003.

Heinl, Robert D., Jr. *Dictionary of Military and Naval Quotations.* Annapolis, Md.: Naval Institute Press, 1966.

Hemmingway, Albert. *Ira Hayes: Pima Marine.* Lanham, Md.: University Press of America, 1988.

Henri, Raymond, Jima G. Lucas, David K. Dempsey, W. Keyes Beech, and Alvin M. Josephy Jr. *The U.S. Marines on Iwo Jima.* New York: Dial Press, 1945.

History of the Iwo Jima Flag Raising, Biographies of the Flag Raisers. Marine Corps Historical Reference Series, No. 14. Washington, D.C.: Historical Branch, U.S. Marine Corps, 1959.

The History of the U.S. Marine Corps Operations in World War II. 2 vols. Washington, D.C.: Historical Division, U.S. Marine Corps, 1966 and 1971. Henry I. Shaw Jr., Bernard C. Nalty, and Edwin T. Turnbladh. *Central Pacific Drive.* George W. Garand and Truman R. Strobridge. *Western Pacific Operations.*

Holmes, W. J. *Undersea Victory: The Influence of Submarine Operations on the War in the Pacific.* Garden City, N.Y.: Doubleday, 1966.

Horie, Yoshitaka. *Tokin Io Jima,* Tokyo: Kobunsha, 1965.

Hough, Frank O. *The Island War: The United Sates Marine Corps in the Pacific.* New York: J. B. Lippincott, 1947.

Huie, William Bradford. *The Hero of Iwo Jima.* New York: Signet Books, 1962.

Hunt, George P. *Coral Comes High.* New York: Harper, 1946.

Huston, John W. *American Airpower Comes of Age: General Henry H. "Hap" Arnold's World War II Diaries.* Maxwell AFB: Air University Press, 2002.

Ienaga, Saburo. *The Pacific War: World War II and the Japanese, 1931–1945.* New York: Pantheon, 1978.

Inoguchi, Rikihei, and Tadashi Nakajima. *The Divine Wind: Japa''s Kamikaze Force in World War II*. Edited by Roger Pineau. 1958. Rpt., Annapolis, Md.: Naval Institute Press, 1994.

Isely, Jeter A., and Philip A. Crowl. *The U.S. Marines and Amphibious War: Its Theory, and Its Practice in the Pacific*. Princeton: Princeton University Press, 1951.

James, D. Clayton. *The Years of MacArthur: Vol. 2, 1941–1945*. Boston: Houghton Mifflin, 1975.

Keiser, Gordon W. *The U.S. Marine Corps and Defense Unification, 1944–47*. Baltimore: Nautical & Aviation Publishing, 1996.

Kerr, E. Bartlett. *Flames over Tokyo: The U.S. Army Air Forces' Incendiary Campaign against Japan, 1944–1945*. New York: Donald I. Fine, 1991.

Kerry, John, and Vietnam Veterans against the War. *The New Soldier*. Edited by David Thorne and George Butler. New York: Macmillan, 1971.

King, Ernest J., and Walter Muir Whitehill. *Fleet Admiral King: A Naval Record*. New York: W. W. Norton, 1952.

Krulak, Victor H. *First to Fight: An Inside View of U.S. Marine Corps*. Annapolis, Md.: Naval Institute Press, 1984.

Lamont-Brown, Raymond. *Kamikaze: Japan's Suicide Samurai*. New York: Sterling Publishing, 1997.

Leckie, Robert. *Okinawa: The Last Battle of World War II*. New York: Penguin Books, 1995.

LeMay, Curtis E., and Bill Yenne. *Superfortress: The Story of the B-29 and American Air Power*. New York: McGraw-Hill, 1988.

Mahan, Alfred Thayer. *The Influence of Sea Power upon the French Revolution and Empire, 1793–1812*. Vol. 1. Boston: Little, Brown, 1892.

———. *The Influence of Sea Power upon History, 1660–1783*. 1890. Rpt., Boston: Little, Brown, 1918.

Marling, Karal Ann, and John Wetenhall. *Iwo Jima: Monuments, Memories, and the American Hero*. Cambridge, Mass.: Harvard University Press, 1991.

McCullough, David. *Truman*. New York: Simon & Schuster, 1992.

Millett, Allan R. *Semper Fidelis: The History of the United States Marine Corps*. 1980. Rpt., New York: Free Press, 1991.

Morehouse, Clifford P. *The Iwo Jima Operation*. Washington, D.C.: Historical Branch, G-3 Division, U.S. Marine Corps, 1946.

Morgan, Henry G., Jr. *Planning the Defeat of Japan: A Study of the Total War Strategy*. Washington, D.C.: Office of the Chief of Military History, 1961.

Morison, Samuel Eliot. *Rising Sun in the Pacific*. Vol. 4 of *History of United States Naval Operations in World War II*. Boston: Little, Brown, 1947–64.

———. *The Struggle for Guadalcanal, August 1942–February 1943*. Vol. 5 of *History of United States Naval Operations in World War II*. Boston: Little, Brown, 1947–64.

Morton, Louis. *United States Army in World War II: The War in the Pacific, Strategy and Command: The First Two Years*. Washington, D.C.: Office of the Chief of Military History, Department of the Army, 1962.

Nalty, Bernard C., and Danny J. Crawford. *The United States Marines on Iwo Jima: The Battle and the Flag Raisings*. Washington, D.C.: History and Museums Division, U.S. Marine Corps, 1995.

Newcomb, Richard F. *Iwo-Jima*. New York: Holt, Rinehart & Winston, 1965.

Potter, E. B. *Nimitz*. Annapolis, Md.: Naval Institute Press, 1976.

Prange, Gordon W., Donald M. Goldstein, and Katherine V. Dillon, eds. *God's Samurai: Lead Pilot at Pearl Harbor*. Washington, D.C.: Brassey's, 1990.

Proehl, Carl William. *The Fourth Marine Division in World War II*. Washington, D.C.: Infantry Journal Press, 1947.

Roberts, Randy, and James S. Olson. *John Wayne: American*. New York: Free Press, 1995.

Ross, Bill D. *Iwo Jima: Legacy of Valor*. New York: Vintage Books, 1985.

Sakai, Saburo. *Samurai!* Edited by Martin Caidin and Fred Saito. Annapolis, Md.: Naval Institute Press, 1991.

Sato, Hiroaki. *Legends of the Samurai*. Woodstock, N.Y.: Overlook Press, 1995.

Sherry, Michael S. *The Rise of American Air Power: The Creation of Armageddon*. New Haven, Conn.: Yale University Press, 1987.

Shigamitsu, Mamuro. *Japan and Her Destiny: My Struggle for Peace*. New York: E. P. Dutton, 1958.

Sledge, E. B. *With the Old Breed at Peleliu and Okinawa*. Oxford: Oxford University Press, 1981.

Smith, Holland M., and Percy Finch. *Coral and Brass*. New York: Charles Scribner's Sons, 1949.

Spector, Ronald. *Eagle against the Sun: The American War with Japan*. New York: Vintage Books, 1985.

Steinberg, Rafael, and the editors of Time-Life Books. *Island Fighting*. Alexandria, Va.: Time-Life Books, 1978.

Strategy. Marine Corps Doctrinal Publication 1–1. Washington, D.C.: U.S. Marine Corps, 1997.

Suid, Lawrence H. *Guts and Glory: The Making of the American Military Image*. Lexington: University of Kentucky Press, 2002.

Sumida, Jon Tetsuro. *Inventing Grand Strategy and Teaching Command: The Classic Works of Alfred Thayer Mahan Reconsidered*. Washington, D.C.: Woodrow Wilson Center Press; and Baltimore: Johns Hopkins University Press, 1997.

Symonds, Craig L. *Historical Atlas of the U.S. Navy*. Annapolis, Md.: Naval Institute Press, 1995.

Tanaka, Yuki. *Hidden Horrors: Japanese War Crimes in World War II*. Boulder, Colo.: Westview Press, 1996.

Tatum, Charles W. *Iwo Jima: Red Blood, Black Sand, Pacific Apocalypse*. N.p.: Charles W. Tatum Publishing, 1995.

Thomey, Tedd. *Immortal Images: A Personal History of Two Photographers and the Flag Raising on Iwo Jima*. Annapolis, Md.: Naval Institute Press, 1996.

Toland, John. *The Rising Sun: The Decline and Fall of the Japanese Empire, 1936–1945*. New York: Random House, 1970.

Ugaki, Matome. *Fading Victory: The Diary of Admiral Matome Ugaki, 1941–1945*. Trans. Masataka Chihaya. Ed. Donald M. Goldstein and Katherine V. Dillo. Pittsburgh: University of Pittsburgh Press, 1991.

Vandegrift, A. A. *Once a Marine: The Memoirs of General A. A. Vandegrift*. Edited by Robert B. Asprey. New York: W. W. Norton, 1964.

Van der Vat, Dan. *The Pacific Campaign: World War II, the U.S.—Japanese Naval War, 1941–1945*. New York: Simon & Schuster, 1991.

Von Clausewitz, Karl. *The Book on War*. New York: Modern Library, 2000.

Weigley, Russell F. *The American Way of War: A History of the United States Military Strategy and Policy*. Bloomington: Indiana University Press, 1973.

Werrell, Kenneth P. *Blankets of Fire: U.S. Bombers over Japan during World War II*. Washington, D.C.: Smithsonian Institution Press, 1996. ·

Wheeler, Keith. *The Road to Tokyo*. Chicago: Time-Life Books, 1979.

Wheeler, Keith, and the editors of Time-Life Books. *Bombers over Japan*. Alexandria, Va.: Time-Life Books, 1982.

Wheeler, Richard. *The Bloody Battle for Suribachi*. 1965. Rpt., Annapolis, Md.: Naval Institute Press, 1994.

———. *Iwo*. Annapolis, Md.: Naval Institute Press, 1980.

Yamada, Fuutaro. *Senchu Ha Fusen Nikki: A Diary of Wartime Younger Generation Who Did Not Fight*. Tokyo: Kodansha, 1985.

Index

Photos and maps are indicated in *italic* type. Military units are indicated in **bold**.

Lejeune, Gen. John A., 157

LeMay, Gen. Curtis: firebombing, 97, 101, 114; Operation Detachment, 53; Pacific strategy, 8–11; problems with the B-29, 30, 102; use of Iwo Jima airfields, 108–10

Lexington battle, 147

Leyte Gulf battle, 100

Leyte. *See* Philippine Islands

Lindberg, Charles, 130

Look, 164

Lowe, Gen. Frank, 181

Lowery, Lou, 130–32

Lucas, Jacklyn, 76

Luftwaffe (German Air Force), 8

Luzon. *See* Philippine Islands

Lydecker, Howard, 177

Lyons, Thomas, 62

MacArthur, Gen. Douglas: Iwo Jima casualties, xv; Operation Detachment, 49–51, 54–55; Pacific strategy, 12–18, 21, 25, 30–34, 37; Seventh War Loan, 144; Tarawa casualties, 18

Manila. *See* Philippine Islands

Mansfield, Mike, 136, 179, 181

Mara, Adele, 176

Marianas Islands, 8–9, 25–28, 30, 33, 41–42, 80, 95–96, 99–100, 102, 104, 107–08, 124, 154. *Also see* Guam, Rota, Saipan, and Tinian

Marine Corps battalions: **3/9**, 88; **2/28**, 129, 132–33, 137–38, 178; **2d Separate Engineer Battalion**, 92; parachute battalions, 58, 137; raider battalion, 58

Marine Corps commands: **V Amphibious Corps**, 51, 58, 61, 64, 71, 83, 120, 136, 150, 152, 154; **1st Marine Brigade**, 180; **Marine Forces Pacific**, 51

Marine Corps divisions: **1st Marine Division**, 14, 16, 89, 181; **3d Marine Division**, 4, 51, 58, 60, 68, 70, 73–74, 77–78, 86, 89, 91, 149–50; **4th Marine Division**, 4, 51, 58, 60, 62, 64, 67–68, 70, 73–74, 86, 89,

91, 149–50; **5th Marine Division**, 3–4, 51, 58, 60, 62, 64, 67–68, 70, 72, 74–79, 86, 89, 91, 133, 137, 149–50

Marine Corps League, 183–84

Marine Corps regiments: **3d Marines**, 70; **27th Marines**, 3; **28th Marines**, 67, 138

Marine Corps War Memorial Foundation, 184

Marine Corps, roles and missions of: amphibious assault, 160–61, 165–66, 175; colonial infantry, 160–61; force-in-readiness, 161–62, 181; H.R. Bill 4214, 170–72; National Security Act, 172–74, 180; National Security Act revisions, 181–82; Senate Bill 758, 171–72. *Also see* Joint Chiefs of Staff, exclusion of the Marine Corps; service rivalry, unification struggle

Marine War Memorial, the: construction of, 178, 182–83; dedication to, 184–85; fight with Air Force over, 187–88; funding for, 183–84; influence of, 186–87; legislation for, 146–47, 172; statistics of, 184

Marshall Islands, 8, 16–18, 84 table 2, 85, 154

Marshall, Gen. George: anger at Gen. Holland Smith, 51; Iwo Jima casualties, 119–20; justifying Iwo Jima, 95; Pacific strategy, 11–12, 14–17, 32–34, 36; Seventh War Loan, 144; unification struggle, 158–59, 164

Matsudo, Linsoki, 80

McDonough, Gordon, 149, 180

McLemore, Henry, 167, 172–73

McNarney, Gen. Joseph, 159

Meat Grinder (Iwo Jima strong point), 4, 68, 73

Meet the Press, 194

Michaels, James, 130

Midway battle, 8

Mindanao. *See* Philippine Islands

Mitchell, Gen. Billy, 23–24

Montoyama: airfield no. 1, 92–93, 107, 152; airfield no. 2, 60, 152; depicted,